SketchUp & LayOut for Architecture

The step by step workflow of Nick Sonder

Written by: Matt Donley and Nick Sonder

SketchUp & LayOut for Architecture
The step by step workflow of Nick Sonder

Published by:
Bizfound, LLC
24 Michael Drive
Bristol, RI 02809
www.bizfound.com

Ordering Information:
Visit **www.sketchupbook.com** for ordering information.

Credits:

   Photography: Vance Fox Photography **www.vancefox.com**

v1.0

Special Thanks to: Bill Keck, Larry Zent, Linda Farmer, Bill & Meg Connors, and the entire SketchUp team.

m**asterSketchup**.com

We dedicate this book to our loving families.

Contents

Introduction   11

Workflow   23

Getting Started   49

Schematic Design   123

A Note From Matt Donley

Through countless phone calls, screen-shares, and hundreds of emails, Nick and I worked together to perfect the workflow that I have documented for you in this book. Since I lack first-hand experience as an architect, I was excited to be able to collaborate with Nick. Nick is an architect out of Truckee, California using SketchUp and LayOut exclusively in his architectural firm. I first learned about his work when the SketchUp team interviewed him in a case study video (**www.sketchupbook.com/sondervideo**), where he showed examples of his amazing custom homes designed using SketchUp and LayOut.

I had the chance to meet Nick at the 2012 SketchUp Basecamp Conference in Colorado. I sat in on his presentation, and I could see then how his work would serve as proof to the world how powerful SketchUp is as an architectural design tool. Up to that point, I had never seen anyone create drawings like that from a SketchUp model. He designed and documented the entire project without ever touching AutoCAD.

Over the next couple of years, we stayed in touch through email and the occasional phone call, but it was not until the next SketchUp Basecamp Conference where we sparked the idea of writing a book together. I had just finished writing my first book, SketchUp to LayOut. I really wanted to create something specifically geared towards architectural design, but I lacked the experience to be able to write it on my own.

By working together on this book, we were able to create something better than what either of us could have created on our own. Nick was able to contribute his years of experience as an architect, as well as his journey in trying and testing out various techniques and workflows using SketchUp and LayOut.

I took the role as the apprentice, asking questions and learning along the way. This was a valuable role to serve, because I was able to experience Nick's workflow from the perspective of a beginner. This enabled me to identify obstacles that other beginners may find challenging. My experience creating tutorials on **Mastersketchup.com**, as well as writing my first book, served me well in communicating Nick's entire workflow in this book.

A Note From Nick Sonder

SketchUp is a program originally developed to be a simple, straightforward 3D program...3D for everyone. In my business, I have always adopted the principles of simplicity. SketchUp brought another avenue to allow me to strengthen this principle. This book details my approach of utilizing native SketchUp techniques, highlighting the strength of simplicity inherent with this design program.

While many plugins offer shortcuts and speed, their application in customized work can lead to complexity in the model. Many of us in the design field were trained with AutoCAD and other complex drafting systems. I actually graduated college when AutoCAD was in its infancy, so I was primarily trained using manual hand techniques. Even though I used AutoCAD for 20 years, the complexity has always left me feeling as though we had stepped too far from the hand-drawing aspect of our field.

Focusing primarily on the native aspects of SketchUp allows me to keep control over the complexity of the model, especially when it comes to layering and composition of groups and components. I have found many plugins automatically create complex layering systems that are often difficult to manage. Much of this stems from what we were all taught with AutoCAD where just about every element had a separate layer on which it was placed. With SketchUp, I looked at how I would organize the model for both editing and presentation. Once you clarify that aspect of your model, you can determine the level of layering needed.

3D modeling has offered designers the ability to literally build the design. One needs to be cautious of this ability as you understand how the project is implemented. The level of detail that you strive for should reflect the deliverables you propose.

I have often been asked if my 3D construction details were derived from my building models. This would be much too cumbersome, as my drawings typically are presented to the contractors and building officials at ¼" = 1'-0". At that scale, the level of detail is somewhat simple. Going to a higher level of detail in that model would create a lot of work that serves no function. Understanding what can be perceived at that scale helps you designate your level of detail. Maintaining this process allows for very efficient models that are much more manageable in every respect, both editing and documenting.

Organization and simplicity allow architects to spend more time designing and less time concerned over producing documentation to convey that design. For my practice, SketchUp and LayOut allowed me to strive for and achieve this goal.

I am confident the workflow presented here, in this book, will allow you to do the same.

Figure 1-1
Sample project designed in SketchUp.

Figure 1-2
Sample project rendered in LumenRT.

Who is the Intended Audience?

Would you like to be able to design and document an entire project using SketchUp and LayOut? Are you wondering if it is possible to completely eliminate traditional CAD from your workflow? This book details an entire workflow, step by step, to show you that it is possible to use SketchUp and LayOut to design at a level of detail and simplicity not easily achievable in traditional CAD software.

Figure 2-1
Projects of any size can be designed in SketchUp and LayOut.

The primary purpose of this book is to show you an efficient method to model and document an entire building using native SketchUp tools, and SketchUp's complimentary program, LayOut. You will be able to build 3D models that can be used for both rendering and construction documentation. You will learn specific techniques for modeling each part of the building, and the workflow of an entire project from concept to completion.

By the end of this book, you can apply what you have learned immediately to your next project. While Nick's work detailed in this book is residential, he has successfully utilized this same process in commercial work including fire stations, office and retail space.

Like a paintbrush, SketchUp is a tool that can be used many different ways. This book will focus on the workflow that Nick has perfected over years of custom home design. Just keep in mind, there is no "one way" to approach a project. We expect and encourage you to adapt this workflow for your own needs and preferences.

Figure 2-2
An example of a project designed using SketchUp and LayOut.

Photo: ©VanceFox.com
Contractor: MD Construction & Consulting

The following pages highlight a few of the projects that Nick has designed using the same workflow you are about to learn using SketchUp and LayOut exclusively. You will be able to produce similar results on your own projects using what you learn in this book.

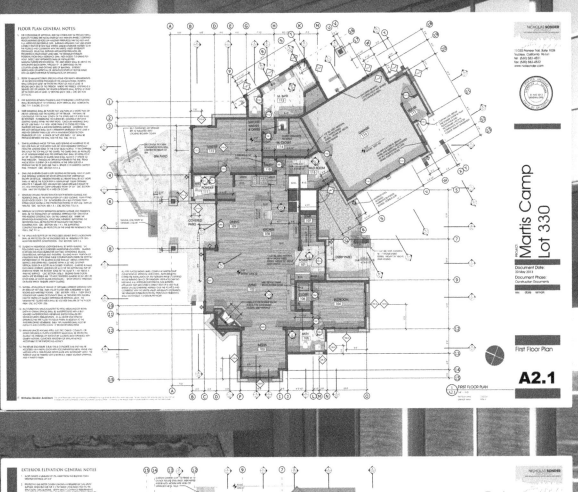

FLOOR PLAN GENERAL NOTES:

NICHOLAS SONDER

11025 Pioneer Trail, Suite 1008
Truckee, California 96161
tel (530) 582-4501
fax (530) 582-4522
www.nicksonder.com

PROJECT:

Martis Camp
Lot 330

Document Date:
20 May 2013

Document Phase:
Construction Documents

rev   date   remark

First Floor Plan

A2.1

Nicholas Sonder Architect

EXTERIOR ELEVATION GENERAL NOTES

NICHOLAS SONDER

11025 Pioneer Trail, Suite 1008
Truckee, California 96161
tel (530) 582-4501
fax (530) 582-4522
www.nicksonder.com

PROJECT:

Martis Camp
Lot 330

Document Date:
20 May 2013

Document Phase:
Construction Documents

rev   date   remark

1 South Elevation

2 Southeast Elevation

Exterior
Elevations

A3.1

EXTERIOR ELEVATION MATERIAL SPECIFICATIONS

Nicholas Sonder Architect

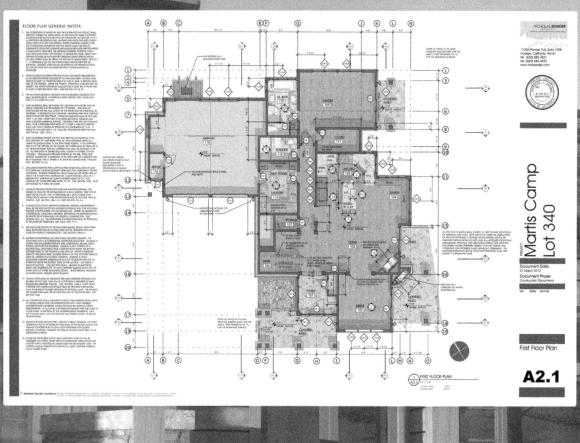

FLOOR PLAN GENERAL NOTES:

NICHOLAS SONDER

11055 Pioneer Trail, Suite 100B
Truckee, California 96161
tel: (530) 582-4521
fax: (530) 582-4522
www.nicksonder.com

PROJECT
**Martis Camp
Lot 340**

Document Date:
31 March 2013
Document Phase:
Construction Documents

First Floor Plan

A2.1

FIRST FLOOR PLAN

EXTERIOR ELEVATION GENERAL NOTES

NICHOLAS SONDER

11055 Pioneer Trail, Suite 100B
Truckee, California 96161
tel: (530) 582-4521
fax: (530) 582-4522
www.nicksonder.com

North Elevation

East Elevation

PROJECT
**Martis Camp
Lot 340**

Document Date:
31 January 2013
Document Phase:
Design Development

EXTERIOR ELEVATION MATERIAL SPECIFICATIONS

Exterior
Elevations

A3.1

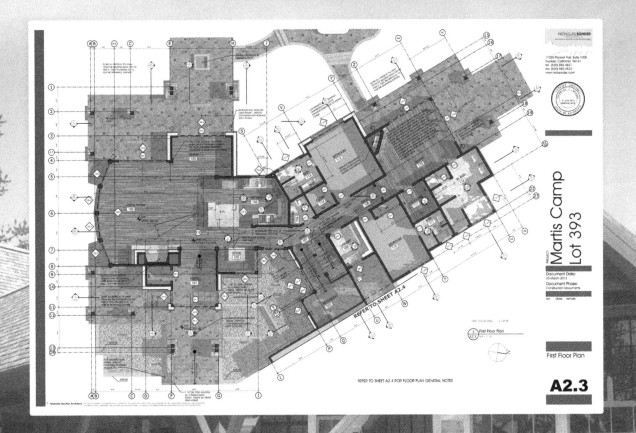

First Floor Plan

A2.3

REFER TO SHEET A2.4 FOR FLOOR PLAN GENERAL NOTES

Martis Camp
Lot 393

Document Date:
23 March 2012
Document Phase:
Construction Documents

EXTERIOR ELEVATION MATERIAL SPECIFICATIONS

EXTERIOR ELEVATION GENERAL NOTES

Exterior Elevations

A3.1

Martis Camp
Lot 393

Document Date:
23 March 2012
Document Phase:
Construction Documents

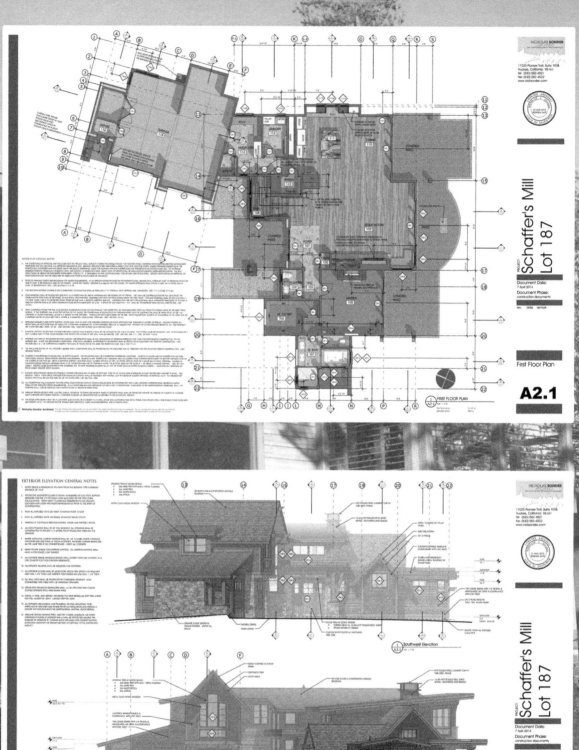

Prerequisites

One concept that is mentioned throughout the book is simplicity. There are a lot of great plugins for SketchUp that can provide additional functionality, but this workflow focuses on native SketchUp tools. A lot of plugins introduce complex layering systems or force you to organize your model a certain way. It is important to have full control over the organization of your model, so we have hand-picked a small selection of optional plugins that can benefit your workflow without adding complexity.

Although this is not a beginner's book on how to use SketchUp or LayOut, we will include step by step instructions where necessary, in order for you to be able to practice specific techniques important to the workflow.

You should be comfortable navigating and modeling in SketchUp. You should understand how SketchUp layers, groups, and components work (Although a small refresher is included in the book.) In LayOut, you should know how to create a new document, insert a SketchUp model, and add some basic dimensions and annotations.

Figure 2-3
An example of a project designed using SketchUp and LayOut.

Photo: ©VanceFox.com
Contractor: MD Construction & Consulting

The book will skip over the basics in order to fit in the complete workflow from start to finish. In most cases, the step by step instructions provided in this book can be followed by even a novice, so do not feel intimidated if you lack extensive SketchUp experience.

If you are brand new to LayOut, and would like a more comprehensive guide on all of LayOut's tools, including a well defined process for preparing your SketchUp model for LayOut, I recommend my first book, SketchUp to LayOut, available at **www.SketchUptoLayOut.com**.

Figure 2-4
Custom home by Nick Sonder designed using SketchUp & LayOut.

Photo: ©VanceFox.com
Contractor: MD Construction & Consulting

What Will You Learn?

Throughout this book, you will learn all of the skills and workflows necessary to model and document an entire project in SketchUp and LayOut. By the end of this book, you will be able to do the following:

✓ Build a quick schematic model to communicate the general design intent, and to work out the general spaces in your design.

✓ Use multiple SketchUp models to split up your project and take advantage of better scene and section cut management.

✓ Create a complete SketchUp model of a building that can be used for generating rendered images or animations, as well as construction documents in LayOut.

✓ Specific techniques for approaching common construction assemblies like floors, walls, windows/doors, roofs, kitchens, and finishes.

✓ Create a site model, which includes landscape elements like trees, vegetation, and driveways, as well as important site survey information such as setbacks and property lines.

✓ Build a library of construction details that can be adapted for each project.

✓ Create and customize SketchUp and LayOut templates in order to save time and increase consistency.

✓ Leverage the use of scrapbooks in LayOut in order to organize your workflow, save time, and reduce redundant work.

✓ Build construction schedules in LayOut.

✓ Completely annotate and dimension a set of drawings in LayOut.

Figure 2-5
Custom home by Nick Sonder designed using SketchUp & LayOut.

Photo: ©VanceFox.com
Contractor: Heslin Construction

Included With Book

Throughout this book, you will see references to a real project that Nick has designed and executed. The project files are included with the purchase of this book, as well as a set of template files that you can customize for your own use.

Download the files at <u>www.sketchupbook.com/files</u>.

Figure 2-6
2D plans are created in LayOut using a 3D SketchUp model.

The following is a list of the files that are included with the book:

Sample Project

The book follows through a sample project from start to finish. You can download the completed project at **<u>www.sketchupbook.com/files</u>** so you can explore the files and see how they are put together.

SketchUp sample files

✓ MC364_Building.skp, MC364_Site.skp, MC364_RCP.skp, MC364_Sections.skp, MC364_Interior Elevations.skp

LayOut sample files

✓ MC364_0_cover.LayOut, MC364_A0_Data.LayOut, MC364_A0_Perspective.LayOut, MC364_A1_Site.LayOut, MC364_A2_Floor plans.LayOut, MC364_A2_

MC364_Reflected ceiling plans.LayOut, MC364_A2_Schedules.LayOut, MC364 A3_Elevations.LayOut, MC364 A4_Assemblies.LayOut, MC364 A5_Interior Elevations.LayOut, A8_Exterior Details.LayOut, A9_Interior Details.LayOut, MPE0_General.LayOut, MPE2_Lighting Plans.LayOut, MPE2_Power & Signal. LayOut

Template Files

In addition to the sample files, you will be given a set of blank SketchUp and LayOut template files that you can customize and use on your own projects. The use of templates is key to this workflow, so you will need to download them in order to follow along in the book.

SketchUp template files

✓ Building.skp, Site.skp, RCP.skp, Sections.skp, Interior Elevations.skp

LayOut template files

✓ 0_cover.LayOut, A0_Data.LayOut, A0_Perspective.LayOut, A1_Site.LayOut, A2_Floor plans.LayOut, A2_Reflected ceiling plans.LayOut, A2_Schedules.LayOut, A3_Elevations.LayOut, A4_Assemblies.LayOut, A5_Interior Elevations.LayOut, A8_Exterior Details.LayOut, A9_Interior Details.LayOut, MPE0_General.LayOut, MPE2_Lighting Plans.LayOut, MPE2_Power & Signal.LayOut

SketchUp Template Files

- Building.skp
- Interior Elevations.skp
- RCP.skp
- Sections.skp
- Site.skp

LayOut Template Files

- 0_Cover.layout
- A0_Data.layout
- A0_Perspectives.layout
- A1_Site.layout
- A2_Floor plans.layout
- A2_Reflected ceiling plans.layout
- A2_schedules.layout
- A3_Elevations.layout
- A3_Sections.layout
- A4_Assemblies.layout
- A5_Interior Elevations.layout
- A8_Exterior Details.layout
- A9_Interior Details.layout
- MPE0_General.layout
- MPE2_Lighting plans.layout
- MPE2_Power & Signal plans.layout

Figure 2-7
SketchUp and LayOut template files provided with book.

Why SketchUp?

The problem with traditional 2D CAD is that you sometimes lose touch with the overall design because you are forced to think from the perspective of flat construction documents. The restrictions of the documentation requirements and the technical limitations of the software take priority over the design itself.

Designing in 3D gives you the freedom to visualize how the project will look in real life. The design becomes the primary focus, and the construction documents become a by-product of the design. That is the way it should be.

There are plenty of 3D design programs out there that automate much of the process of designing a building, but you sacrifice the design once again because you are forced to learn and abide by complicated technical processes in order to get the software to do what you want. Creating anything custom further complicates the process, or is simply not possible.

Where SketchUp shines is in its ability to create accurate 3D models quickly in an easy-to-use interface without forcing users to learn complicated tools or workflows. SketchUp has a unique way of prioritizing the design, and LayOut provides the conduit to communicate your design on paper.

This book reviews the entire project workflow for a custom home in Truckee, California. This project was selected because of its complexity and high standards required by California building code. While your projects may not require the same type of documentation as this project, you will be able to see just how capable SketchUp and LayOut are at designing complex construction projects.

Overview

A project takes shape throughout six distinct phases of design: Pre-Design, Schematic Design, Design Development, Construction Documentation, Bidding negotiation, and Construction Administration. This book will focus on the phases where SketchUp and LayOut are implemented: Schematic Design, Design Development, and Construction Documentation. Each project starts with plenty of design flexibility and becomes more refined as you get further into the project.

Design Phases

1. **Schematic Design Phase** - At the start of the project, general design ideas are gathered by the design team and the client. Hand sketches may be used to communicate the general design intent of the project and to define important preferences of the client. Then, the existing site conditions are modeled and an initial building model is created. An existing site plan, conceptual floor plans, and several perspective views of the model will be exported and presented to the client at this phase.

2. **Design Development Phase** - Once a general design is developed, it is further refined and detailed. Several documents are created as required by the specific project. Throughout this phase, feedback is collected from the client and the SketchUp model and LayOut drawings evolve.

3. **Construction Documentation Phase** - In this phase, the project is refined even further, and details are finalized as the rest of the construction documents are created.

The Schematic Design phase sets the pace for the rest of the project. Both the SketchUp model and LayOut files evolve through each following phase. A significant amount of the book dedicated to an organized and successful start in Schematic Design.

The whole point of this workflow is to reduce the number of technical obstacles that get in your way when you are trying to design. The simplicity and organized nature of this process allows for revisions to be made easily. You continue to build upon the existing models and documents you create as you progress through the project. You are never starting from scratch as you progress into the next phase of design. (**Figure 3-1**)

An important thing to note is that each phase of design requires new LayOut documents to be created, while other times you are just updating documents that you have already created from a previous phase. For example, you will create floor plans in Schematic Design, but you will not add dimensions to the floor plans until you get to the Design Development phase.

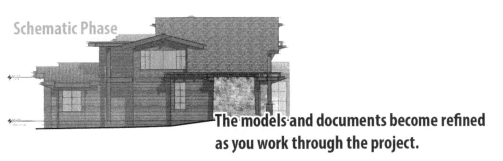

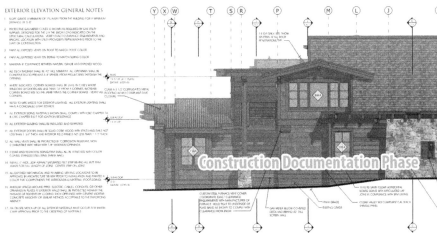

Figure 3-1
Each phase of design builds upon the files from the previous phase.

The book is laid out to guide you through Schematic Design step by step, showing you how to start with your existing site model, create existing site plans, then create your schematic model of the building.

When you get to Design Development, the book will focus on specific examples of the level of detail required in the model for this phase of design. You won't see the types of documents required in Design Development, since it varies for each project and location. Instead, all of the LayOut documents prepared after the Schematic Design phase will be discussed in the Construction Documentation chapters.

Project Organization

When you first learned how to use SketchUp, you modeled a project all within a single SketchUp file. However, in this workflow, a completed project will be made up of **multiple SketchUp models, and multiple LayOut documents.** There are many advantages to working in this manner, but it mainly comes down to file size, organization, speed, and convenience.

✓ You can take advantage of preconfigured templates customized to the specific type of model or document you are creating.

✓ The file size of each individual model and document will be greatly reduced, allowing for better speed and performance, greater flexibility in filesharing, and it gives you the ability to delegate parts of the project to other members on your team.

✓ It is much easier to access individual drawings for revisions and updates. Exporting individual PDF files based upon the discipline required is very easy.

✓ Your SketchUp models will be more organized by limiting the number of scenes to only those that are relevant to the specific type of model you are working on.

✓ Section cut organization is easier, because section cuts will be contained within separate SketchUp models, keeping your main model clutter free.

There are some disadvantages to splitting your model into multiple files. It will require more organization just to simply keep track of the different files, you will have to copy redundant job information in LayOut for your title blocks, and exporting files and combining documents will be more tedious. But it is simply too complicated to confine a project of this magnitude and detail to one LayOut file and one SketchUp file.

When you use multiple files for each project, patterns start to emerge with each new project. By standardizing your workflow, templates can be used in both SketchUp and LayOut to reduce the amount of time you spend setting up and configuring the project. This provides you even more time to focus on the design, and less time fussing with software.

Templates have become a critical part of the workflow, and you can download a complete set of SketchUp and LayOut templates with the book for you to use and follow along. Let's take a closer look at the templates included in the book, what they will do for you, and how to work with them.

Starting With a Template

When talking about SketchUp and LayOut templates, we are actually not referring to the feature which allows you to select a template when you first open SketchUp or LayOut. What is preferred is to have a sample folder on your computer that contains a set of files needed for a project which you can copy and paste into a new project folder. When you begin the project, you just open the files you copied from the sample folder.

> **TIP** The disadvantage of using a genuine template (you can create your own by going to **File > Save As Template**) is that once you have created a new file from template, you then need to go **File > Save As**, navigate to your project folder, type in a name, then save. When you are creating a single file, this is no big deal. But when you have multiple files which require you to do this, it can become very tedious.

By simply copying a set of files from one folder to another, you have gotten everything done in one shot, and the files are already named appropriately. It just saves a lot of time when you have multiple files which make up a single project.

In SketchUp, each template model should include the following features: (Figure 3-2)

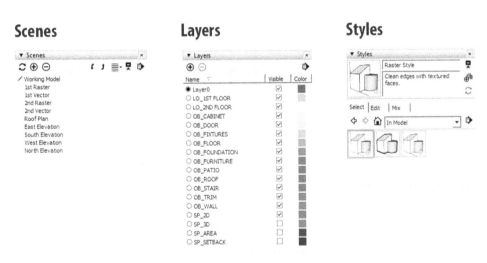

Figure 3-2 Templates should include default scenes, layers and styles.

What should be included in a SketchUp template or a LayOut template? In general, you want to include any elements that you know will appear in every project. But you also want to include things like scenes, layers, section cuts and styles in order to reduce any redundant work that would be required on every project.

✓ **Preconfigured scenes** - These scenes might include utility scenes that recall your optimum settings for modeling, such as a certain style, layer visibility, and camera position. SketchUp scenes are also critical for setting up viewports in LayOut. Scenes save camera view, style, section cuts, layers, and other settings. You will need to create at least one scene for each viewport in LayOut. Saving scenes in a template for viewports that occur on every project can save you a lot of time.

✓ **Preconfigured styles** - Your template SketchUp model should include the styles that you are most likely to use in your project. Styles are what define the look of your model, including edges, faces, and background. You should not have to recreate styles every time you start a new project. (Styles can also be saved on your computer for future use, and do not necessarily need to be saved in a template.)

✓ **Section cuts** - Some section cuts are identical from job to job, and you might be able to have some pre-existing section cuts strategically placed within your model templates. They might require a little nudge here or there, but the bulk of the work will be completed.

✓ **Layers** - Include default layers appropriate to the type of model the template represents. Layers help you organize the visibility of objects within your model.

In LayOut, you will want to include the following features in your templates: (Figure 3-3)

Figure 3-3
Temporary guide boxes are helpful for aligning viewports and other objects.

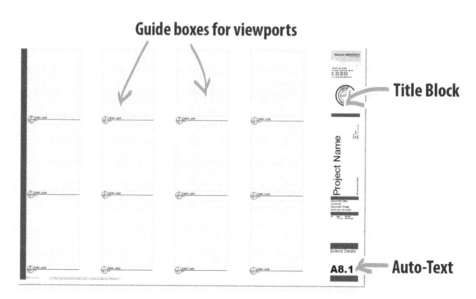

Guide boxes for viewports

Title Block

Project Name

Auto-Text

✓ **Title block** - The title block is perhaps the most obvious thing to include in your template. Although project specific information will need to be copied into each file, page names, guides, and detail labels can typically be prepopulated.

✓ **Auto-Text Tags** - Auto-Text Tags can be used to automate text boxes in LayOut, such as dates, page numbers, page names, file name, and other custom variables.

✓ **General notes, schedules** - If there are specific notes or schedules that occur on every page set in your documents, include them in your template file or scrapbook so they are always available.

✓ **Styles** - You can preconfigure the default tool settings for text, shapes, dimensions and labels so that they will be ready to go when you create your new document.

✓ **Guides** - Use shapes to create guides to help you snap viewports to. This can help you keep a consistent layout among all of your documents, and help you insert viewports faster.

Figure 3-4
LayOut floor plan templates.

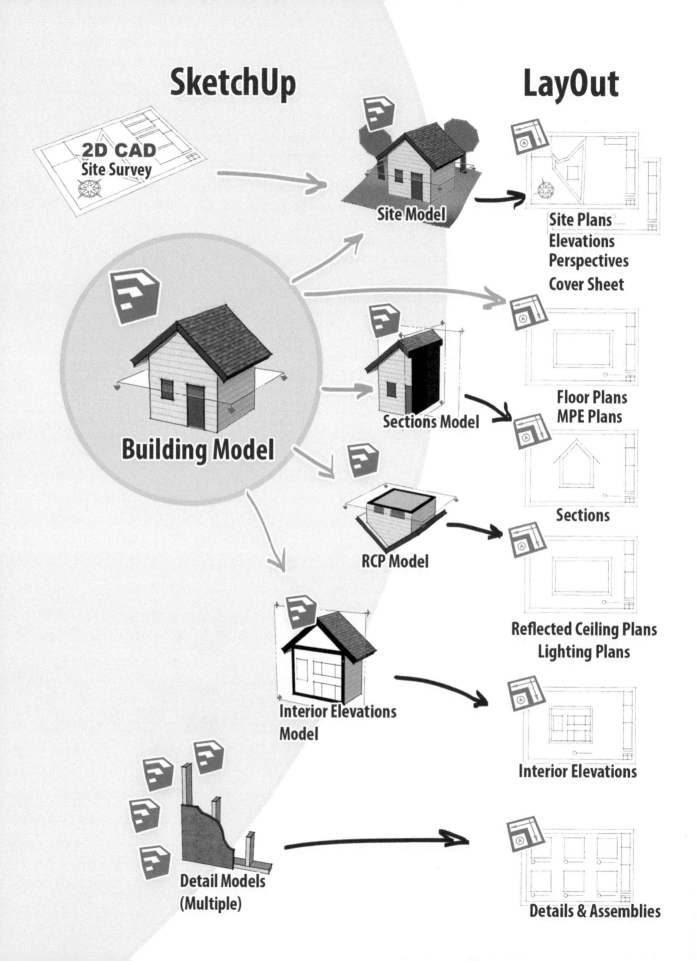

SketchUp

LayOut

2D CAD
Site Survey

Site Model

Building Model

Sections Model

RCP Model

Interior Elevations
Model

Detail Models
(Multiple)

Site Plans
Elevations
Perspectives
Cover Sheet

Floor Plans
MPE Plans

Sections

Reflected Ceiling Plans
Lighting Plans

Interior Elevations

Details & Assemblies

Project Map

The image on the left shows a general overview of the various files used in a single project and how they relate to each other. The SketchUp models you will use in your project have specific scenes to generate the viewports that are inserted into each LayOut document. Each SketchUp template has a specific purpose and has many presets in place to save you time.

✓ **Building Model** -The building model is your main SketchUp model that contains the building and all the elements inside it. This model does not include any of the site elements; **it is only the building** itself. This model will be used to create many viewports directly in LayOut, including the floor plans and power & signal plans.

The building model is also imported into many other SketchUp models as a component to prepare additional scenes for other types of LayOut documents. Whenever the building model is imported, **it is never edited from inside that model**. You must always revert back to the original building model to make changes, then reload it into the other models. You will review much more on this later on.

✓ **Site Model** - The site model includes the terrain, utilities, site survey data, and landscaping. The building model is imported into the site model and placed on the lot precisely at the location and elevation where the building will be constructed.

The site model is used to create viewports in LayOut for the existing site plans, site analysis, site plans, cover sheet, perspectives, and some details.

✓ **Sections Model** - This model is used to generate sections of the building. It is preconfigured with various section planes aligned in different directions for you to import the building model into and move the section plans to intersect with the building at the desired location.

✓ **Reflected Ceiling Plan Model** - The reflected ceiling plan model (or RCP model) has the building model imported into it and flips it vertically in order to create the proper reflected orientation. It includes section cuts in it to be used in the lighting plans in LayOut. The RCP model template is set up with section cuts already in place that you will adjust to the correct height needed, depending upon your model.

✓ **Interior Elevations Model** - This model has the imported building model and does not contain any additional geometry. Its main purpose is to provide a clean model environment to place section cuts into and to save scenes for the interior sections you will need in LayOut.

✓ **Detail Models (MULTI)** - Multiple detail models will be created on an as-needed basis in order to illustrate the various construction assemblies in your project. Over time you will build your own library of typical construction details that you will be able to use on multiple projects. In other situations you might need to create a project-specific detail or use your building model to show a specific part of the model to create a detail viewport in LayOut.

As you can see, the most important model is the building model, because it is being imported into most of the other models you are creating. When you import the building model into another file, you do not ever edit the building from within the model it was imported. You always want to go back to the original building model, make your edits there; then you can update the model reference in all of the models in which you have imported the building. More information on this will be provided in a later chapter.

LayOut Files

Figure 3-5
LayOut
template
files
included
with this
book.

LayOut Template Files

- 0_Cover.layout
- A0_Data.layout
- A0_Perspectives.layout
- A1_Site.layout
- A2_Floor plans.layout
- A2_Reflected ceiling plans.layout
- A2_schedules.layout
- A3_Elevations.layout
- A3_Sections.layout
- A4_Assemblies.layout
- A5_Interior Elevations.layout
- A8_Exterior Details.layout
- A9_Interior Details.layout
- MPE0_General.layout
- MPE2_Lighting plans.layout
- MPE2_Power & Signal plans.layout

There is a separate LayOut file for each page set in a project (**Figure 3-5**). By having separate documents for each type of page you need, you will have the opportunity to customize the template more specifically to the type of page you are creating. For instance, you can place general notes, guides to help align viewports, detail markers, and other elements that typically occur on that page set. This will save you time on each project because these elements will already be in place, reducing the amount of overall work required for a project.

✓ **Cover** - This LayOut document will contain your cover page. You might want the title block to look slightly different than the interior pages of your other documents, so set up the template to reflect that.

✓ **Project Data** - The project data sheet contains boilerplate information such as abbreviations, but also specific information such as design team contact info, sheet index, building area and site coverage info.

✓ **Exterior Perspectives** - This LayOut template includes multiple pages showing exterior perspective viewports of your site plan model.

✓ **Site Plans** - Another multi-page document, the site plan LayOut file includes viewports of your site model and communicates information such as property lines, building orientation, elevations, contours, grading, utilities, landscaping, etc.

✓ **Floor Plans** - The floor plans document will contain floor plans for each floor of your building, as well as the roof plan. The viewports in this model will be created directly from scenes of the main building model. One page will be used for each floor plan generated.

✓ **Reflected Ceiling Plans** - The reflected ceiling plans will show a mirrored view of the ceilings in plan view. The viewports are created from a special SketchUp model which imports the building model and generates the reflected ceiling scenes.

✓ **Door & Window Schedules** - This LayOut document is created entirely in LayOut, and does not show any SketchUp model viewports in it. By using the annotation tools in LayOut, you will manually create the window and door schedules for your project. After creating a schedule, save it in a scrapbook for future use.

✓ **Exterior Elevations** - Exterior elevations are created with viewports of the main building model, showing parallel projection views of each side of the building. The viewport is then annotated with column lines, elevation markers, section markers, and door & window labels.

✓ **Building Sections** - These pages show the various sections of the building, created from a special SketchUp model that contains section cuts of the building.

✓ **Assemblies** - The assemblies pages are created from a variety of different SketchUp models which show typical construction assemblies that occur throughout your project. Some of them may be customized specifically for this project, while others may be copied from a generic detail library.

✓ **Interior Elevations** - These pages are used to show elevations of the interior.

✓ **Exterior Details** - Multiple exterior details are shown in this page set. The details are created from multiple detail models, separate from the main project models.

✓ **Interior Details** - Multiple interior details are shown in this page set. The details are created from multiple detail models, separate from the main project models.

✓ **MPE General Notes** - The MPE (mechanical, plumbing, electrical) general notes sheet.

✓ **MPE Lighting Plans** - Reflected ceiling plan viewports are used on these pages, and lighting symbols and wiring diagrams are inserted from within LayOut.

✓ **MPE Plans** - The MPE (mechanical, plumbing, electrical) plans include floor plan viewports to show the placement of all electrical, plumbing, and mechanical equipment and connections.

These are all examples of typical pages found in a set of construction documents for a custom home. You may find that you do not need as much information, or that you need to create additional pages in order to fully communicate the design of the building or to meet requirements of your local building officials.

Before starting a project, you should go through the provided LayOut templates and customize them with your preferences and company information. This is information that will remain the same on every project, like your logo, company name, address, contact info, etc (**Figure 3-6**). You will find more detail on how to work in LayOut in a later chapter.

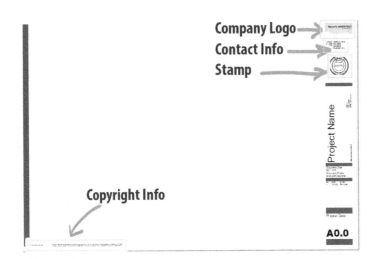

Figure 3-6
Customize
the provided
templates to
match your
company
info.

Once you have corrected the information on one title block, you can copy those objects to the other LayOut files. You may also find general notes that you would like to edit in the A0-Data.layout file, or on the A2-schedules.layout file. Explore each template and customize it to your own needs. The whole point is to make these your own.

Rendering

Rendering is the process of using a third-party software or plugin to create a more photorealistic image or animation of your 3D model using more advanced lighting physics than what is available in SketchUp alone. Renders can help convey a different sense of emotion and a more rich visualization of a design than what a standard SketchUp image or animation can achieve. (**Figure 3-7**)

In general, there are three types of renders that you can create:

✓ **Images** - Still shots captured from the render software that show your model under different lighting conditions.

✓ **Animations** - A preconfigured video animation of a fly-through of your model.

✓ **Live renders** - An interactive 3D render allowing users to navigate through the model in real time while seeing the lighting effects and other animated entourage.

While images and animations are great for capturing specific views of your model, live renders are great for allowing people to explore your model on their own. This is great not only for the project owner, but for building partners as well.

LumenRT, for example, can create a stand-alone exe file called a LiveCube, that can be sent to anyone who wants to navigate the model. It is great because there is no software to install; they just need a computer powerful enough to view it. Alternatively, you could send a SketchUp model directly and have them install the SketchUp viewer to view the model. (**www.sketchup.com/products/sketchup-viewer**)

There are a number of different rendering software packages available, each with a varying degree of cost, complexity, learning curve, and output. Here are a few examples, in no particular order:

- ✓ **Kerkythea** - **www.kerkythea.net**

- ✓ **V-Ray** - **www.chaosgroup.com**

- ✓ **Visualizer** - **www.getvisualizer.com**

- ✓ **Thea Render** - **www.thearender.com**

- ✓ **Twilight** - **www.twilightrender.com**

✓ **LumenRT** - <u>www.lumenrt.com</u>

✓ **Lumion** - <u>www.lumion3D.com</u>

✓ **Supodium** - <u>www.suplugins.com</u>

Level of Detail

Do you model all the nails in your building? Probably not. That is unnecessary information to include in the model. It is below the level of detail required for your drawings. But where do you draw the line? How do you define a clear level of detail for your model? In a set of construction drawings, you will need to show a few different levels of detail.

Imagine having to model every single stud, sheet of plywood, and shingle on a building. How long would it take you to move a window over a few inches?

One of the most valuable concepts you should learn from this book is how to define the level of detail required in your models. The less complicated your model is, the easier it is to create and change. On the other hand, a basic model is ugly, and does not communicate your design intent well enough.

You need to find a balance. The first step to figuring out the level of detail is to think about what information needs to be communicated in the current set of drawings you are working on.

Defining Level of Detail

The best way to keep your project simple and flexible is by modeling to the lowest level of detail acceptable. The level of detail required on a set of drawings will be determined by what scale the viewport is set to, what dimensions need to be communicated, and what visual elements need to be included in order to fully define the design intent.

Imagine a plan set to a 1/4" scale. At this scale, certain details are simply too small to discern, so they should be omitted. For instance, consider a wall assembly, with siding, sheathing, studs, and interior gypsum board modeled. If you viewed a section cut of a wall shown at 1/4" scale, you would not be able to distinguish the edges that make up the sheathing or the wall studs. Depending upon the thickness of your edges, they may even appear as one thick line.

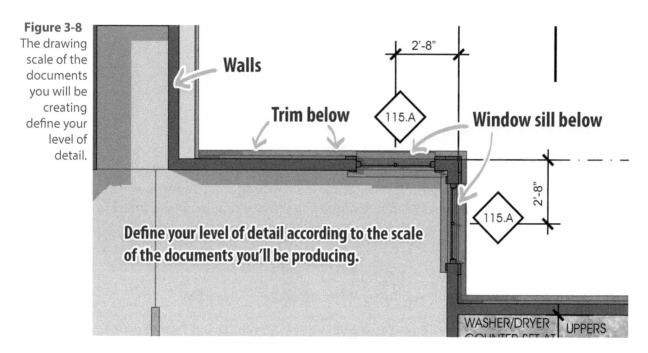

At this scale, it is simply unnecessary to show that much detail because you can not see it. You also need to consider what dimensions need to be communicated on the drawings. Since the framing crew will need to reference the plans in order to build the structure of the building, the model should represent the rough framing dimensions of the building. In the case of the walls, you should represent them as a single extruded rectangle equal to the thickness of the wall framing.

That means you are not going to draw the studs, the plywood, or the wall finishes, you are just going to show one simple extruded rectangle for the walls (**Figure 3-8**). What if you need to show construction details set to a larger scale? Build separate construction detail models with a higher level of detail.

The level of detail also becomes more refined as you move through a project. In Schematic Design, your model will be very conceptual. As you progress into Design Development, the model will become much more detailed as design decisions are being finalized.

When you get to sections of this book that describe how to model specific parts of a building, you will see illustrations that compare the level of detail of the SketchUp model with what that assembly looks like in real life. Apply these examples to other parts of the building to determine your own acceptable level of detail while modeling.

Separating Detail Models

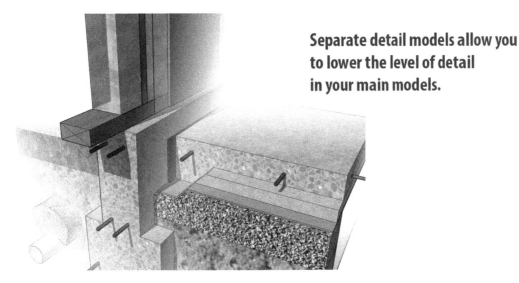

Separate detail models allow you to lower the level of detail in your main models.

Figure 3-9
Detail models can be used to illustrate construction assemblies.

The easiest way to enable a lower level of detail in your main model is to start using separate detail models when you require construction assembly drawings. A detail model is a small model that contains an example construction assembly. You illustrate it in a "cut-away" sort of fashion, to reveal each part of the assembly. (**Figure 3-9**)

Having separate detail models gives you more flexibility in creating sections, because you can actually model the cut-away instead of trying to use section cuts or clever workarounds to reveal the detail in your main model.

Over time you will build a collection of detail models that you can reuse for new projects. If a specific project calls for a slightly different detail, you can make a copy of that model specifically for that project and customize it as needed.

Organization

An efficient project workflow depends on a well organized SketchUp model. Model organization is managed through the use of layers, groups, and components. Layers let you control the visibility of objects, while groups and components manage the structure of the objects in your model.

Layer Principles

In SketchUp, layers behave much differently than other types of programs you may have used. If you have used layers in other programs such as Photoshop or AutoCAD, you understand that layers help organize a project, toggle visibility, and help prevent accidental changes to objects by locking or hiding a layer. They also limit the scope of object manipulation to one layer at a time.

In 2D, you can think of layers as sheets of transparent paper stacked on top of each other. By changing the active layer, you change which "sheet of paper" you are drawing on or manipulating. This is really useful because you can hide layers you are not working on in order to isolate certain parts of the project, and you can prevent objects on other layers from being inadvertently edited.

LayOut works very similar to this idea, with the added benefit of being able to use shared layers, which give you the option of displaying the same objects on all pages in your project. Perfect for creating title blocks.

In SketchUp, layers behave much differently. **SketchUp layers only affect object visibility.** So, if you have two sets of entities assigned to different layers, all of the entities have the potential of being affected by modifications you make to the model, regardless of whether or not one of the layers is hidden. Layers do not protect entity structure; they only toggle entity visibility.

In order to protect the structure of various collections of entities in your model, you need to use groups and components. You can create a group or component by selecting a set of entities (faces, edges, groups, components, etc.), then **right-clicking** > **Make Group** or **Make Component**. Then you can assign those groups and components to different layers in your model in order to have control over their visibility. Layers are assigned to objects from the **Entity Info dialog** layers dropdown menu.

Copies of components are identical to each other. Any changes made to one are duplicated in all other instances of that component. Groups, however, are unique to each other. If you copy a group and make a change to it, the original group is unaffected. Components are ideal for objects that you know will repeat throughout your model. For example, balusters, light fixtures, trees, etc.

> **TIP** Since layers do not protect the structure of entities that are assigned to them, you should always have layer0 set as the active layer and only assign layers to groups and components that you create.

Layer Naming

As you browse through all of the SketchUp templates provided with the book, you will notice a pattern to the layer names in each model. Layers start with a two-letter prefix, followed by an underscore, then a descriptive name. Layers are categorized into three major layer types in order to organize the list of layers and make it easier to understand the layer's purpose. (**Figure 3-10**)

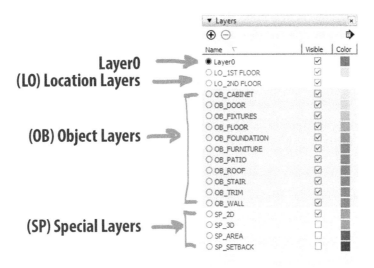

Figure 3-10
The three types of layers used in the provided templates.

✓ **(LO) Location Layers** - These are parent layers that are used to collect sub-groups and components into a defined location, level, area, or phase. Location layers are helpful when working on multi-level buildings because you can quickly hide the 2nd floor while you work on the 1st floor, for example. Location layers can also be used to represent different phases of construction, such as existing, demolition, and new construction.

✓ **(OB) Object Layers** - Anything assigned to an object layer represents a physical 3D object in the model. Example object layers include OB_TREE, OB_WALLS, OB_TERRAIN, etc.

✓ **(SP) Special Layers** - All other layers are categorized as Special layers. These layers represent construction boundaries, or anything else that does not represent a physical object in the model. You may use a special layer to assign entities such as guides, labels, dimensions, or any other special SketchUp object.

This layer-naming convention is very flexible, allowing you to customize it to your own needs. When creating layers, think of them in terms of categories instead of individual objects. Consider how you would want to control the visibility of different types of objects, then create layers for them.

Assigning Layers

When assigning layers, there is a typical hierarchy of groups that are created in order to help in the process of assigning layers. You are probably most familiar with using groups and components to collect loose entities, but groups can also be used for the sole purpose of collecting other groups or components to assign them to a single layer.

With the building model, for example, the building should be divided up into the main LO layers, to define each level of the building. Within each location group, you should have multiple groups that are assigned to the appropriate object type layer. Each of the object type groups should contain all the groups of that object type. (**Figure 3-11**)

Figure 3-11
Use a series of parent groups assigned to LO layers to organize your models sub-groups.

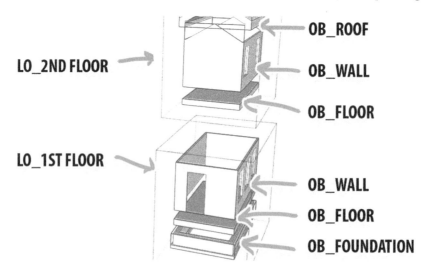

LO_2ND FLOOR → OB_ROOF, OB_WALL, OB_FLOOR

LO_1ST FLOOR → OB_WALL, OB_FLOOR, OB_FOUNDATION

In other words, instead of selecting each roof group and assigning them to the OB_ROOF layer one by one, leave them assigned to layer0, but place them inside a parent group and assign that to OB_ROOF. Now, instead of having multiple groups in your model assigned to the same layer, you have a single parent group assigned to it. If you ever need to add another roof group to the model, just enter the parent OB_ROOF group, and the layer assignment will be inherited from the parent group. (**Figure 3-12**)

Figure 3-12
Parent groups can pass down layer assignment to child groups.

All objects located on a specific building level are grouped together, assigned to an LO layer.

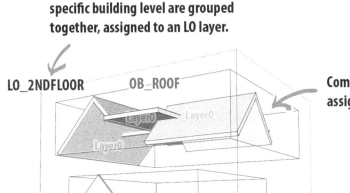

LO_2NDFLOOR   OB_ROOF

Common objects grouped together, assigned to an OB layer.

OB=WALL

Using a layering system like this provides you much more flexibility and control over visibility, while reducing redundant layers. For example, instead of duplicating object layers for each level of the building (1stfloorwalls, 2ndfloorwalls, 3rdfloorwalls), You just use a single object type layer (OB_WALL), and place the group within the appropriate location layer group(LO_1ST FLOOR or LO_2ND FLOOR or LO_3RD FLOOR).

It is important to note that you should not get hung up on layer assignments while you are modeling. It is ok if you do not assign everything to a layer at the moment you model it. Constant interruption can hinder creativity, so do not worry about it at first. Just make sure you are actively creating groups and components with the layer structure in mind.

Take a break from modeling once you get to a certain point and go through the model and make sure everything is assigned to the correct layer. Alternating between modeling and organizing is a perfectly acceptable way to model.

Outliner

The **Outliner panel** shows you every group and component in your model. You can access the **Outliner panel** under **Window > Default Tray > Outliner (Window > Outliner on Mac)**. The Outliner can be used to navigate through the various groups and components in your model, but it is most useful if you rename the groups to something descriptive so you can identify them by name.

In the sample files provided, you will notice that most of the parent groups have been renamed to match the layer they have been assigned to so you can navigate the model from the **Outliner panel (Figure 3-13)**. Many of the screen shots in the book also show a well labeled Outliner. In reality, when working on an architectural project like this, the Outliner is rarely used to navigate the project, so it is not worth spending the time to label groups and components.

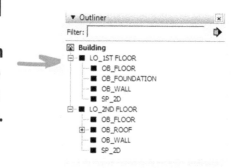

Figure 3-13
Parent groups have been renamed to match the layers they are assigned to.

As long as you organize your model well enough and assign your groups and components to the appropriate layers, you will be able to navigate your model very easily by interacting directly with the model and toggling layer visibility.

The only time you need to label groups and components is when you are modeling something in SketchUp that has unique parts which make up an assembly that does not have an obvious layer category. For example, if you were modeling a custom cabinet, you could rename each group or component to describe which part of the cabinet it is. In this case, it would not make sense to create a layer for each part of the cabinet to assign to a single group or component, so it is preferred to use the Outliner directly for organization.

Keyboard Shortcuts

SketchUp and LayOut both offer the ability to speed up your workflow by using keyboard shortcuts to activate certain tools and actions. It is worth training yourself to use these keyboard shortcuts to activate tools instead of clicking on the tool icon, or activating it through the menus. With keyboard shortcuts, you just tap a specific letter or combination on the keyboard to activate a certain tool.

After a little practice, they become second nature. You will rest your left hand on the keyboard, and the right hand on the mouse, ready to activate any tool you need. (Opposite if you are left handed, of course.)

To help you learn the default keyboard shortcuts, they are noted throughout the book in parenthesis every time a tool is mentioned. The tool's icon is also placed in the margin and all tools are mentioned in **bold** to help with recognition.

For example, if the **Push/Pull tool (P)** is mentioned, you will see the icon, the keyboard shortcut, and the tool name for easy identification. If the tool does not have a keyboard shortcut by default, there will be no letter in parenthesis.

Custom Keyboard Shortcuts

SketchUp and LayOut both allow you to define your own custom keyboard shortcuts. It is recommended to set up a few custom shortcuts in SketchUp in order make common actions quick to execute.

To define a custom SketchUp keyboard shortcut, follow these steps: (Figure 3-14)

1. In SketchUp, go to **Window > Preferences > Shortcuts (SketchUp > Preferences > Shortcuts on Mac).**

2. In the **Filter field**, start typing in the name of the tool or action you would like to assign a shortcut to, until you see it appear in the list. Select the tool or action in the list.

3. Type in a letter or combination of letters into the **Add Shortcut field**, then click the **Plus** button.

4. Click **Ok** to finish.

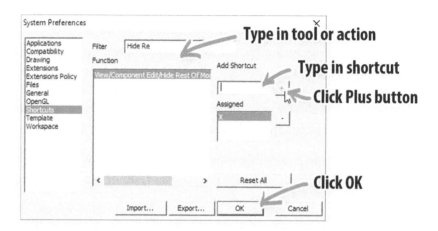

The following custom keyboard shortcuts are very handy to have configured:

✓ **View > Edit > Hide Rest of Model** - Assign this view toggle to the letter **X**. This toggles the visibility of the rest of your model while you are editing a group or component. It is very useful to be able to switch back and forth from this view.

✓ **Edit > Paste in Place** - Assign **CTRL+SHIFT+V** (**Command+SHIFT+V** on Mac) to Paste in Place. You will use this command quite a bit to move objects in and out of groups and components without changing their physical location in model space.

Add your own custom keyboard shortcuts for tools that you use most often.

Before you begin modeling your design ideas, you should first begin by modeling what currently exists on site. Understanding the project site is essential to a successful architectural solution. Modeling the site first allows you to become familiar with the site's features and constraints. The existing site model is an important starting point for your project.

In this section of the book you will learn how to create the existing site model and build an existing site plan in LayOut.

Objectives

Schematic Design starts with an assessment of all existing site conditions. Modeling these constraints gives you a basic canvas to start your design. With the site model and site plans created, you can then start the schematic model of the building.

The main objectives of the existing site model are as follows:

✓ Assess existing site conditions, then create a model of the existing site.

✓ Import site survey info into SketchUp and LayOut.

✓ Configure site plan LayOut template for future phases of design.

✓ Generate existing site plans in LayOut.

✓ Use existing site plans to brainstorm design ideas for the building.

Site Plan

You will create an existing site model in SketchUp using information from your site survey, and you will generate an existing site plan in LayOut. You will use this set of plans to help design the floor plan of your building and to build your model. The existing site model will eventually be transformed into the proposed site model, and you will add your building model to it.

Figure 4-1
Existing site plan and analysis.

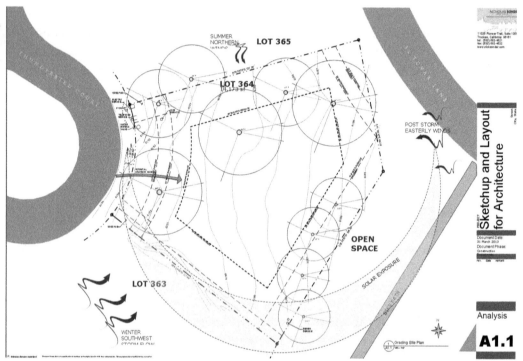

You can also create a site plan analysis, as pictured above (**Figure 4-1**). A site analysis takes into account prevailing winds, sun exposure, and other environmental influences on the site.

Predesign Information

When starting any project, you typically have a number of constraints established. These are things like property lines, setbacks, site characteristics, zoning restrictions, utilities, adjacent or existing construction, trees, roads, view direction, etc. Local, state, and national building codes also have an impact on design, along with schedule and budget.

In addition to existing site constraints, you will want to discover what your client's expectations and requirements are so that you can incorporate them into your design. Find out what is important to them and what they would like to see in the design of their building.

Site Survey

The site survey is an assessment and measurement of a number of features on the project site. The existing site conditions will play a major part in the design of the building. Typically, you would hire a surveyor to conduct the survey and generate the survey documents for you (**Figure 4-2**).

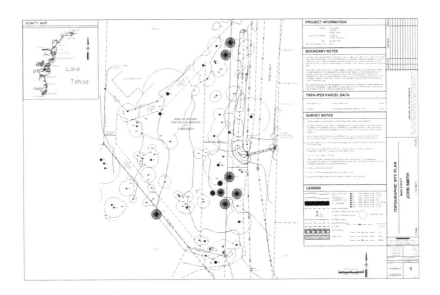

Figure 4-2
A sample site survey showing contour lines, trees, and site boundaries.

Your surveyor should be able to provide a CAD file survey of which you will be able to import into SketchUp. It is highly recommended that you use this CAD file to import into SketchUp, but if you only have access to a paper copy of a survey, you can use that too. You will have to import it into SketchUp as an image, and manually recreate the entities. You will learn how to work with each file type in the next section.

The site survey will be used to build your existing site model. The site survey should include the following information:

✓ **Property lines** - This is the boundary of the property.

✓ **Property setbacks** - These are boundaries defined by local zoning to establish a minimum setback from the property line from which you can build.

✓ **Site contours** - Contour lines represent the elevations of the terrain. You will use this information to produce the 3D terrain in SketchUp.

✓ **Roads** - Existing or planned roads are important to know because they will help you determine where the driveway needs to be located in relationship to the road and the building.

✓ **Utilities** - The location of utility hookups, along with any existing utility lines that run to the site.

✓ **Adjacent buildings** - You will need to know the location of any existing construction, so you can see how it will affect your project.

✓ **Trees** - Trees and other vegetation should be located on the site survey in order to indicate which trees are to be removed or preserved on the site.

✓ **View** - If the site has any particular view direction (mountains, waterfront), that should be noted on the survey as well, so you can take that into consideration while you design.

✓ **Compass** - North should be located on the site survey so you will be able to take the position of the sun into consideration with your design.

Client Program

Perhaps one of the most important pieces of information you need to collect is from your client. What are their expectations and requirements? What type of design do they like? Are there specific elements that they want to see in their project?

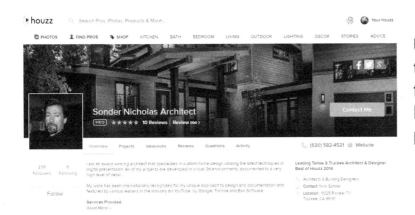

Use Houzz.com to collect ideas from clients to learn their style preferences.

Figure 4-3
Houzz.com profile page.

Things like family size, lifestyle, accessibility, architectural style preference, business needs, room size and building size are all things that should be discussed with your client prior to beginning design.

Sometimes it is hard for a client to communicate their preferences to you. One great strategy for helping a client identify what they want is to have them create an account on **Houzz.com.** Houzz is a website where people can browse thousands of pictures of buildings, and collect them into their own personal portfolio that they can share with you (**Figure 4-3**).

This is a great way for you to identify their preferences, and to open a discussion about the design of their project.

Other Information

In addition to the site survey and the client program, there is other information that you may need to collect, depending upon the project.

For instance, you may require a geotechnical report to investigate soil conditions, or you may need to conduct a hydrology study to determine how you need to manage runoff.

You will also want to discuss schedule and budget. It is not our goal in this book to teach you how to be an architect, so you will need to draw from your own experience on what information you need to make your design decisions. So let's focus back on the SketchUp side of things and start modeling the existing site model.

Starting a New Project

The first step to starting a new project is to create a new project folder on your computer. At this point, you should have downloaded the provided SketchUp and LayOut templates, and you should have already customized the LayOut template title blocks to match your company information.

Project Folder

You are going to simply copy the template folder, and paste it as a new project folder (**Figure 4-4**). The SketchUp and LayOut templates inside are now going to become the project files for your new project.

Figure 4-4
Copy your template folder each time you want to create a new project.

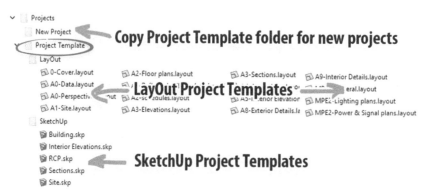

We are not going to tell you how to organize you project folders, as we are convinced that most people are set in their ways with how they handle that and you are likely to already have a system in place. So do not get hung up on the simplicity of what we are showing you here. You are likely to have other folders in your main project folder for submittals, subcontractors, exports, etc.

One quick thing worth mentioning is the importance of having a backup plan in place. Look into Window's File History feature, or Mac's Time Machine feature, which are both excellent, hands-off local backup solutions worth getting set up for hourly, daily, and weekly automated backups.

When you start a new project, it is perfectly normal to jump right into modeling, which is the topic of the next section. First, let's just review the LayOut templates so you can get the title block configured correctly for the project for each file.

Title Blocks

After making a copy of the templates for a project, the project name and client info will need to be copied between all of the template files for that project (**Figure 4-5**). The cover template title block is laid out differently than the interior pages, so you will need to fill in that information manually.

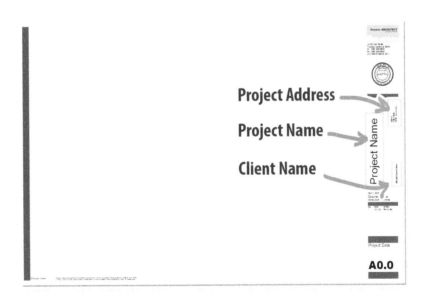

Figure 4-5
Title block information will need to be copied between all project LayOut documents.

To copy project info between templates, follow these steps: (Figure 4-6)

1. Open A0-Data.layout, and **double-click** on each text box that you need to change and type in the project info. Tap ESC to apply the changes in each text box.

2. Drag a selection box from right to left over the text boxes that you need to copy. Press CTRL+C (Command+C on Mac) to copy them.

3. Open another template that needs the project info. Drag a selection box over the text boxes you need to replace, then tap **DELETE**.

4. Press **CTRL+V** (**Command+V** on Mac) to paste the text boxes from the first template into this one. (Notice how they paste into the same layer and location on the page.) Repeat this process for each project template. Since you are pasting elements onto the shared layer TITLEBLOCK, you only need to paste them onto one page, since shared layers display the same elements on all pages.

Figure 4-6
How to copy and paste title block information between documents.

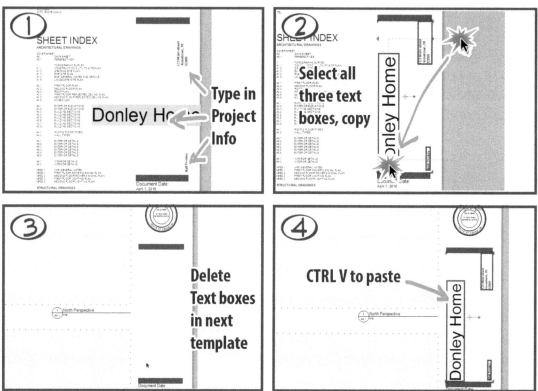

Page numbers will change automatically, and page names will display whatever you type into the **Pages panel (Figure 4-7)**. This is done through the use of a LayOut feature called Auto-Text Tags, which will be reviewed in more detail in a later chapter. For now, just know that you do not need to edit those text boxes directly.

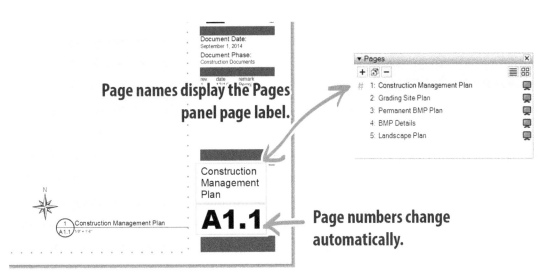

Figure 4-7
Page names and page numbers are controlled using Auto-Text Tags.

Once you have the project templates saved with the project specific information, they will be ready when you start to create the documents. This may feel redundant, but you only have to do it once per project. Creating separate LayOut files per project is very helpful, as explained before.

In the next section, you will begin the project model, so go ahead and save all your work and close down LayOut for now. You now get to work on the fun part of creating the model in SketchUp.

Existing Site Model

Once you have collected your predesign information, you can begin building the existing site model. Modeling the existing conditions is very helpful in giving you a canvas from which to begin your design. It will serve as a communication tool that you can use with your client in order to discuss the important elements of the design. It is also a vital part of the documentation package that you will eventually provide to your contractor as the existing site transforms to the developed site.

Your existing site model will include the following elements (Figure 4-8):

✓ 3D terrain of the existing site, generated from the site survey.

✓ Imported Google Earth geolocation, for accurate solar analysis and confirmation of site characteristics.

✓ Existing trees on site represented as 3D components.

✓ Roads

✓ Edges to represent property lines, setbacks, utilities, etc.

Figure 4-8
A completed existing site model with imported site survey entities, 3D terrain, and trees.

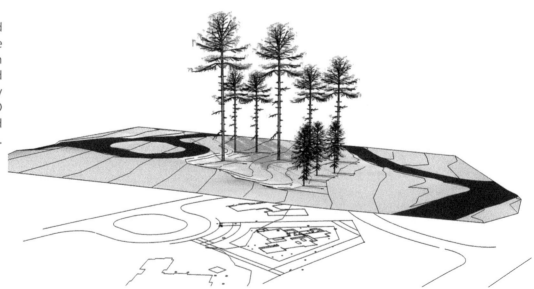

Once you have created this site model, you will send it to LayOut to create your site plan. Nick likes to model the existing site first, as it helps him become familiar with the site features, optimizing his time on the first site visit.

Do not underestimate the importance of the site model. The level of detail and accuracy invested into the site model now will pay off down the road since most issues during construction tend to be related to the site.

SketchUp Site Model

To begin, open the site model template **Site.skp** that you copied into your new project folder. This template will include all the necessary layers for the various elements you will be importing from the site survey (**Figure 4-9**). It will have scenes preconfigured that you will bring into LayOut to generate the existing site plans. We will review the scenes when it comes time to prepare the model for LayOut, so for now let's just take a look at the layers included in the template.

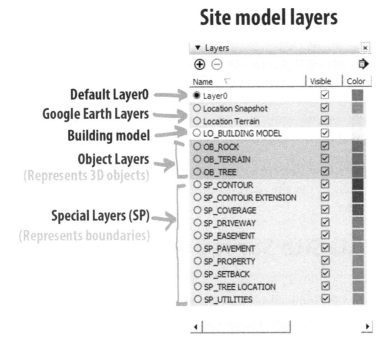

Figure 4-9
Site model template layers.

✓ **Layer0** - The default SketchUp layer, which should always be active.

✓ **Google Earth layers** - These are the layers that the Google Earth terrain will be assigned to when you geolocate your model.

✓ **LO_Building Model** - When the building model is imported onto the site, you will assign it to this layer for easy visibility control of the entire building.

✓ **Object layers** - All physical objects such as 3D terrain, trees, and rocks are assigned to an object layer. Add more object layers as needed if you are modeling additional object types.

✓ **Special layers** - Each site survey entity gets its own layer. Most of these layers represent boundaries on the site such as property lines, setbacks, and easements.

There are numerous SP layers in this template, which represent each boundary type that you will be importing from the site survey. Each boundary will be isolated in a scene that you will bring into LayOut as a viewport.

Now that you have a fresh site model to work in, you will start by importing the site survey. You can import either a CAD survey, or a scanned image or PDF. The process is different depending upon the resources available.

Ideally, you should have a site survey delivered to you from your surveyor in 3D CAD format. This will have each contour line elevated in 3D at the appropriate height. This will save you some work as you import it into SketchUp. A 2D CAD file will work too; you will just have to manually move the contour lines to the appropriate height in SketchUp. (Although, you should wait until you have created contour extensions before elevating the contours. You will learn more about this a little later on.)

If you do not have a CAD file of the site survey, you can model it from scratch, as long as you have a paper version of the site survey. Both methods of creating terrain in SketchUp will be reviewed next.

Importing CAD Site Survey

Before attempting to import a DWG file into SketchUp, it is usually best to open the file in a CAD program and do some cleanup to the file. SketchUp will automatically discard things such as dimensions, text, hatching, etc. It can help to purge any unused layers and delete all unnecessary entities that you will not be using in the SketchUp model. Take note of the DWG units, because you will need to tell SketchUp what unit of measurement in which to import the CAD file.

If you are unable to clean up the CAD file before importing into SketchUp, or would just prefer to do the cleanup in SketchUp, we will go over how to do that next. You might prefer cleaning up the CAD file in a blank SketchUp file first, then importing the results to your site template model. (This will prevent you from losing your template layers when you purge the model.)

To import a CAD survey into SketchUp, follow these steps: (Figure 4-10)

Step by Step

1. Inside SketchUp, go to **File > Import**.

2. Change the **Files of type** drop-down menu to select **AutoCAD Files** (*.dwg, *.dxf)

3. Click on **Options**. If you know the unit of measurement the CAD file was drawn in, you can select it in the **Units** drop-down menu. Do not worry if you are unsure; you can always double-check and scale the imported CAD once it is in SketchUp. However, **SketchUp will import more accurately if you select the correct scale during the import, as opposed to rescaling the model after importing.**

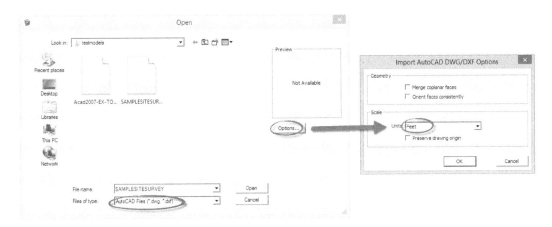

Figure 4-10
Import window and CAD import options

4. Select the CAD file you would like to import, and click **Open**.

5. Once the import is complete, you will see a summary window of what was imported, which you can close. If you do not see the imported entities in your workspace, press SHIFT+Z to zoom extents. (**Figure 4-11**)

Figure 4-11
CAD site
survey
imported
into
SketchUp.

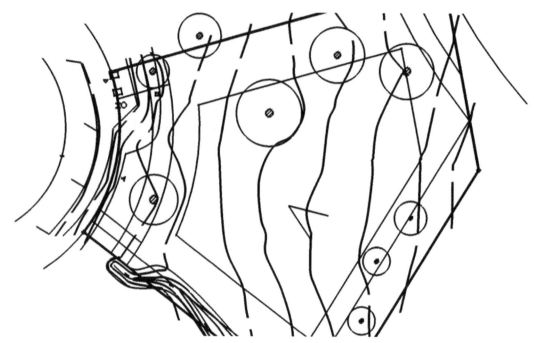

Once you have the survey imported to SketchUp, you need to verify that it is at the correct scale.

Step by Step

To scale an imported CAD file, follow these steps:

1. With the **Tape Measure tool** (**T**), measure a known dimension in the model. (Make sure you select endpoints, not edges when measuring.) Look at the **Measurements toolbar** in the bottom right corner to confirm that the imported CAD was scaled correctly.

2. If the scale is wrong, immediately type in the correct dimension, and press **ENTER.** If SketchUp asks if you want to change the scale of your model, click yes. (Alternatively, re-import the CAD file at the correct unit.)

TIP If you are ever in a situation where you want to only scale one object in your model, without affecting anything else, just make sure the object is in a group or component. If you use the Tape Measure scale method while inside a group or component, it will only affect the entities within it.

Organizing the Site Survey

After you have imported your site survey, you will need to spend a little bit of time working through your model and organizing the imported data. When you import a CAD file, all of the CAD layers come with it. What you will do is step through each element that you want to keep, then assign it to your own layer system.

Each CAD file is going to be different, so it would be impossible to show you how to organize every type of CAD file, but here are some common characteristics of an imported CAD file:

✓ When you import a CAD file, SketchUp automatically places all of the imported entities within a component. Within that component, everything will most likely exist as a loose entity, assigned to a layer. CAD blocks will be converted to components as well.

✓ You will likely have a big mess of entities all assigned to various layers. Since SketchUp layers do not protect geometry, you will need to isolate the entities from each CAD layer, and group them together.

✓ The imported layers are the key to determining what the elements represent. You should review the layer system with your surveyor, so you know what each one represents.

Color by Layer

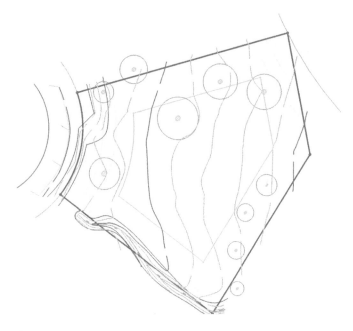

Before you begin organizing the imported CAD, it is helpful to make some changes to the SketchUp style, so that the edges are colored according to the layer that is assigned to them. (**Figure 4-12**)

To color edges by layer, follow these steps: (Figure 4-13)

1. Open the **Styles dialog**. **Window > Styles**.

2. Select the **Edit** tab, then select the **Edges button**.

3. Click the **Color** drop-down menu, and select "By Material".

4. Select the **Modeling** button, and check "Color by layer."

Review the colors assigned to each layer in the **Layers dialog. Be aware that if the layer color matches the color of your background, you will not be able to see the object.**

> **TIP** These are temporary overrides to your current style. If you would like to save the changes you have made to the style, or save this configuration as an entirely new style, you will need to click Update or Add New in the **Styles dialog**.

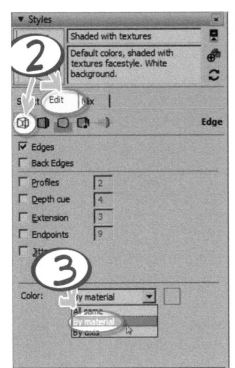
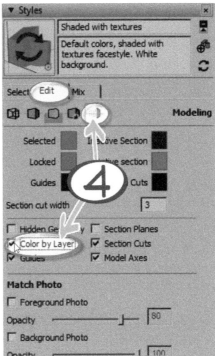

Purging the Model

Your CAD import may contain extraneous components, materials, and layers that add clutter to your model, so the next thing you will want to do is purge your model. **Although you can purge layers by clicking the details button in the Layers dialog, it will not eliminate layers that are used by any component definitions that have been imported.** The best way to purge your model is to use the **Model Info dialog**.

WARNING! - When you purge your model, you will lose any layers that do not have any geometry assigned to them. If you are using a template model with a predefined layer structure, that means you will most likely lose many of your template layers. So, if you are cleaning up a CAD import in SketchUp, it is usually best to do it inside a blank SketchUp model, then copy and paste the results into your site model template.

To purge unused layers, follow these steps: (Figure 4-14)

1. Open the **Model Info dialog** by going to **Window > Model Info**.

2. Click on **Statistics**.

3. Click **Purge Unused**.

Figure 4-14
Purging your
model will
eliminate
extra layers,
components
and more.

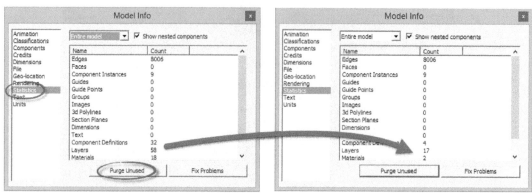

Once you have purged the model, it is likely that you are going to still have extra entities in the model that you do not need. You will have to manually go through your model to find these objects and delete them.

A quick way to identify and delete entities you do not want is to select one of the edges you want to delete, and look at the **Entity Info dialog** to see which layer it has been assigned. In the **Layers dialog**, select that layer, and click the **Minus sign**. SketchUp will ask what you want to do with the contents, so you can just select "Delete Contents" and click Ok.

Grouping/Layering Entities

You now need to go through the model, find the entities you would like to keep, and group them together according to the layer to which they are currently assigned.

By grouping entities together, then assigning that group to a custom layer, you can be assured that when the layer is hidden, the entities are protected inside a group or component and will not be unexpectedly altered.

> **TIP** If you prefer, you can choose to keep the imported entities on their assigned layer. Just be sure to understand that layers do not isolate the structure of entities; they only toggle the visibility of them.

Since you do not want to use the same layer naming structure from your surveyor, you will be grouping them and assigning them to your own layers, then deleting the imported layers, moving all loose entities to layer0.

During this process of organizing your imported entities, you will need to have the **Entity Info dialog** open, as well as the **Layers dialog** open.

> **TIP** If you had cleaned up the CAD survey in a separate SketchUp file, you should copy and paste in place the entities into your site model at this point.

To reorganize the imported CAD entities, follow these steps: (Figure 4-15)

1. **Right-click** on an entity > **Select** > **All on same layer.**

2. **Right-click** on the selection, select **Make Group**.

3. In the **Entity Info dialog**, assign the new group to the appropriate layer.

4. Delete the old layer, and when it asks what you want to do with the assigned entities, choose "Move contents to default layer". This will reassign all loose entities from that layer to layer0.

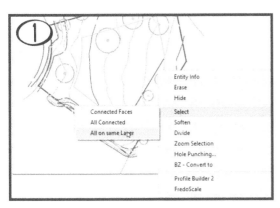

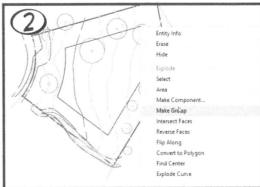

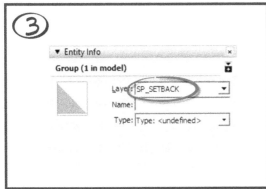

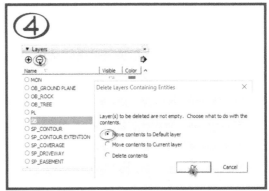

Figure 4-15
Group similar entities, assign layer, purge old layer.

Repeat this for each type of entity you would like to keep in the model. When you are complete, you should have all of the various site survey elements grouped and assigned to their own layer. (**Figure 4-16**)

At this point, you can purge your model again, then take a look at any remaining layers in your model, and determine if they contain any entities that you would like to keep. If not, go ahead and delete those layers and their contents.

Figure 4-16
Your final organized CAD import should be separated by group, and assigned to different layers.

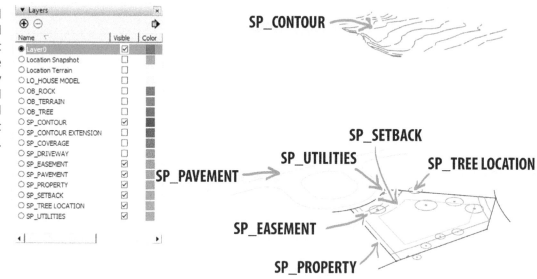

Importing Non-CAD Site Survey

If your site survey is on paper, PDF, or if you are otherwise unable to obtain the CAD file, you will need to import it into SketchUp as a jpeg. The biggest limitation of using a jpeg or PDF survey is that there are no vector entities to use as snap points, so your survey will not be as accurate as using a CAD survey. You will be using the image for reference while tracing over it to create the property lines, setbacks, contours, etc, right inside SketchUp.

To insert a jpg site survey, follow these steps: (Figure 4-17)

1. Inside SketchUp, go to **File > Import.**

2. Change the **Files of Type** drop-down menu to select **JPEG Image** (*.jpg).

3. Make sure **Use as image** is selected.

4. Select the jpg image of the site survey. Click **Open**.

5. **Double-click** somewhere in the SketchUp workspace to place the image.

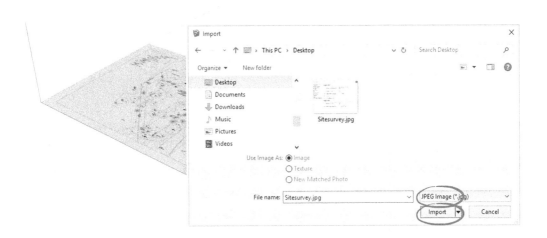

Figure 4-17
Importing a
site survey
as an image.

The imported image will be placed inside your SketchUp model, but it will not be set to the correct scale. What you need to do next is use the **Tape Measure tool** (T) to measure a known distance on the survey, and type in the correct dimension in order to scale the entire model.

To scale your imported jpeg, follow these steps: (Figure 4-18)

1. Activate the **Tape Measure tool**(T).

2. Find the longest known dimension on the survey, and click on each end of the dimension in order to measure it. (Using the longest dimension gives you more accuracy when scaling.)

3. Immediately type in the known actual dimension, and press ENTER.

4. SketchUp will ask if you want to resize the model. Click **Yes**.

You will want to create a new layer to place the survey image on, perhaps SP_ SURVEY. The template is configured to be used with a CAD survey, so that layer is not included in the template.

Figure 4-18
Resize your
SketchUp
model to
full scale by
measuring
a known
distance on
the survey
image.

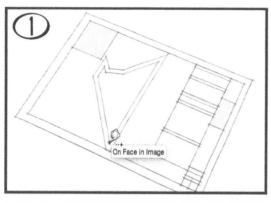

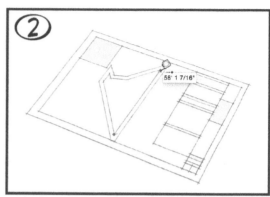

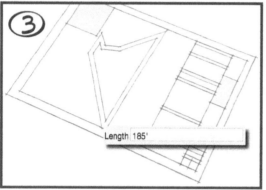

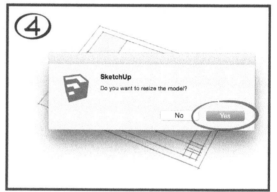

Drawing Boundaries

You should now have a model with a full size site survey which you can now trace over to create all of your various property lines, setbacks, and contours. The objective is to use the written headings and dimensions to draw the lines in SketchUp, using the imported jpeg as reference. There are a few things you can do to make this task easier:

✓ While tracing over the site survey, it can be helpful to align your camera to top view, and set it to parallel projection. Go to **Camera > Standard Views > Top, and Camera > Parallel Projection.** To navigate your model while in this camera mode, you can zoom by scrolling your mouse wheel, and pan by holding the middle mouse button and the **SHIFT** key at the same time.

✓ By default, north is set along the green axis. The green axis is pointing "up" when viewing your model in the standard Top view. If you need to change the orientation of the default north, it is recommended to use the Solar North plugin from the SketchUp team. We will go over north orientation in more detail later on.

Solar North (Free)

The free Solar North plugin, developed by SketchUp, gives you a visual indication of where north is oriented in your model. It also provides a tool to realign north with any reference in your model. Alternatively, you can define north by a degree angle.

www.sketchupbook.com/solarnorth

✓ You are going to be working with angle measurements to set the headings. By default, SketchUp displays angles to a precision of 0.1. You can increase the precision of angle units to 0.001 by going to **Window > Model Info > Units > Angle Units > Precision. (Figure 4-19)**

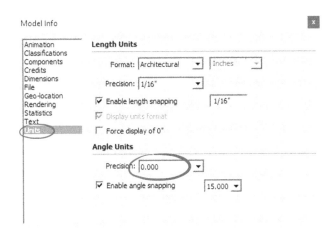

Figure 4-19
Increase the precision of angle units for more accurate headings.

✓ As you trace over the image, your connected segments may generate a face, which obscures the survey from view. Go to **View > Face Style > X-Ray** to turn on X-Ray mode. This will make it easy to see the survey, without having to delete the faces just yet. (Faces are required for using the **Offset tool** (F), so it is handy to be able to keep them temporarily. Eventually, you will delete all the faces and just keep the edges.)

Your survey will likely include compass direction in **degrees, minutes, and seconds.** You will have to convert them to degrees in order to feed them into SketchUp.

Decimal Degrees

SketchUp is not able to read Degrees, Minutes, Seconds directly, so they have to be converted to decimal degrees. But even if you were to convert the headings to decimal degrees, SketchUp's highest level of precision is 0.000°, so you might lose some accuracy with your headings.

Degrees(°), minutes('), and seconds(") takes a degree reading, then divides the next degree by 60 minutes (1° = 60'), and divides the next minute by 60 seconds (1' = 60"). So, for example, consider the following:

N76° 16' 36"W

1. Convert the seconds to decimal minutes. N76° **16 + (36/60)'**W = N76° **16.6'**W

2. Convert minutes to decimal degrees. N76° **(16.6/60)'**W = **N76.276666°W**

2DXYSite Survey ($25)

LOT 102
9961 FT²
0.23 Acres

For faster input of degrees, minutes, seconds, the 2DXYSite Survey plugin accepts direct heading input. It creates more accurate headings by ignoring SketchUp's limited angle accuracy, and instead uses trigonometry behind the scenes to calculate the end point of the heading.

www.sketchupbook.com/2DXY

Whether you are using native SketchUp tools or using a plugin, do not worry too much if your image is not lining up perfectly with your dimensioned edges. It is hard to accurately scale an image, but it really does not matter since it is just for reference. What is important is that you are using the written dimensions and headings to draw the boundaries.

To draw lines using decimal degrees, follow these steps: (Figure 4-20)

Example: N76° 16' 36"W, 29.86'

Convert degrees, minutes, seconds to decimal degrees. **N76.277°W.**

1. Use the **Line tool** (L) and draw a line 29.86' long, aligned in the direction of the heading. (In this case, along the green axis pointing North. If it were a South

heading, you would draw the line in the opposite direction.)

2. With the **Rotate tool (Q),** click on the starting point of the line to define the pivot point along the blue axis, then click again along the line to start the rotation.

3. Rotate the line towards the direction of the quadrant indicated by the heading. In this example, West, so rotate counterclockwise. Type in 76.277 ENTER.

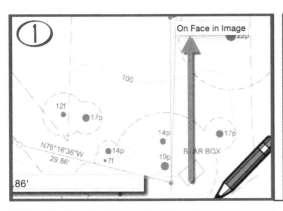

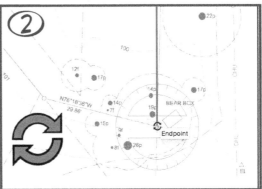

Figure 4-20 Use the Rotate tool after drawing the line to orient it correctly without having to create a guide first.

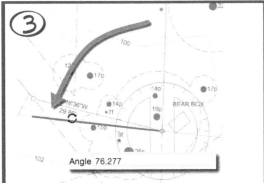

Repeat this process for the next line, and continue until you are back at your starting point. You will most likely notice that your starting and ending points do not line up exactly. That could be caused by inaccuracy with the survey readings or the low precision of SketchUp angles. You will have to make a small adjustment to one of your lines in order to get them to meet up.

Use these additional tips for creating boundaries: (Figure 4-21)

✓ Once you have your initial boundary drawn, use the **Offset tool (F)** to create setbacks quickly.

✓ If some boundary lines have different setbacks than others, use the **Tape Measure tool** (T) to create a guide from the boundary line. Then, grab the **Line tool** (L) and use the guide as reference to intersect with the existing offset.

Figure 4-21
Use the Offset tool, Tape Measure, and Line tool to create your boundaries.

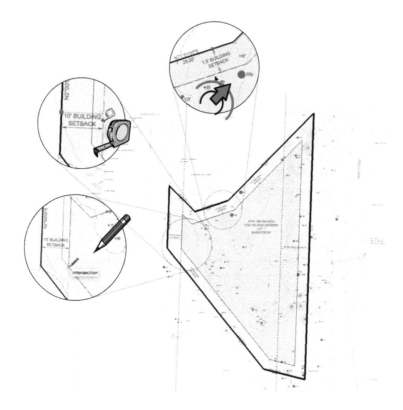

Organizing Elements

As you are tracing the information on your survey, you want to be sure to create groups for the following elements:

✓ **Property lines** should be grouped together and assigned to the SP_PROPERTY layer.

✓ **Setbacks** should be grouped together and assigned to the SP_SETBACK layer.

✓ **Contour lines** should be grouped together and assigned to the SP_CONTOUR layer.

✓ **Easements** should be grouped together and assigned to the SP_EASEMENT layer.

✓ **Utility** locations should be grouped together and assigned to the SP_UTILITIES layer.

The individual entities should be on layer0 (You should always have layer0 as your active layer), but you should assign the groups to an appropriately named layer so you can turn the visibility on and off.

Geolocating the Site

Once you have your site survey imported and cleaned up, the next step is to geolocate your model using the built-in Google Earth features. Geolocating does a few things:

✓ **Imports satellite imagery of your site** - SketchUp will import a satellite image of your site from Google Earth and place it in your model.

✓ **3D terrain from Google Earth** - In addition to the satellite image, a separate 3D mesh will be imported using approximate terrain height data from Google Earth. (The 3D terrain is generally not accurate enough to rely on, as heights can differ drastically from your survey.)

✓ **Accurately located on Earth** - Geo-locating your model actually associates a latitude, longitude, and cardinal direction with your model so you can cast accurate shadows using SketchUp's shadow settings.

✓ **Accurately scaled** - The imported Google Earth image is accurately scaled, so you can use it to cross-check your survey data and make sure it matches.

The imported satellite image will be helpful for confirming road locations, landmarks and adjacent construction with the corresponding elements on the site survey.

To geolocate your model, follow these steps: (Figure 4-22)

1. In SketchUp, go to **File > Geo-location > Add Location.**

2. Type in the address of your job site, or use the map to zoom into the area manually.

3. Click the **Select Region** button to create a crop box around the area you would like to import into your model. The crosshair is the anchor point of the import, and will be placed at the origin in your model. Try to aim the crosshair to the approximate location of your axes origin, so you will not have to move the imported

Google Earth terrain very much from its insertion point.

4. Click the **Grab** button to import.

> **TIP** You will not be able to see the map texture if you still have the Color by layer style activated. Remember, styles affect how textures are displayed, so you have to change to a style that shows textures.

Two new layers will be added to your model, and you will see a flat, 2D image of your site, in addition to a group that contains a 3D terrain mesh from Google Earth. If you do not see the 3D terrain, double-check to make sure the Location Terrain layer is enabled.

Figure 4-22
Geo-locate your model with Google Earth Data.

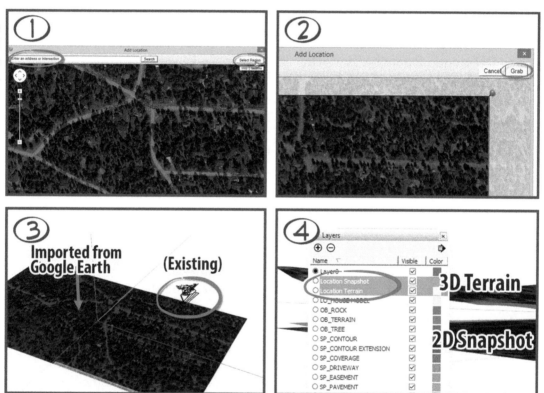

> **TIP** If you are using the provided template, the Google Earth layers will already exist in your model. The reason is because, whenever you add new layers to your model, those layers will become visible in any existing scenes you have in the model. The layers were included in the template so this would not happen.

While the 3D terrain is very cool, it is typically only accurate to within +- 20'. Since that is not going to be helpful to us, you can just go ahead and delete the 3D terrain group because it is just going to get in the way.

Once the Google Earth image is imported into your model, it will need to be rotated to match your site survey orientation. **You do not want to rotate your site survey to match the Google Earth image because then all of your template scenes will need to be realigned.**

If you would like to use geolocation to cast accurate shadows onto your model, you will also need to recalibrate the north direction within your model. By default, north is aligned with the green axis. Keep in mind that the north direction is saved in scenes as a shadow property, so if you need to change north away from the default green axis, you will also need to update all your scenes. **If you have no interest in creating accurate shadows in your model, you can simply move/rotate the Google Earth image to match your survey and ignore which way SketchUp thinks north is facing.**

Vertical North Alignment

When you are dealing with a site survey and a Google Earth image, you need to make sure that their relative north directions match. Then, in order to cast accurate shadows, you need to tell SketchUp which way is north in relationship to its axes.

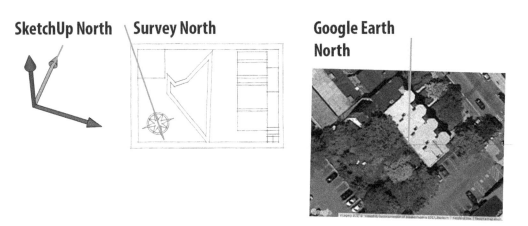

SketchUp North **Survey North** **Google Earth North**

Figure 4-23
There are three north orientations you must coordinate in your model.

✓ The default north direction in SketchUp is aligned with the green axis. In the site template provided with this book, each scene is saved with this default north orientation. If your site survey does not have a vertical north alignment, skip ahead to the next section to learn how to align north.

✓ Google Earth images are cropped parallel to north/south and east/west. You can use the edge of the image to align with north in your survey.

✓ If your site survey north direction is already aligned with the green axis, all you need to do is rotate the Google Earth terrain and 2D snapshot along the origin so that it is parallel to the green axis.

If your site survey has north pointing along the green axis, follow these steps to align the Google Earth image to north: (Figure 4-24)

Figure 4-24
Align the imported Google Earth image to match the site survey north direction.

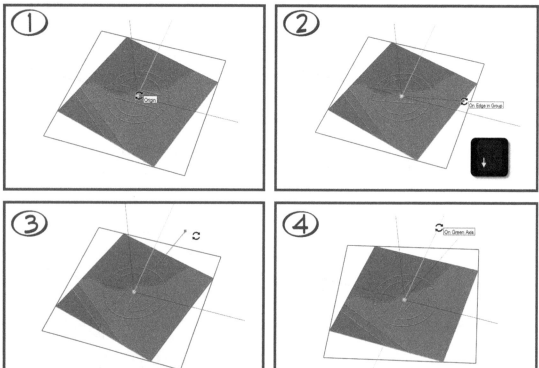

You need to rotate the Google Earth image so that its edges are aligned with the green axis (north). You want to rotate around the axes origin, since that is the reference point for the location. Turn on Hidden Geometry so you can reference the edge of the Google Earth image.

1. Select the image. With the **Rotate tool** (**Q**), click on the origin to define the pivot point.

2. Hover over the edge of the image and tap the **down arrow.** This will lock a perpendicular reference to the edge of the image.

3. Click to start the rotation.

4. Hover over the green axis and click to finish. Your Google Earth import is now aligned with your site survey north and with the saved north position in each scene.

Use the **Move tool** (**M**) to move your site survey entities to align with the Google Earth image.

North is not Vertical

If your site survey has a north direction other than along the green axis, and it is important to you to have accurate shadows in your site model, you will need to do a few more steps.

If your site survey north direction is not along the green axis, follow these steps:

1. Since each scene is saved with the north orientation along the green axis, you need to clear the shadow settings from the scenes so they can be reconfigured. Select all scenes (hold **SHIFT**, click the first scene, then click the last scene, then uncheck the shadows box.) (**Figure 4-25**)

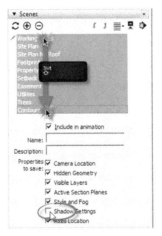

Figure 4-25
Select multiple scenes and toggle the Shadows Settings to update them in one step.

2. Using the Solar North plugin, realign north to your site survey's north direction. Make sure you have a line in your site survey that represents its north direction; you will be referencing it in the next step. (**Figure 4-26**)

Figure 4-26
The Solar North plugin can change the North direction in your model.

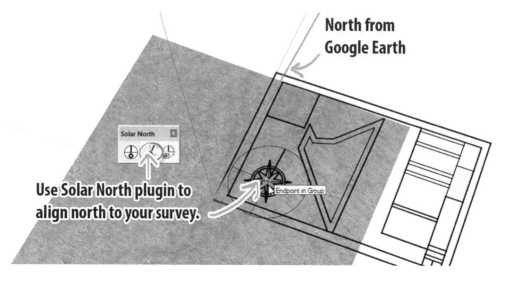

3. You need to rotate the Google Earth image to match the new north orientation. Start the rotation at the axis origin so you retain the correct sun projection. Hover over an edge of the image and tap the **down arrow** to reference parallel to it, and click to start the rotation. (**Figure 4-27**)

Figure 4-27
Hover over an edge and tap the down arrow to align.

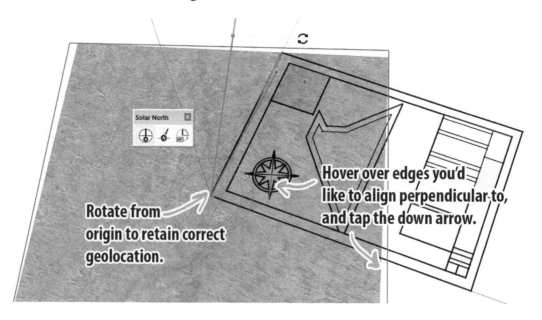

4. Hover over the edge in your site survey that points north, and tap the **down arrow** to lock a parallel reference for the rotation. Click to finish the move.

5. To save the new north orientation, select all scenes, then check the shadows settings box so it will save with the scenes. You can go back later and adjust the time and date settings for each individual scene to get a good shadow projection on your model.

> **TIP** North direction is a shadow property, which is a setting that can be saved in a scene. This means that if you set the north orientation using the Solar North plugin, the orientation may be lost if you have a scene saved with shadow settings. This also means you could set multiple "north" orientations and save them in different scenes in order to have more control over the direction of your shadows.

Review the imported terrain. Look for discrepancies between what you see here and your site survey. You can trace over any objects you want to include in your site plan but were not included in the site survey. Roads and adjacent structures are good examples of things you can trace over using the Google Earth snapshot. (**Figure 4-28**)

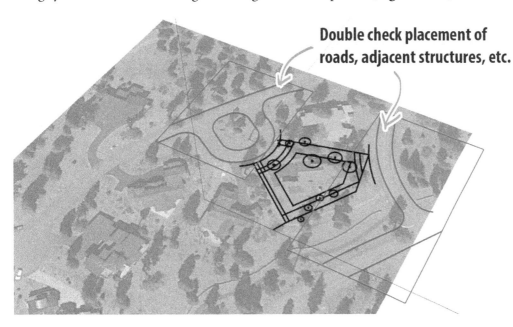

Double check placement of roads, adjacent structures, etc.

Figure 4-28
Google Earth images are great for confirming placement of site survey entities.

Optimizing Contour Lines

 SketchUp has a built-in tool called **From Contours** that will generate a 3D terrain in one click, just by selecting the contours you would like to generate the terrain from. However, before generating the 3D terrain from the contour lines, there are a few things you will need to check:

✓ You might want to manually extend the contour lines past the boundaries of what the site survey included. This will allow you to create a larger 3D terrain that extends beyond the scope of your site survey. (**Figure 4-29**)

 ✓ Examine each contour line and make sure there are not any broken segments. If there are, use the **Line tool** (**L**) to reconnect them.

Extending Contour Lines

Again, this process is completely optional, but it will make your perspective views look better because you will have more of the land visible in the scene, instead of the ground just dropping off randomly. **You want your terrain to be large enough to fill the entire page in LayOut when it is set to the scale you specify.**

If your contour lines are already elevated to their appropriate heights, extending those lines can be challenging. It would be nearly impossible to draw a line on the same plane as a contour line without some sort of reference surface. If you were drawing along an axis, it would be easy because you could use the arrow keys to lock axis. Since the contour lines are somewhat organic and are at various angles, you need to take a different approach.

What you will do is create a large, temporary rectangle on which you can drape a copy of the contour lines (You will use the **Drape tool**). With the contour lines on a flat surface, it becomes easy to manually draw additional lines extending the context of the site. Then, all you have to do is select each line segment and move it up along the blue axis, referencing the height of the original contour lines.

If your contour lines are flat on the ground plane, you will need to elevate them manually once you have created the contour extensions.

> **TIP** Your model axis origin does not need to represent sea level. If your project is several thousand feet above sea level, it is recommended that you move your contour lines down to within 1,000 ft of the axis origin. For example, if a certain contour line is elevated to 6,542', you should set it to 542' from origin in your model instead of 6,542'. By reducing the distance between the ground plane and your terrain, you will make it easier to navigate your model, easier to measure elevations, and you will reduce camera clipping which occurs on large-scale models.

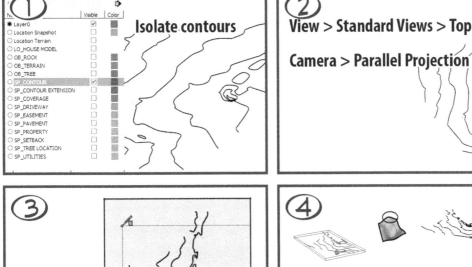

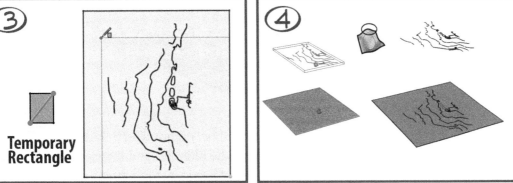

Figure 4-30
Creating a copy of your elevated contour lines onto a flat surface.

Step by Step To drape your elevated contour lines to a flat surface, follow these steps: (Figure 4-30)

1. Toggle your model layers, so that only the contour lines are visible.

2. Go to **Camera > Standard Views > Top**, then **Camera > Parallel Projection**.

3. With the **Rectangle tool (R)**, draw a rectangle under the contour lines, representing the span of the extensions you want to create.

4. Activate the **Drape tool** by going to **Tools > Sandbox > Drape**. Click on the contour group to identify what you want to drape, then, click on the rectangle to tell SketchUp where you want to drape the contours. (**Figure 4-31**)

Figure 4-31
Your original contour lines remain unharmed when using the Drape tool.

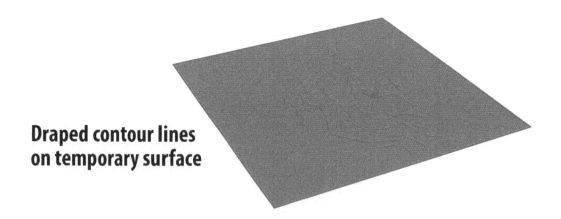

Original Contour lines in group (Unharmed)

Draped contour lines on temporary surface

Your original contour lines will not be affected, so do not worry about that. The **Drape tool** "drapes" a copy of the entities along the blue axis and intersects them with the surface below. (You might want to orbit out of top view for a moment in order to see the results of the **Drape tool**. Otherwise, you will not notice much of a difference since you are looking directly from above.)

At this point, you will want to turn off the SP_CONTOUR layer, so you are just working with the flat contour lines.

To create contour line extensions, follow these steps: (Figure 4-32)

1. The first thing you need to do is make sure the draped contour lines and the surface are protected within their own group, so your new lines do not stick to them. Drag a selection box around the entire rectangle, **right-click > Make Group**.

2. Back in top view, use the **Line tool (L)** or **Freehand tool** to create new edges that extend off of the ends of your existing contour lines. Since these areas are beyond the scope of the project boundaries, precision is not critical. The whole purpose of doing this is to visually extend the area of the terrain, so use your best judgement.

3. Once you have created all of your extension lines, select all of them, and reassign them from **layer0** to **SP_CONTOUR EXTENSIONS**.

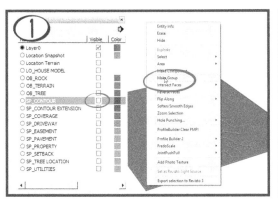
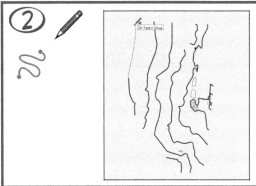
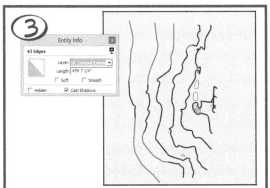
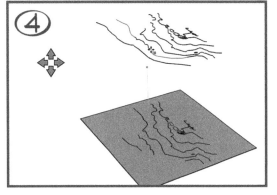

Figure 4-32
Create your contour line extensions, assign them to SP_CONTOUR EXTENSIONS, then move them up to your original contour lines.

You are probably saying "But wait! I thought you were never supposed to assign entities to anything other than layer0?" While that is typically true, you need to make an exception here, because the extensions will need to be placed within the original contour lines group in order to generate a 3D mesh, but you still need to be able to turn the visibility of the extension lines off, separately from the survey contour lines. Assigning the edges to their own layer is the only way to accomplish this.

4. Orbit out of top view, then turn on the SP_CONTOUR layer. Select each of the extension lines you have created, one elevation at a time, then use the **Move tool** (M) to move them along the blue axis to the height of the appropriate contour line.

5. To finish up, tap **CTRL+X** (**Command+X** on Mac) to cut all of the extensions, then **Edit > Paste in Place** while inside the contour line group. You can now delete the temporary rectangle you created below. (**Figure 4-33**)

Figure 4-33
One of the few exceptions to the layer0 rule. Assign the contour extension entities to their own layer.

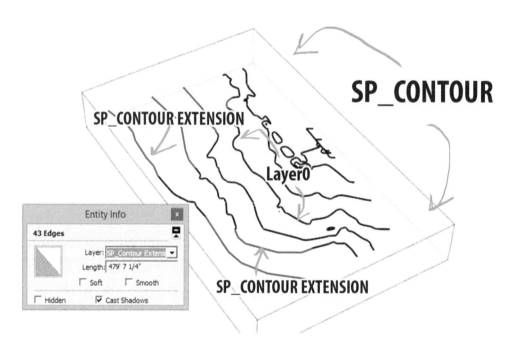

Sandbox Tools

SketchUp includes a set of tools called the Sandbox tools for working with terrain. You have already used the **Drape tool** to drape contour lines. You will be using more of these tools a little bit later on to help generate the terrain and drape edges onto surfaces. For easier access to the sandbox tools, you can add the Sandbox toolbar to your workspace. You can access the Sandbox toolbar at **View > Toolbars > Sandbox**. (**Figure 4-34**)

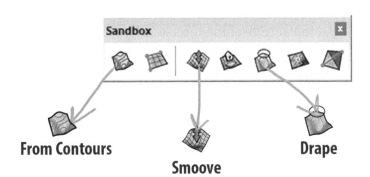

Figure 4-34
The sandbox toolbar.

The tools you will be using the most are:

✓ **From Contours** - The **From Contours tool** allows you to select a set of elevated contour lines, then generate a terrain mesh from them.

✓ **Smoove** - The **Smoove tool** gives you the ability to change the height of specific parts of a mesh.

✓ **Drape** - The **Drape tool** projects a selection of edges down onto a surface or mesh. This is great for draping roads and tree locations.

Generating Terrain from Contours

Whether you import contours from CAD or draw them manually, you still need to convert those contour lines into 3D terrain. This can be done using the native SketchUp tools. The tool you are going to use is part of the Sandbox toolset, and it is called **From** **Contours.**

To generate terrain from contour lines, follow these steps: (Figure 4-35)

1. Open the group your contour lines are contained in. Select all contour lines (Click and drag a selection box around all contour lines).

2. Click on the **From Contours** button in the Sandbox toolbar. (If you do not see the sandbox toolbar, **right-click** on your toolbar and enable Sandbox.)

3. A new terrain will be generated and placed into a group in your model.

The terrain is placed inside a new group, inside the contour lines group. You need to remove it from the contour lines group, so select the terrain group, press **CTRL+X** (**Command+X** on Mac) to cut, then exit the contour lines group and go to **Edit > Paste in Place** to paste the group outside of the contour lines group.

4. Select the terrain, and assign it to the layer **OB_TERRAIN**.

Figure 4-35
Generating terrain mesh from contour lines uses SketchUp's sandbox tool From Contours.

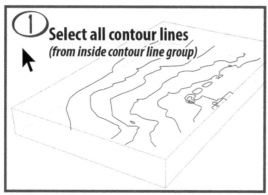

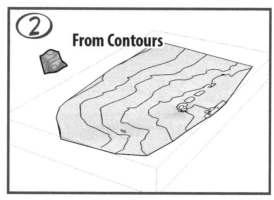

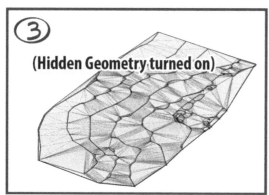

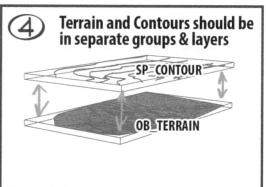

Toposhaper (Free)

Toposhaper is a powerful terrain generation and cleanup tool that produces a cleaner mesh than the Sandbox tool **From Contours**. Toposhaper averages the contour lines so the terrain will not follow the contours exactly as modeled. This plugin is not hosted on the SketchUp extension warehouse. It is downloaded from Sketchucation.com with a free account.

www.sketchupbook.com/toposhaper

Once your terrain is generated, go to **View > Hidden Geometry** to view the mesh that was created. If you find some spots that do not look quite right, take a look at your contour lines again and make sure they are at the correct elevation. Sudden changes in elevation can sometimes create strange results in your mesh. You might need to manually edit the terrain, which will be reviewed in a later chapter.

> **TIP** If you are happy with your terrain, it is a good idea to create a copy of the entire mesh, and place it far above the original, along the blue axis. You can place it on a special layer and hide it for now. If you ever need to repair a part of your existing terrain, you will be able to use it to copy "bandages" back to the original.

It is important to understand that there is nothing special about geometry produced by the Sandbox tools, meaning the results are just edges and faces. If you had manually drawn all those lines, it would be exactly the same thing as what is produced by the Sandbox tools.

Also, even though you have generated a mesh from your contour lines, you do not want to delete the contour lines. You will display them in LayOut on your existing site plan. At this point, however, you do not need them visible in your model, so you can turn off that layer.

Hiding Terrain Edges

Figure 4-36
Hide terrain perimeter edges so they do not appear to be a boundary.

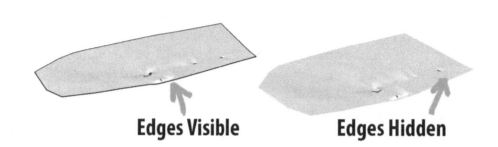

Edges Visible   **Edges Hidden**

Once your terrain is generated, you will want to hide the perimeter edges of the terrain so they do not appear when you bring it into LayOut. The edges of the terrain are not meant to represent any type of boundary or border, it just happens to be where the terrain ended. By hiding the terrain boundary edges, you will prevent them from being mistaken as a boundary in LayOut. (**Figure 4-36**)

Step by Step

To hide the perimeter edges of a terrain, follow these steps. (Figure 4-37)

1.   With the **Select tool** (SPACE), click on the terrain until you can select its faces and edges.

2.   **Double-click** on the face to select it and its bounding edges.

3.   To deselect the faces so that you are left with only the edges selected, hold down the **SHIFT** key and click on the face.

4.   Go to **Edit > Hide** to hide the selected edges.

Alternatively, if your terrain extends beyond the scope of the LayOut page, you don't have to worry about this. If the edges of the terrain are beyond the viewport boundary, you won't see them anyways. (**Figure 4-38**)

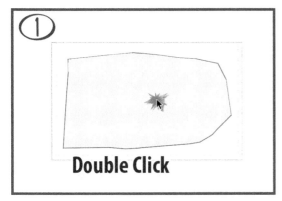

Double Click

Shift-Click Face

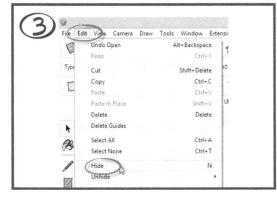

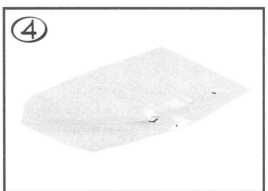

Figure 4-37
Select all connected entities, then SHIFT+click the surface to remove it from the selection.

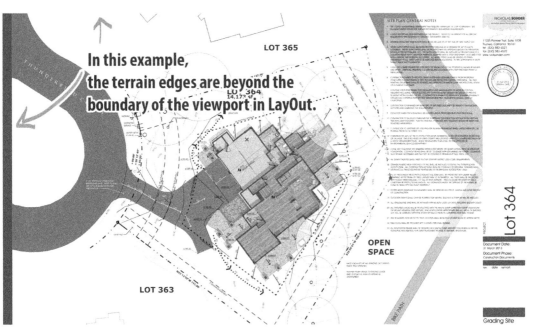

Figure 4-38
When the terrain extends beyond the viewport, you do not need to hide the edges.

Draping Entities Onto Terrain

Once you have your 3D terrain generated, there are a few things you will want to drape onto your terrain. The **Drape tool** can be used to take edges and project them onto the 3D terrain. (**Figure 4-39**)

One example is tree locations. The site survey should indicate the location of trees. You might want to drape the tree locations onto the 3D terrain in order to help place 3D trees in your model more easily. (Just drape the tree trunk location, do not drape the drip line. You do not want the drip line to show up on your terrain, you will be placing 3D trees in the model to show that.)

Another example is roads. Most times, you can get away with simply draping the road outline onto the terrain and painting it a different color to distinguish it from the ground. Your site survey contours will most likely account for the grade of the road, letting you skip having to manually model the road. (For driveways, you might need to model the grade for accuracy. You will review this in a later chapter.)

Figure 4-39
The Drape tool can be used to drape tree locations onto the terrain surface.

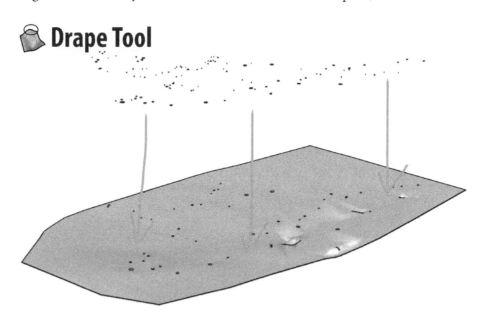

Drape Tool

TIP Once you drape entities onto a mesh, it becomes very difficult to make any changes to the draped entities.

To drape entities onto a terrain, follow these steps: (Figure 4-40)

1. Make sure the entities you want to drape onto the terrain are aligned with the terrain along the blue axis. (The height does not matter, it just needs to be aligned along the blue axis. It could be above or below the terrain.) If you are planning on applying a different color to the draped area, you will need to make sure it is a closed segment. (Meaning, a face exists within the connected edges. You can retrace over an edge with the **Line tool** (**L**) to repair a missing face).

2. Select the group or entities you would like to drape onto the terrain.

3. Activate the **Drape tool**, click on the terrain to drape the selected entities.

Figure 4-40
Drape a road onto a terrain mesh.

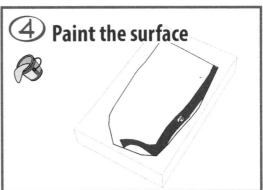

The entities will be copied and projected onto the surface of the terrain, within the terrain group.

Trees and Vegetation

There are a few different options for placing trees and vegetation in your site model, and the method you choose is up to you. What you are trying to achieve is a balance between computer performance and an acceptable representation of the tree in both the model and in LayOut.

Figure 4-41
3D modeled trees look great with their high detail and accurate shadows, but come with a performance cost.

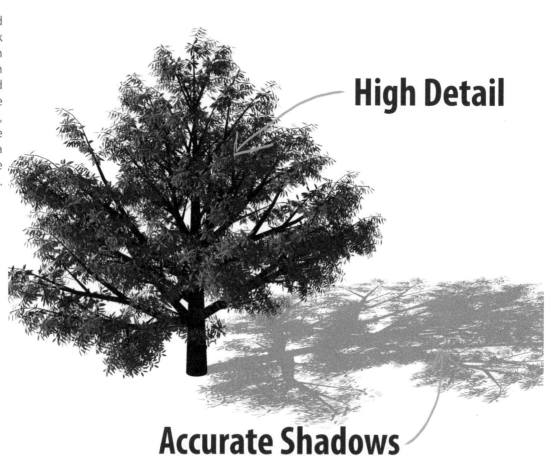

High Detail

Accurate Shadows

Credit: Jeffrey C. (3D Warehouse)

✓ **3D Tree models (Figure 4-41)**- These trees are modeled in 3D, and tend to look great in perspective camera mode. They also have very accurate shadow projections. However, most times, they do not translate well in plan view, and they add a lot of geometry to your model, slowing your model down and increasing file size.

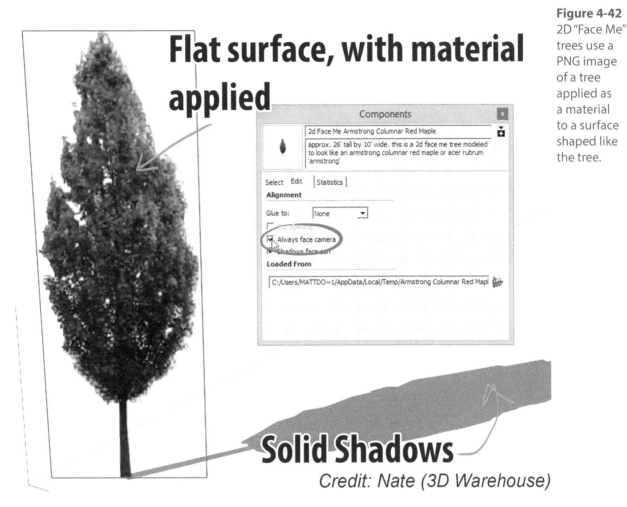

Credit: Nate (3D Warehouse)

✓ **2D "Face Me" Models (Figure 4-42)**- These trees are actually flat surfaces with an image applied to the face, that will automatically rotate to face the camera as you orbit around the model. The surface is cut out to the shape of the tree, and the edges are hidden, so the tree casts a shadow shaped like the tree. The advantage of using these types of components is that they are typically smaller file size, and there are a variety of styles you can use (photorealistic, illustrated, sketchy, etc). They tend to look best when viewed from the side but lose their appeal when viewed from above or at an angle. When viewed from a top view perspective, they are completely useless because the image is aligned vertically.

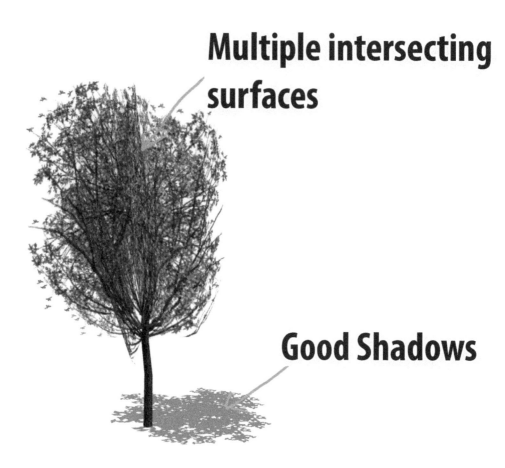

Multiple intersecting surfaces

Good Shadows

Credit: Alan Fraser (FormFonts)

✓ **Lightweight 3D tree models** (**Figure 4-43**)- A sort of hybrid between a highly detailed 3D model, and a simple 2D "Face Me" component. One technique for creating trees is to use a combination of 2D semi-transparent materials oriented in a way to create the illusion of a 3D tree. It gives you a great looking tree from any perspective, and sometimes includes a special layer that you turn on when viewing in plan view.

✓ **Rendering Software** - If you plan on using something like Lumion or LumenRT, you will likely want to add trees and vegetation inside their program instead of inside SketchUp. Both programs have special tools for inserting trees that are optimized for display inside the renderer. They will even blow in the wind during animations. LumenRT offers proxy components that you can place inside SketchUp. Proxies are "placeholder" components that look great in SketchUp, but are automatically replaced once imported into LumenRT. Best of both worlds.

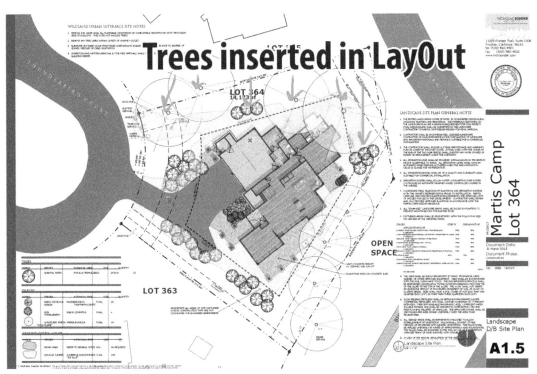

Figure 4-44
Trees can be placed in LayOut from the Scrapbook panel.

✓ **LayOut tree symbols (Figure 4-44)**- Yet another approach you can take is to use the LayOut scrapbooks to insert tree and plant symbols on your site plan drawings manually. In order to do this accurately, you will need to have some sort of guide to snap to in the SketchUp viewport. Your site survey should include tree locations, which can be used as reference to snap symbols. Once you have them inserted, you can hide the tree symbols in SketchUp, update the scene, then update the viewport in LayOut.

Tree Graphics From SketchUp

An alternative way to show tree graphics in LayOut is to set up your tree components to have a 3D and 2D version within the component inside SketchUp (**Figure 4-45**). This will allow you to toggle which version is visible depending upon how you are viewing the model.

Whenever you have an object that has two different versions, you will use two special layers called SP_3D and SP_2D. The flat graphical version of the tree will be in a group or component assigned to the SP_2D layer, and the 3D version of the tree will be in a group or component assigned to the SP_3D layer.

Both of those objects will be contained within a parent component which is assigned to the OB_TREE layer. Position the 2D object about five feet above the base of the tree, so it does not intersect with the terrain below when viewed from above.

Figure 4-45
A tree component with a flat tree symbol placed on a special layer to be used in LayOut.

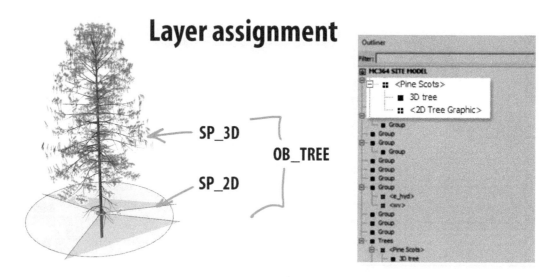

TIP If you do not want to assign each individual tree component to the OB_TREE layer, you can collect all of your tree components inside a parent group, and only assign the parent group to OB_TREE. Leave the tree components on layer0.

Organizing the model this way gives you complete control over what is visible.

✓ If you want the 3D trees visible, turn on OB_TREES and SP_3D.

✓ If you want the flat 2D trees visible, turn on OB_TREES and SP_2D.

✓ If you do not want any trees visible, turn off OB_TREES.

Inserting Trees on the Site

The process for inserting trees onto your site will depend upon the type of trees you want to use.

> **TIP** When inserting trees into your model, using the same tree component multiple times will help you save file size. To help make those components look unique, use the **Scale tool (S)** to make each tree a different size. The rotation handles available with the **Move tool (M)** will let you easily rotate a tree to a different orientation. You can also **right-click** on a tree, flip along the red or green axis to mirror it. Randomizing components in this way can help make each instance look unique.

Use your site survey as reference for tree sizes and locations, then drop your 3D trees on top of the marks. Once all the trees have been imported, move them down along the blue axis until they intersect with the site terrain. (**Figure 4-46**)

Figure 4-46
Site model with 3D trees placed on the terrain.

Model Review

In your model so far, you should have the following:

✓ **Site survey** entities imported, grouped, and assigned to their "SP" layer. Site survey entities should all be on the ground plane, except for the elevated contour lines.

✓ **3D terrain** generated from the site contour lines and any contour extensions you have created manually. The terrain should be large enough to span past the boundaries of the viewport you will be creating in LayOut.

✓ **Trees** and other objects should be placed in the model to represent the existing site conditions.

Figure 4-47
Schematic model Outliner and Layer organization overview.

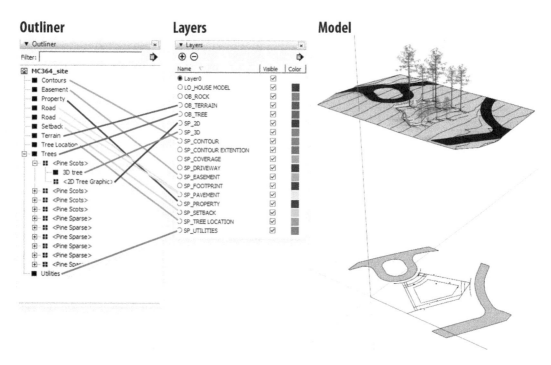

Existing Site Plans

The existing site plan is a single page document that shows the existing site terrain, trees, obstructions, property lines, etc (**Figure 4-48**). You may choose to create the existing site plan as a site analysis plan, which takes into account sun position throughout the year, prevailing wind direction, views, etc.

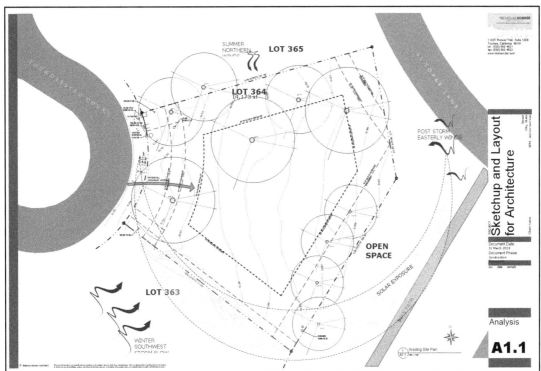

Figure 4-48
The Existing Site Plan site analysis page.

The site plan is compiled by creating multiple scenes in SketchUp isolating the various elements you want to display. The scenes you create in SketchUp are going to be assigned to viewports in LayOut, so you need to set the camera perspective, style, and layer visibility for each viewport you want to create. You will then add annotations and objects in LayOut to complete the drawing.

One characteristic of SketchUp is that you cannot assign different line weights or styles to edges within a single scene. Instead, you will need to isolate entities within their own scenes and bring them into LayOut separately. If you want to have even more control over the style of edges in your viewports, you can explode them into LayOut entities (**Figure 4-49**). This will allow you to use LayOut's **Shape Style panel** to edit the color, stroke, and style of the lines. This is exactly what you will be doing for all of the boundary lines.

Figure 4-49
Boundary
viewports
are
exploded
once inside
LayOut.

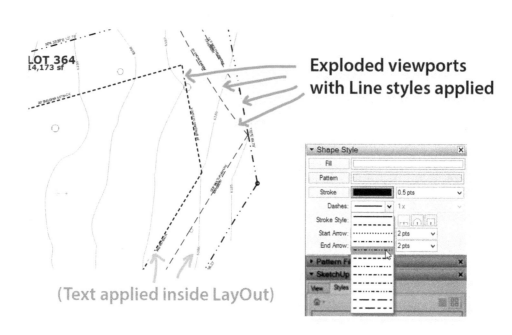

While exploding viewports is typically a big no-no because it breaks the link between your SketchUp model and LayOut, you make an exception here because these lines are typically things that will never change throughout a project. The added flexibility of being able to customize the style of the edges makes it worth it.

The whole process of taking a CAD survey, processing it in SketchUp, then bringing it into LayOut to explode is tedious. However, the process can become more efficient if you use the templates provided with this book. By using the template, all of the scenes will be created already, saving you a ton of time. However, if for some reason you are not using the template, we are going to review how to create a scene for LayOut in the next section.

Just keep in mind that when you are using the template, **there will be additional layers and pages that are not being used for the existing site model**, but will be used on later phases of the project. You can just ignore them for now. For the existing site plan we are only going to focus on the first page in the LayOut document.

> ## Ever Evolving
>
> The existing site plans show the project site, without the proposed building. However, you will eventually use this same LayOut file once you start modeling the building to generate the proposed grading plan and other site plans.
>
> You will want to save a copy of the existing site plan LayOut file and SketchUp file for the record, but you will actually use the same files to continue to evolve throughout the life of the project. This saves you from having to recreate files at each phase.

Scenes for LayOut

In the provided templates, all of the scenes are already created for you. If you are starting from scratch, or need to add your own scenes, you will need to create scenes manually. In this section you will review how the site template scenes were created so you can understand the process behind creating scenes.

The scenes you will be creating are: Site Plan scene, Property line scene, Setback scene, Contour scene, Tree location scene, and the Utility location scene. These will all be scenes viewed from the same Top view perspective, but you will hide different layers in order to make certain entities visible in each scene. The first scene you will create is the Site Plan scene.

To prepare the Site Plan scene in SketchUp, follow these steps:

1. In SketchUp, go to **Camera > Standard Views > Top.**

2. Go to **Camera > Parallel Projection**.

3. Press SHIFT+Z to zoom extents.

4. In the **Styles dialog**, select the style you would like to use for sending the model to LayOut.

5. In the **Layers dialog**, uncheck all layers except Layer0 and OB_TERRAIN.

6. In the **Scenes dialog**, click the plus button to add a scene, making sure all check boxes are enabled so all properties get saved with the scene. Rename the scene to something that will make it easy to identify, for example, **Site Plan**. (**Figure 4-50**)

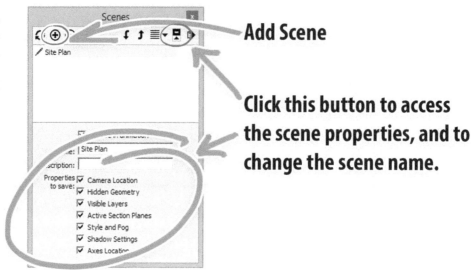

Figure 4-50
Make sure all scene properties are saved in each scene.

Repeat this process for each additional scene, but **make sure that you do not change the position of the camera.** That way, all of these scenes will be aligned perfectly with each other. Essentially, you will just be toggling layers for each of these scenes. Create the following scenes: (**Figure 4-51**)

- ✓ Property Lines

- ✓ Setbacks

- ✓ Contours

- ✓ Trees

- ✓ Utilities

Although it is possible to align viewports manually inside LayOut once the viewport scale is set, it is much easier to have the scene cameras aligned in SketchUp in the first place. This eliminates having to do any manual alignment so you can just copy and paste viewports on top of each other.

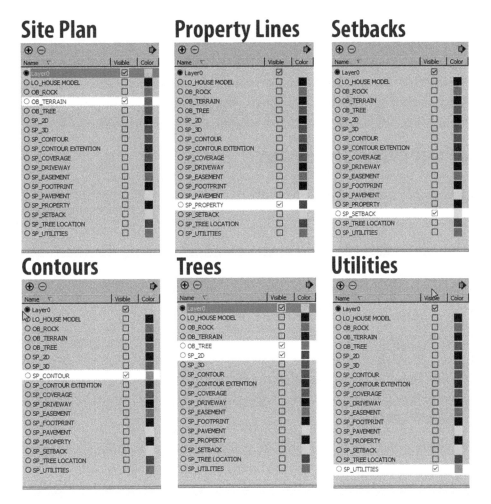

Figure 4-51
Save each of these scenes with these layers turned on (in addition to layer0)

With your scenes saved, save your SketchUp model. You can now go to LayOut and import the model to create the site plan.

LayOut Site Plan

The site plan is created by taking all of the scenes you just created in SketchUp, and laying them on top of each other as viewports in LayOut. This technique is called **Stacking Viewports**. By stacking viewports, you are taking multiple viewports of the same SketchUp model at the same camera perspective, but with different layers or styles applied to them.

One of the challenges of stacking viewports is that it becomes difficult to select individual viewports once they have been placed on the page, so it is important to create layers in LayOut for each viewport you will be placing on the page. By assigning each of the viewports to its own layer, you give yourself more control by being able to lock or hide layers. The site plan template included with this book has layers already set up. If you are not using the provided template, you can add your own layers easily.

Adding Layers in LayOut

In LayOut, the various settings, properties, and tools are located in panels that are docked to the right hand side of the workspace. You can expand or collapse each panel by clicking on the title bar. If you find that you are missing a specific panel, you can enable it from the **Window menu**.

To add new layers to a LayOut document, follow these steps:

1. In the **Layers panel**, click on the **Plus icon**. **+**

2. **Double-click** on the layer name to rename it.

3. Click and drag layers to shuffle the visible order of their contents on the page. Objects assigned to layers appear on the page in the order in which they are arranged in the **Layers panel**.

With the site plans, there are some elements that are going to duplicate on each page, such as the property lines, setbacks, easements, trees, and title block info. Other elements are unique to each page. LayOut gives you a great way to manage duplicate elements by using **shared layers**.

A shared layer will display the same entities on every page that has that layer visible. Do you want your title block to appear on every page? Just put it on a shared layer. Make sure that layer is visible on every page. If you do not want your title block to appear on your cover page, just hide that shared layer on that page, and those elements will remain hidden.

Template Layers

Open the **A1-Site.layout** template. There are layers in place for the various viewports you will be inserting, as well as for the annotations you will add inside LayOut. (**Figure 4-52**)

The layers are divided into two major types:

✓ Layers that contain objects that are unique to specific pages in the document.

✓ Layers that are shared on multiple pages in the document.

The first layer, Page Notes, is for entities that are related to specific pages in the document. It is not a shared layer, so anything you place on this layer will only appear on the page it was placed onto.

The layers for the various survey entities are placed on a shared layer, so that you can toggle them on or off depending upon which page you are on. In the templates, shared layers are labeled with CAPITAL letters, and non-shared layers are in lower case.

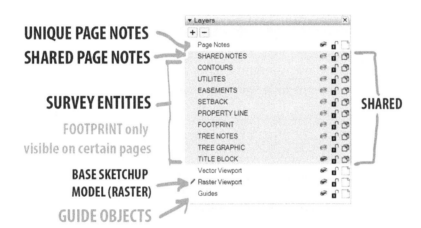

Figure 4-52
Site plan template layers being used on this page.

Viewport Layers

The site plan is unique due to the number of viewports that you will need to insert into it. Most other documents you will create only require a couple of viewport layers. Since you want to isolate each survey entity, they must have their own layers. (**Figure 4-53**)

Figure 4-53
Site plan
template
layers that
are being
used for
viewports.

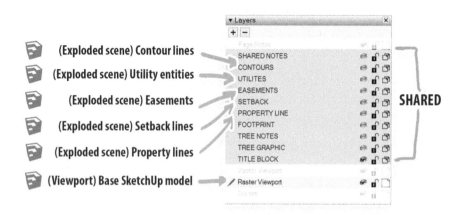

Figure 4-53
Site plan template layers that are being used for viewports.

The other layers are for inserting LayOut objects. Let's review each layer, starting at the bottom, and going up from there:

✓ **Guides** - The Guides layer contains shapes that help you align viewports as you insert them. You can delete or hide this layer once you have placed your viewports.

✓ **Raster Viewport**- A raster viewport, assigned to Site Plan scene, set to Ortho, at 1/8" = 1' (Or whichever scale is appropriate to your project.) This layer is not shared because the site plans eventually show different scenes on each page.

✓ **Vector Viewport** - While you will not use this layer in the existing site plan, this layer is used to show a vector rendered viewport of the building walls on some of the other site plan pages.

✓ **TITLE BLOCK** - Shared layer, contains all title block elements that remain the same on each page, including page names and page numbers through the use of Auto-Text Tags.

✓ **TREE GRAPHIC** - Shared layer, tree symbols inserted from the LayOut scrapbook. They are placed manually using the draped tree locations on the site terrain as reference. If you inserted tree symbols in SketchUp directly, this is the layer on which you would place that viewport.

✓ **TREE NOTES** - Shared layer, text indicating tree size.

✓ **FOOTPRINT** - Shared layer, dashed line shape created in LayOut, outlining the footprint of the building for use on certain pages.

✓ **PROPERTY LINE** - Shared layer, exploded viewport showing property lines, text labels.

✓ **SETBACK** - Shared layer, exploded viewport showing setback lines, text labels.

✓ **EASEMENTS** - Shared layer, exploded viewport showing easement lines, text labels.

✓ **UTILITIES** - Shared layer, exploded viewport showing utility lines, stubs, meters, vaults, and text labels.

✓ **CONTOURS** - Shared layer, exploded viewport showing contour lines, text labels.

✓ **SHARED NOTES** - Shared layer containing all text and annotations related to the shared site plan elements. (Page specific annotations will be on a separate non-shared layer.)

✓ **Page Notes** - All other annotations unique to a page belong on this layer.

Whenever you add elements to a page, you want to make sure you are adding them to the correct layer. Simply click on the layer name you would like to make active, and any elements you add to the page from that point forward will be assigned to that layer. You can tell which layer is currently active by the **Pencil icon** next to the layer name.

You can assign objects to a different layer by **right-clicking** on it > **Move to Layer**.

Existing Site Plan

To build the existing site plan, you need to insert a viewport of the site, set it to the correct scale, then insert and explode all of the viewports for the various survey entities you would like to show.

Let's start with the main site viewport, placed on the Raster Viewport layer.

To insert a viewport, follow these steps: (Figure 4-54)

1. In the **Pages panel**, select page **Existing Site Plan**.

2. In the **Layers panel**, click on the **Raster Viewport** layer. (Selecting it will make it the active drawing layer.)

3. To insert your first viewport, go to **File > Insert,** and select the site model you

want to place into LayOut.

Figure 4-54
Select a
layer before
inserting a
viewport.

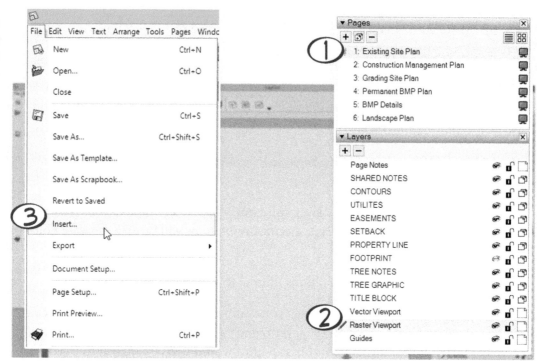

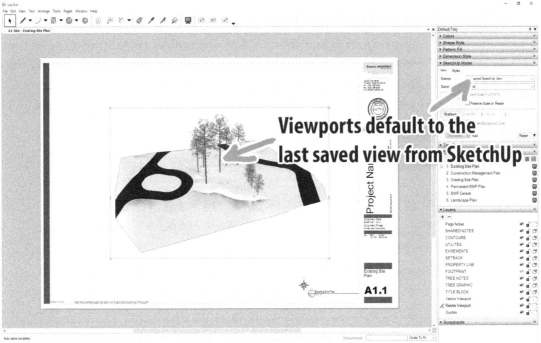

Viewports default to the last saved view from SketchUp

Figure 4-55
Viewports display last saved view when inserted into LayOut.

LayOut will place a viewport of your model on the current page and layer, showing you the last saved view of the model. If you expand the **SketchUp Model panel**, you will see "Last Saved SketchUp View" in the Scene drop-down menu. (**Figure 4-55**)

> **TIP** You very rarely would want to leave a viewport set to "Last Saved SketchUp View." If you were to go back to the SketchUp model at any time to make changes to it, and you updated the model reference in LayOut, viewports set to Last Saved SketchUp View would change to whatever view you had left the model at when you saved it. You should always assign a scene to a viewport, or at least override the Last Saved SketchUp Viewport by entering Model Space or making some other change to the viewport settings.

You will now assign a scene to the viewport, and set the scale and size of the viewport window.

To configure a viewport scene, size, and scale, follow these steps: (Figure 4-56)

1. Select the viewport.

2. In the **SketchUp Model panel**, select the Site Plan scene.

In the image below, notice how many properties change when you assign a preconfigured scene to a viewport. Not only does the camera perspective and SketchUp style change, but other viewport settings change as well. The Ortho button turns on, so do Shadows and Fog. That is because those are all properties that you saved to the scene in SketchUp, so when you assigned that scene to the viewport, the corresponding properties change in order to match the scene settings.

Figure 4-56
Assigning a scene to a viewport applies all of the scene properties to the viewport.

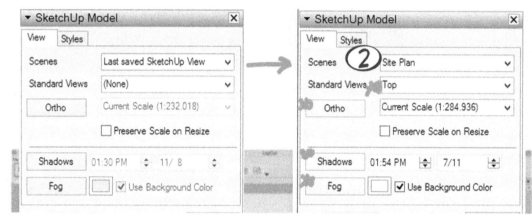

3. In the Scale drop-down menu, select an appropriate drawing scale for the viewport. Note: The current scale will appear in the drop-down menu between its two closest scales. (**Figure 4-57**)

4. Once your scale is set, confirm that the **Preserve Scale on Resize** checkbox is checked. This will make sure the scale does not change when you resize the viewport.

5. Click and drag the boundaries of the viewport window, if needed, so the entire model is visible. If you need to pan the viewport, just click and drag the viewport using the **Select tool** (SPACE).

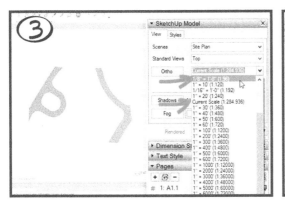 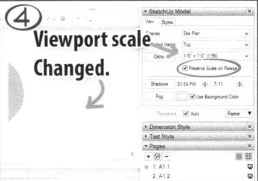

Figure 4-57
Set the viewport scale, and resize the viewport to fit the page.

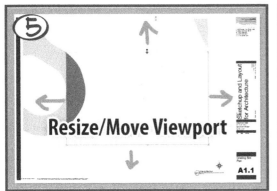 

TIP If you **double-click** on a viewport to enter model space in order to pan the camera view, the viewport will become detached from the SketchUp scene because you have overridden one of the scene properties (in this case, the camera position). Any future updates you make to the scene properties will not update in the viewport unless you reassign the viewport to the scene. When you have overridden a scene, you will see (Modified) in the scene drop-down menu. The best way to avoid this is to simply click and drag the entire viewport, then readjust the viewport boundaries as needed.

You will also notice the render mode drop-down menu in the **SketchUp Model panel**. For this base viewport, you will want to make sure it is set to **Raster** mode.

Exploding Boundary Lines

In SketchUp, you created a scene for each of the survey boundary lines you want to show on the site plan. In LayOut, you will want to create a viewport for each of those scenes. Since you made sure to save the scenes from the same **camera perspective** in

SketchUp, you can simply copy and paste the first viewport you created, and it will align perfectly when you reassign the new scene to it.

To stack additional viewports into LayOut, follow these steps: (Figure 4-58)

Step by Step

Figure 4-58
Copy and
paste
viewports,
then assign
to a different
scene.

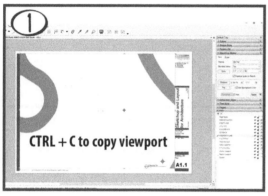
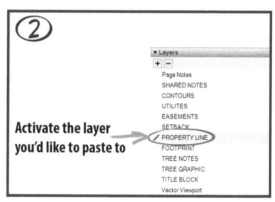

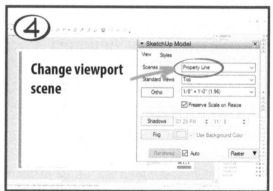

1. Select the existing viewport on the page. Press **CTRL+C** (**Command+C** on Mac) to copy.

2. In the **Layers panel**, click on the PROPERTY LINE layer to make it the active drawing layer.

3. Press **CTRL+SHIFT+V** (**Command+SHIFT+V** on Mac) to paste a copy of the viewport onto the current layer. (Not holding **SHIFT** would paste it onto the same layer from which it was copied.) You may not notice a difference at first, and that is because the pasted viewport is assigned to the same scene so it looks identical.

4. Go to the **SketchUp Model panel**, select the Property Line scene from the scene drop-down menu. Now you will notice the viewport looks different than the

viewport underneath it. You do not have to set the size or scale of this viewport, because those settings have been copied from the first viewport.

You want to explode this viewport so you will be able to customize the line style using the LayOut shape settings. **If you explode a viewport while it is in Raster mode, the viewport will be converted into an image.** That is not what you want. You want to convert the entities in the viewport into LayOut shapes, so you first need to make sure the viewport is in **Vector mode**.

5. In the **SketchUp Model panel**, select Vector in the **Render** drop-down menu.

6. **Right-click** on the viewport, and select **Explode**. (**Figure 4-59**)

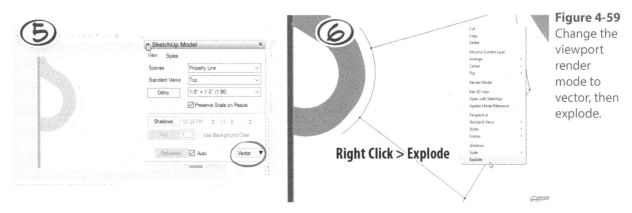

Right Click > Explode

Figure 4-59
Change the viewport render mode to vector, then explode.

The viewport will now be exploded, so all of the entities that were in the viewport are now converted into LayOut shapes. Now, you can select them, and go to the **Shape Style panel** to change the line style, stroke, and color.

With the PROPERTY LINE layer still active, switch to the **Text tool** (T) and add text to indicate the property line headings.

Repeat this process for each boundary scene you created in SketchUp. Continue copying the original Site Plan viewport to an appropriate layer, reassign the scene, set to Vector render, then explode it and apply a line style to the boundaries. Add notes and annotations as they relate to each layer.

Tree Graphics From Scrapbooks

If you did not use tree components in SketchUp that look acceptable in plan view, you can insert tree graphics manually in LayOut. In order to insert trees in this manner, you need to know where the trees are located on the site. When importing the survey into SketchUp, you should have isolated the tree locations in their own scene and inserted a viewport into LayOut assigned to the TREE NOTES layer. Make sure that layer is visible so you can reference the tree locations when you place the tree graphics.

Figure 4-60
Trees can be represented in LayOut using scrapbook symbols.

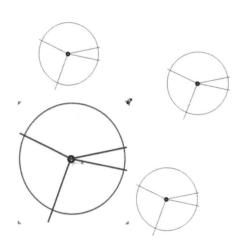
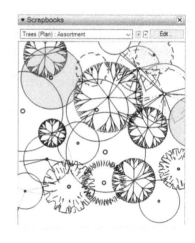

Step by Step

To insert tree graphics from a scrapbook, follow these steps: (Figure 4-60)

1. Activate the TREE GRAPHIC layer.

2. Go to the **Scrapbooks panel**, and choose Trees (plan) from the drop-down menu.

3. When you click on one of the graphics with the **Select tool** (SPACE), your cursor becomes a stamp tool. Place a tree on your page.

4. With the **Select tool** (SPACE), click and drag the tree's boundary to resize it. Hold down the **SHIFT** key to scale proportionally. You can estimate the size, since drip lines are not a precise measurement anyway.

5. If you need to, reposition the center grip to the center of the tree. Then, click and drag the tree over one of your tree locations until it snaps to the center point. (If you have trouble snapping to the center, hover the snap point over a circle perimeter for a moment, then try to find its center.)

   Once you have placed one tree, it is easy to copy similarly sized trees to other locations using the **Select tool** (SPACE) while holding down the **CTRL** (**Option** on Mac) key.

Tips & Tricks

Aligning Text

When you are inserting labels for the various boundaries, you might find it difficult to rotate and align your text labels, especially when you have a viewport of your terrain model underneath. What happens is the text tries to snap to all the hidden end points in the terrain, making it nearly impossible to align accurately to the boundary line. Here are some tips to help you align text to any edge.

To align text to a boundary line, follow these steps: (Figure 4-61)

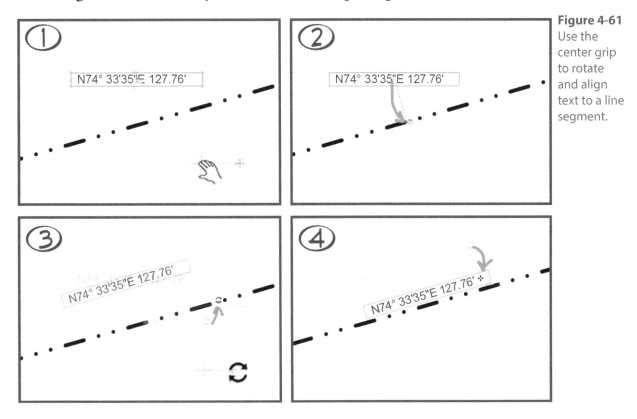

Figure 4-61
Use the center grip to rotate and align text to a line segment.

1. **Right-click** in a blank area of your document and confirm **Object Snap** is on, and **Grid Snap** is off.

2. In the **Layers panel**, hide all the layers except for the one you are currently working on. This will simplify your workspace, giving you confidence that you are

snapping to the correct lines. LayOut will not snap to objects when their layers are hidden.

3. Drag the center grip onto the line with which you want to be aligned. Then, grab the rotation handle and rotate it until it snaps to the line. You will now be perfectly aligned. You can then click and drag, or use the arrow keys to move the text into position.

4. If you need to enter a degrees symbol °, press **ALT 248 (Option+SHIFT+8 on Mac)**.

Page Numbers and Detail Labels

If you are not utilizing Auto-Text Tags to label your pages, you should place your page numbers and detail labels on the page-specific layer for that page. You might not want to use Auto-Text if you have non-sequential page numbering, or if you use a complicated prefix logic.

If you are using Auto-Text, LayOut can number your pages automatically for you, and you should place the page number Auto-Text only once on a shared layer. Typically placed on the TITLE BLOCK shared layer, this will make the page number appear on every page.

LayOut provides a custom Auto-Text variable for page numbers, which will automatically display whichever page it is currently on, even when the text is on a shared layer. In addition to that, you can set a custom page number prefix using a custom Auto-Text tag named <PageSet>. You can create and edit your own Auto-Text by going to **File > Document Setup > Auto-Text**. (**Figure 4-62**)

Figure 4-62
Auto-Text controls the page numbers in the title block.

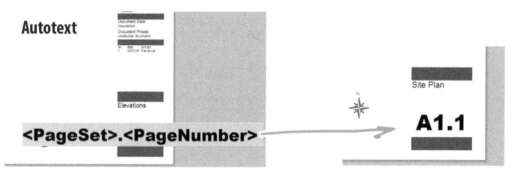

Applying Styles to Lines

When you explode a vector rendered viewport, it is converted into LayOut entities. This gives you much more flexibility over the style of the lines. You can edit the style of a LayOut shape using the **Shape Style panel**. First, you need to select the shape you want to edit. (**Figure 4-63**)

Property Line Style Example

Black — 4 pts Stroke — 0.5x Dash Scale

Figure 4-63
With the boundary lines exploded, you can apply a style to them in LayOut.

Lock Layers

Sometimes it can be difficult to select a specific object on a page when you have multiple overlapping objects. It can be helpful to go to the **Layers panel** and lock or hide layers that you do not want in your selection. SHIFT+click or CTRL+click (Command+click on Mac) to quickly select multiple layers at one time. (**Figure 4-64**)

Figure 4-64
Lock layers in order to make it easier to select objects on the page and to prevent accidental editing.

Contour Elevation Labels

When adding text to indicate contour line elevations, you may want to add a break in the contour line in which to insert your text label. You can do this using the **Split tool. (Figure 4-65)**

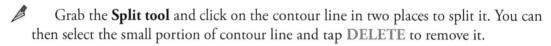

Grab the **Split tool** and click on the contour line in two places to split it. You can then select the small portion of contour line and tap DELETE to remove it.

Use the **Text tool (T)** to create your elevation label, then position and rotate the text using the rotation handle. You want the text to be parallel with the section of contour line you are labeling, and it should be positioned right on top of the line.

Export PDF

Once you are ready to print your site plan, go to **File > Export.** You only need to export the first page, so under Pages select "From 1 to 1". The default settings work well as is. Click export to review your site plan in your pdf viewer, then print it out on paper.

You can also, obviously, print directly from LayOut, but it is a good idea to get in the habit of producing a pdf record of the file before printing, so you always have a digital record of each version of the file that you print.

The Site Visit

With your site plan in hand, the next step is to take a trip to the site with the client, in order to double-check your information, take notes, pictures, and start thinking about the design. (**Figure 4-66**)

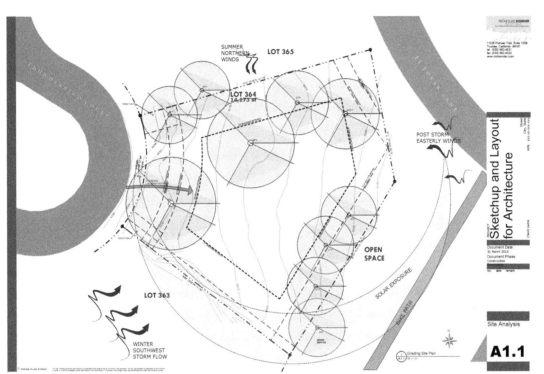

Figure 4-66
Use the completed site plan to start planning your building design.

You will want to pay attention to things like sun location, water runoff, driveway access and garage location. If you are in a cold climate, having the garage on the southeast side of the building will encourage snow melting on the driveway. Are there specific trees that you want to keep on the property? Are there any other natural obstructions that you must work around? While having this discussion, take notes directly on your site drawing.

Now is also the time to begin the discussion with your client as to preferences in the design. Is there a particular view that the client would like to see from within the building? What are some of their preconceived notions about what the building will look like? It is your job to discover these program elements and to weigh their importance in the overall design.

Objectives

The schematic model of the building is a basic model used to define the **general massing and layout of the project's spaces and characteristics**. It is a low level of detail model, giving you the ability to make fast changes to the design at the early stages of the project.

This is the most important phase in the design process. By the end of the Schematic Design phase, you should have developed a floor plan that works well on the site, and a design that meets your client's expectations. In the phases that follow, you will add detail and further refine the model. One of the reasons Schematic Design is so important is that you will refine the same model in the next phase so you are not starting from scratch.

You do not need to worry about overlapping groups, or having your roof lines perfectly intersect with the walls. While it is acceptable to have a low level of detail, it is still important to model with dimensional accuracy to show the correct scale of the model.

The main objectives of the Schematic Design Phase are as follows:

✓ Using the constraints of the existing site and the clients preferences, create a schematic model of the building.

✓ Work through all major design decisions and end up with a final schematic model ready to bring into the Design Development phase.

✓ Create a set of schematic documents, including a proposed site plan, floor plans, perspectives, and elevations.

In this phase, it is important to understand that you are not modeling the building to a high level of detail. Throughout the entire project, the objective is to model at a **level of**

detail that is appropriate to the scale of the design decisions that are being made in that phase. Since this phase will have many changes, sometimes drastic, it is important to keep a low level of detail in order to better facilitate those changes. (**Figure 5-1**)

Figure 5-1
Schematic Design models have a low level of detail.

Figure 5-2
A close look at the level of detail of a Schematic Design model.

Schematic Design Drawings

Figure 5-3
Schematic
Design
phase
exterior
perspective
drawings.

There are a number of documents you will be creating in the Schematic Design phase. They will include the following pages:

✓ **Exterior Perspectives** - Images of the exterior of the building, on the site model (**Figure 5-3**).

✓ **Proposed Site plans** - Plan view of the site, with the building, showing the property lines and setbacks.

✓ **Floor plans** - One page for each level of the building, as well as a roof plan. There are no dimensions on these floor plans. The purpose of these plans is to show the layout of the building.

✓ **Exterior Elevations** - One elevation for each side of the building with annotations showing the floor height for each level of the building and a datum elevation directly related to the site model.

Building Model

Every person is different in how they prefer to explore design ideas. Some people like to sketch ideas using pencil and paper; other people like to model their ideas directly inside SketchUp. It is up to you to decide how you would like to collect your thoughts and inspiration for the design of your building.

Conceptual Floor Plans

One way to brainstorm floor plan ideas is to use the existing site plans to overlay a conceptual floor plan of the building (either by hand, or using SketchUp or LayOut) (**Figure 5-4**). Once you have gotten the floor plan thought out, you will begin with modeling the 3D building. In the image below, Nick used tracing paper overlaid on top of the existing site plan in order to sketch ideas for the floor plan by hand.

Figure 5-4
Conceptual
floor plan
sketches
drawn over
an existing
site plan
printout.

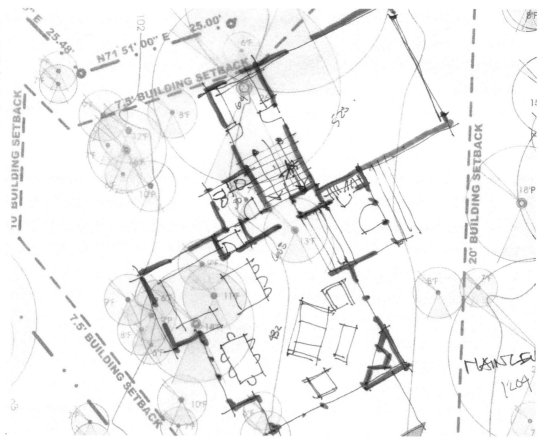

Multiple Project Models

One of the key features of this workflow is using separate SketchUp models to help keep individual file size down, focus your attention on a specific part of the project, and organize section cuts and scenes.

The site model is saved as one SketchUp file. The building model is saved as a separate SketchUp file. The building model is then imported into the site model as a component (**Figure 5-5**). This allows you to update the site model with any changes made to the building by simply reloading the building component.

What are the benefits of using separate models in a project?

✓ Instead of having one model with an overwhelming number of scenes, you have the ability to thoughtfully organize sets of scenes as they pertain to specific models.

✓ Each model is created from a template that is created specifically for that model, saving you time by having scenes, layers, and other redundant settings preconfigured.

✓ It is an insurance policy against accidental modification of other parts of your model. If you mess up one file, you have not lost your entire project.

✓ When working with a team, it is much easier to share workload when the project is split into multiple files. One person can be working on the site model while you continue to make changes to the building model.

✓ When there are many section planes in a model, they can be difficult to organize. With separate SketchUp models, section planes can be inserted in a separate, dedicated model, where the building is imported as a component. It is much easier to model the building when you do not have to worry about section planes getting in your way.

The site model will be used to create the following LayOut viewports: **Existing site plans, perspective images, site plans.**

The building model will be used to create the following LayOut viewports: **Floor plans, roof plan, and exterior elevations.** (The building model will eventually be imported into other models to create building sections, reflected ceiling plans, and interior elevations.)

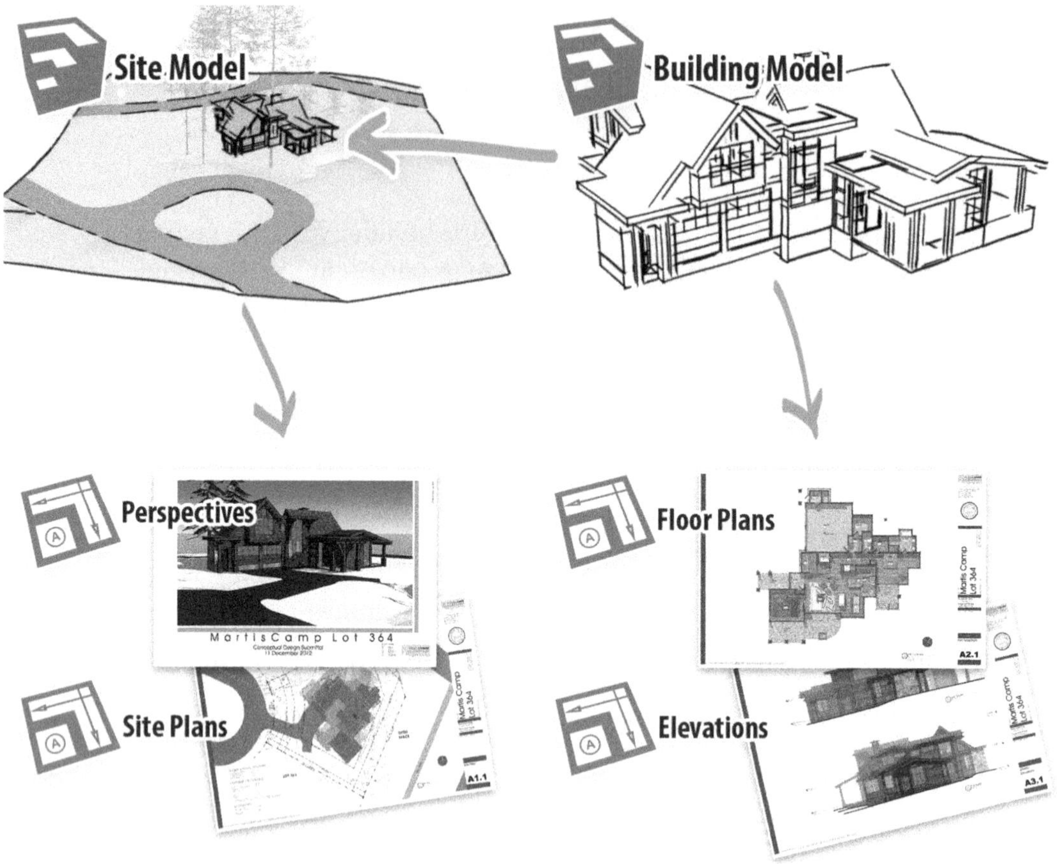

Figure 5-5
The building model is imported into the site model.

Although the building model will end up as a separate model, **you are going to start off by modeling right inside the site model.** There are many advantages to being able to reference all the elements in the site model to get your building design started. Once the major elements are established, you will cut and paste it into the building model template.

Floors

The floor area of your building will be the first thing you model. For this initial step, you will use simple rectangles to represent the overall floor area of the building. The overall exterior dimensions of the floor space should be equal to the rough framing dimensions.

Where do you begin? Start with known constraints, then work from there. For example, if your building has a garage, it should be one of the main elements in the design due to its importance for both access and impact on the building massing. Since the garage location is determined by road position, site grade, driveway access, and sun position, you should have a pretty good idea where the garage needs to be positioned.

> **TIP** Before you begin modeling the building inside the site model, save a backup copy of the site model and label it as the existing site model backup. Even though the site model began as an existing site model, it will evolve with the project and become the proposed site plan. Save a backup in case you need to refer back to the existing site model for any reason.

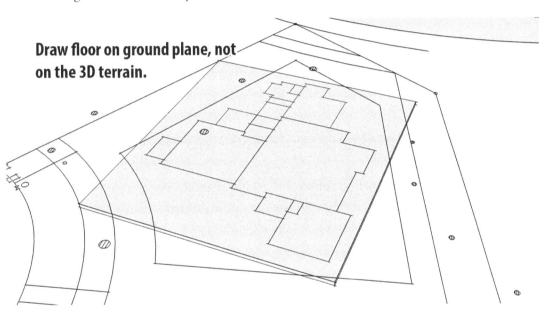

Draw floor on ground plane, not on the 3D terrain.

Figure 5-6
Start modeling the building on the ground plane of the site model.

To start modeling the floor, follow these steps: (Figure 5-6)

1. Start by drawing a rough rectangle on the ground plane and make it a group.

2. Move the rectangle to within your setback lines, then use the **Rotate tool** (Q) to rotate the rectangle to the correct orientation. This rectangle represents the first corner of the building.

3. Use the **Axes tool** to temporarily reset the model axes to be aligned with the building. (This will be helpful as you continue to model the floors, but the axis will reset back to default when you activate a scene.)

Step by Step

Floor layout Methods

There are many ways to lay out a floor plan, and you will likely have your own preferences for how you like to work. However, it is important to make sure you extrude the rectangle to the appropriate floor thickness before you subdivide the surface for each room.

You could start with an oversized rectangle, and draw your rooms starting from one corner. Use single edges to divide the interior spaces. Once you have achieved a successful layout, use the **Push/Pull tool (P)** to erase any extra surfaces on the exterior of the building. (**Figure 5-7**)

Figure 5-7
Create floor plan on extruded rectangle.

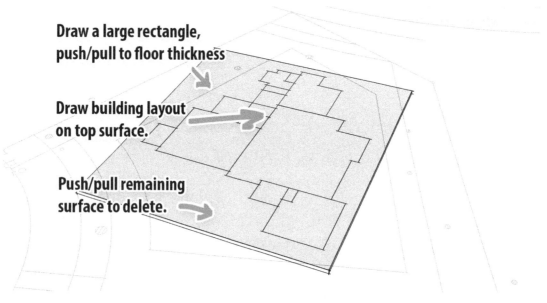

Draw a large rectangle, push/pull to floor thickness

Draw building layout on top surface.

Push/pull remaining surface to delete.

Another approach would be to start with a small extruded rectangle, then build off of it to expand the floor into the shape of the building. Again, at this phase, you can simply use single edges to divide the interior spaces. (**Figure 5-8**)

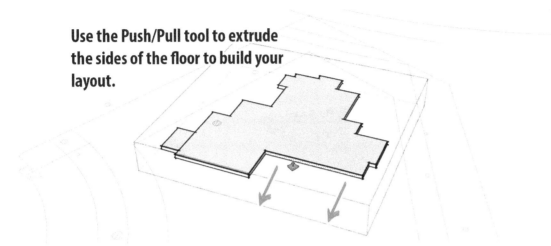

Use the Push/Pull tool to extrude the sides of the floor to build your layout.

Tips for Floor Plan layout

✓ **Line tool with arrow keys** - Using the **Line tool** (L), you can tap an arrow key to lock axis, allowing you to move the mouse to other parts of your model to reference a length or to type in a length manually. Locking axis is a good habit to ensure you are drawing on axis every time.

✓ **Tape Measure tool** - Use the **Tape Measure tool** (T) to create guides for aligning objects. Once you are done, you can quickly erase all guides from the **Edit menu**.

✓ **Overlapping lines** - Do not worry if you have to overlap lines while creating your layout. You can easily erase them before offsetting and extruding your walls.

✓ **Check setback lines** - You can check your compliance with the setback lines by going to **Camera > Parallel Projection**, then **Camera > Standard Views > Top**.

✓ **Parallel alignment** - While drawing a line, using the protractor, or the **Rotate tool** (Q), you can lock a parallel alignment by hovering over an edge in your model and tapping the down arrow.

Floor Level of Detail

The floors in your model should have a very low level of detail. They are going to simply be an extruded mass, representing the entire floor framing assembly. The thickness of your floors should be equal to the actual dimension of the floor framing, including the subfloor (**Figure 5-9**). You do this because when you dimension the model in LayOut, you want the measurements to represent the framing dimensions.

Figure 5-9
The level of
detail of a
floor object
compared
to actual
construction.

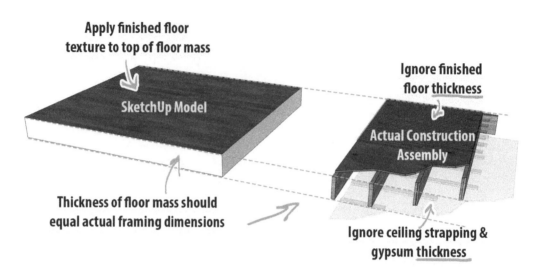

**Apply finished floor
texture to top of floor mass**

SketchUp Model

**Ignore finished
floor thickness**

Actual Construction
Assembly

**Thickness of floor mass should
equal actual framing dimensions**

**Ignore ceiling strapping &
gypsum thickness**

TIP You might notice that in the final construction documents, the finish floor material is shown on the floor plans. Are you ignoring the thickness of the finish floor material in the model? Yes!

Although you dimension the floor assembly to equal the thickness of the rough framing and the subfloor, you fake the appearance of the finish floor by applying a finish floor material directly to this surface. You gain the value of being able to identify finish floor material without adding complexity to the modeling and documentation process.

Setting Floor Height

When you have got a basic floor plan established, you will want to move the floor group vertically, in order to see how it sits on the site plan. This will give you a different perspective on your layout, and you might need to make changes to it depending upon how it interacts with the site contours.

When you move the floor, you will want to move a copy of the setback lines too. The setback lines will serve as an alignment tool once the building is extracted into its own model.

Step by Step

To copy the floor & setback lines into the terrain, follow these steps:

1. With the **Move tool** (M), tap the **up arrow** and tap CTRL (Option on Mac) to lock the blue axis and copy the floor group and setback lines vertically to intersect with your 3D terrain. Hover over different spots on the terrain to reference that height. Place it roughly to the height you want.

2. Take a look at the Measurements toolbar to see what height the floor landed at, and type in a new dimension so the floor is pinned to an absolute dimension. (Not some random height you happened to pick with your mouse.) (**Figure 5-10**)

3. Delete the old floor group from the ground plane area. (It is ok to have multiple setback line groups since setbacks are not things that typically change throughout a project, and they are only ever viewed in a scene from above.)

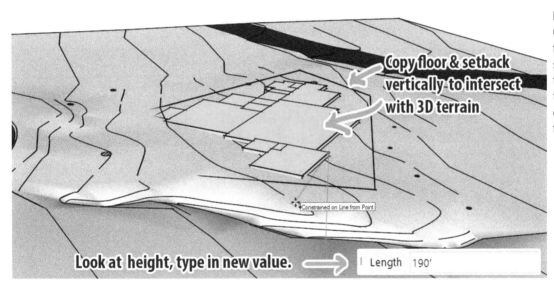

Copy floor & setback vertically to intersect with 3D terrain

Constrained on Line from Point

Look at height, type in new value. ⟹ | Length 190'

Figure 5-10
Copy the floor and setback up to the 3D terrain to establish floor height.

At this point, continue to analyze the model, and make adjustments to your floor plan accordingly.

Use the **Tape Measure tool** (T) to measure the distance between a point on the building and the terrain (**Figure 5-11**). You can do this by measuring from a point on the floor group (instead of an edge), tap the **up arrow** to lock the blue axis, and reference a point on the terrain in line with the building. Go to **View > Hidden Geometry** to see the terrain more easily.

Figure 5-11
The Tape Measure can be used to compare heights between the terrain and the floor.

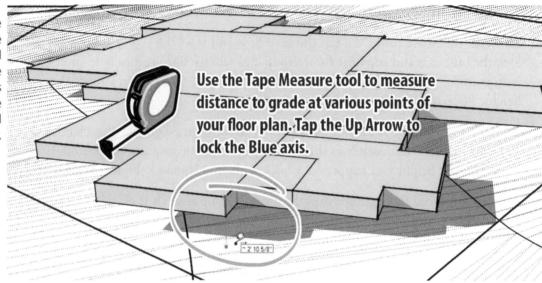

Use the Tape Measure tool to measure distance to grade at various points of your floor plan. Tap the Up Arrow to lock the Blue axis.

Figure 5-12
Project with multiple levels coordinated with a sloped grade.

On projects like this, use the Tape Measure tool to check multiple points on the model to see how the building relates to grade.

Patio Stairs Stairs Lower level

Photo: ©VanceFox.com
Contractor: MD Construction & Consulting

Extracting Part of a Group

Have you created your floor plan, then discovered that you need to have a split level plan because of the site slope? Perhaps you want to extract part of a floor to distinguish it as a different construction assembly. You do not have to start over, you can easily extract a part of a group.

To extract a part of an existing group, follow these steps: (Figure 5-13)

1. Select the surfaces you would like to extract from the group, press **CTRL+C** (**Command+C** on Mac) to copy them.

2. Delete the floors from the existing group using the **Push/Pull tool** (**P**). **Exit the current group.**

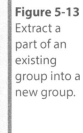

3. **Edit > Paste in Place** to paste the copied surfaces outside of the original group. Turn them into a group right away, then move them to the new height and extrude the floor thickness.

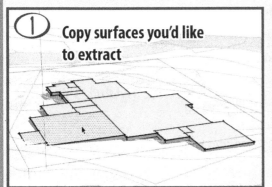

① Copy surfaces you'd like to extract

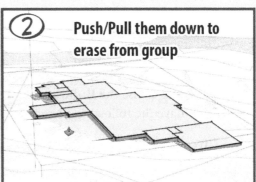

② Push/Pull them down to erase from group

Figure 5-13
Extract a part of an existing group into a new group.

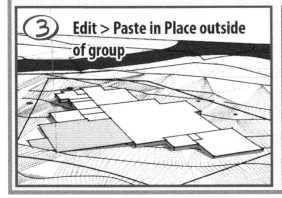

③ Edit > Paste in Place outside of group

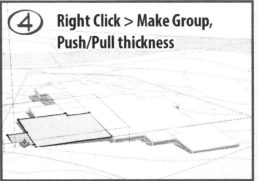

④ Right Click > Make Group, Push/Pull thickness

Extracting the Building Model

After the initial analysis of the relationship between your floor plan and the site, you will want to stop modeling the building from within the site model, and extract it into its own SketchUp file. You will then import that file back into the site model as a component, and reload it when you want changes to be reflected in the site model.

Why can't you just continue modeling the building inside the site model?

✓   You do not have any layers in the site model for the building, and you do not want to have to deal with the site model layers. In the building template model, the layers will be preset for the building.

✓   You are at the point where you can begin to focus on the building itself, without worrying about how the building relates to the site. For this reason, it is better to be working in a model where you do not have to see anything other than the building.

✓   Depending upon the complexity of your project, the site model file size may be too large to continue modeling the building. If you are experiencing performance issues, modeling the building in its own file will help you model faster.

✓   The site model includes scenes related to the site. You want to have a separate model with scenes dedicated for the floor plan, roof plan, and elevations.

You are going to use the **Building.skp** template model for the building. This template will have the following presets: (**Figure 5-14)**

✓   **Layer** structure is preset for the building model to make it easier to organize the model.

✓   **Scenes** will be included for the working model, as well as all the scenes that you will be bringing into LayOut for the viewports.

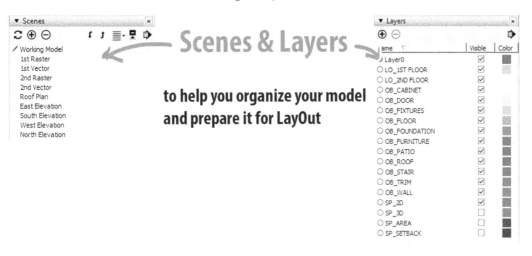

Figure 5-14
The building
template
scenes and
layers.

✓ Also, specific **styles** are included in the template for use while modeling and for each type of scene that you will be exporting to LayOut.

We are going to review the template in more detail later, but for now open up the **Building.skp** file. Make sure you open the file into a new instance of SketchUp, and not from the **File menu** of your currently active SketchUp model. You actually want to have both the site model and the building model open at the same time, because you will be referring back to the site model while you are modeling the building.

In order to have some sort of reference to the site within the building model, you are going to copy the setback lines along with the floor group from the site model into the building model.

To copy the floor plan into the building model, follow these steps: (Figure 5-15)

1. In the site model, make sure the axes are aligned to the floor group.

2. Select the setback lines and the floor group(s) and press **CTRL+C** (**Command+C** on Mac) to copy.

3. Go to your building model, press **CTRL+V** (**Command+V** on Mac) to paste. Click on the model origin (where the three axes intersect) to place the objects into the model. Save the building model.

Copy floor & setback lines from site model, paste into building model template.

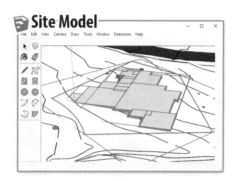
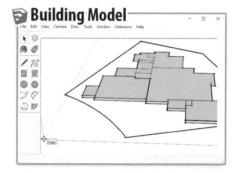

4. Go back to the site model, delete the floor groups (but keep the setback lines).

5. Go to **File > Import** to import the building model back into the site as a component (**Figure 5-16**). Click anywhere to place it initially, then grab one of the endpoints in the setback line and snap it to the setback line in the site model to perfectly align the building to the site. (**Figure 5-17**)

6. Assign the imported building to the LO_BUILDING MODEL layer in the site model.

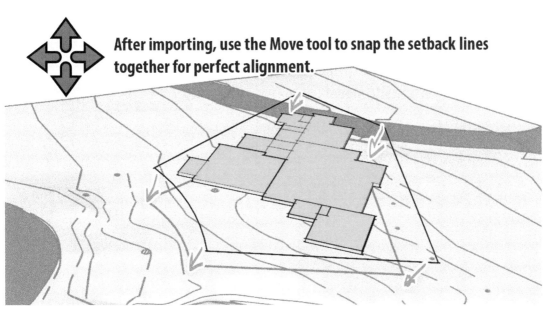

After importing, use the Move tool to snap the setback lines together for perfect alignment.

Figure 5-17
Position the imported building model by aligning the setback lines.

Changing the Building

The most important thing to understand about having a separate site model and building model is that you should never open or edit the building component **from inside the site model**.

When you need to make changes to the building, you need to open up the building model separately from the site model, save the changes, then reload the building model into the site model. (**Figure 5-18**)

Figure 5-18
The building
model
should be
reloaded
into the site
model when
changes are
made.

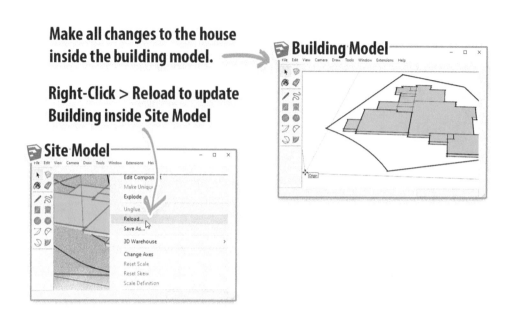

Figure 5-18
The building model should be reloaded into the site model when changes are made.

Step by Step

To reload the building model into the site model, follow these steps:

1. Make changes to the building model (for example, adjust the height of the floors), then go to **File > Save**.

2. Inside the site model, **right-click** on the building component **> Reload**. Select the updated building model skp file (It should already be preselected), and click Open.

The building component will then update with any changes you have made to the building model. This is the only way you want to update the building model.

It is important to note that once you have initially imported your building model into your site model and aligned their setback lines, you should not change the position of the setback lines (in either model). If you do, (for instance, if you decide to change the orientation of the building and need to rotate the setback lines again), you will need to realign the imported building model again.

To prevent accidental movement of the setback lines, you may consider locking them (Right-click > Lock).

Continue modeling the building from inside the building model, adding another floor group if there is a second floor to the building. (**Figure 5-19**)

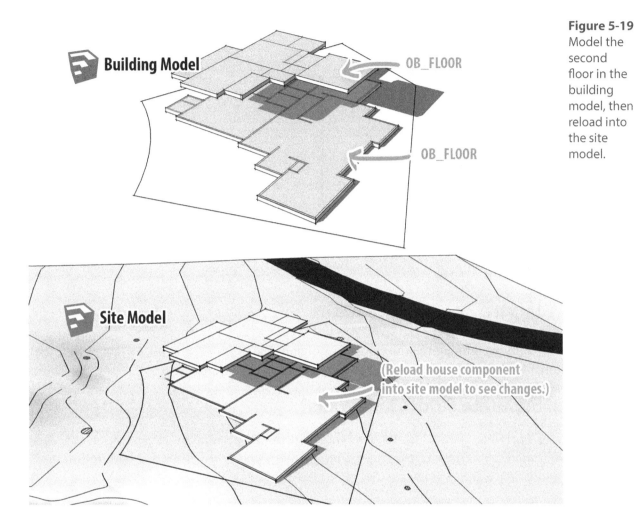

Hiding Trees to be Removed

Once you have positioned the building where you want it to be on the site, you will be able to see which existing trees on site will need to be removed.

In the site model, turn on the OB_TREES layer, and select the trees that you want to remove with the **Select tool** (SPACE) while holding down CTRL (Option on Mac) to select multiple. **Right-click > Hide (Figure 5-20).** The reason why you hide the trees instead of erase them is so you have the ability to unhide them if a change is made to the structure that would allow the tree to remain.

Figure 5-20
Hide trees
that will
need to be
removed
from the
site.

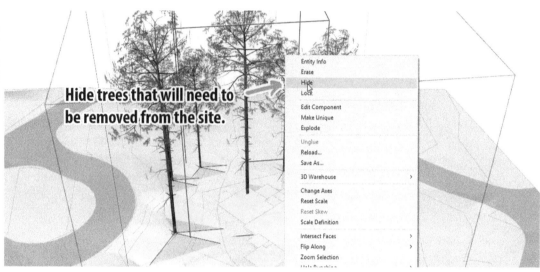

Walls

Continue refining the interior spaces of your building. When you are happy with the initial layout, you can then offset the walls so you can extrude them to the proper height.

Separate Floors and Walls?

Depending upon which method you are planning on using to create section cuts of your model, you may or may not be able to model your walls and floors within the same group.

The reason for doing this is to benefit from the seamless surface between the floor and walls when viewed from the exterior of the building. Otherwise, you would have an ugly seam at the bottom of the wall that you would have to address by hiding the edges within the wall group and floor group.

In the example project in this book, the walls for the first floor will be extruded up from the first floor object. There is no separate group for the walls, they will be within the same group as the floor. There is a single object layer called OB_FLOOR/WALL which has been assigned to the group.

If you are using a section cut method which requires you to hide the floors while having walls visible, you will need to have them in separate groups assigned to OB_WALLS and OB_FLOORS.

Walls Extruded From Floor

If you are going to be extruding walls directly from your floors, make sure you are inside your floor group and draw the wall outlines directly on the top of the floor surface. Once you are done, use the **Push/Pull tool** (P) to extrude the walls up to their heights. Assign the group to the OB_FLOOR/WALL layer. (You may need to rename the existing OB_WALL layer if OB_FLOOR/WALL layer does not exist already.) (**Figure 5-21**)

Extrude walls directly from the floor group to prevent seam between walls and floor

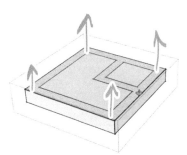
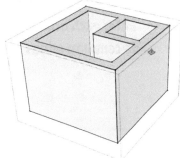

Figure 5-21
Walls can be extruded directly from the floor group.

Walls Separate From Floor

If you need to have the walls as a separate group from your floors, you may still want to draw your wall outline directly inside the floor group. The reason for this is when you eventually apply floor materials to the floor, you will need the floor to be subdivided by each room so you can apply different materials to each room. This is also helpful when calculating areas of each room. (**Figure 5-22**)

Instead of extruding the walls up from the floor, select the wall area inside the floor group, press CTRL+C (Command+C on Mac) to copy it, then exit the floor group. Go to **Edit > Paste in Place** to paste the wall outline outside of the floor group. Make it a group then extrude it up to the height of the wall.

Figure 5-22
If walls are modeled separately, you will need to hide common edges to prevent a seam from appearing.

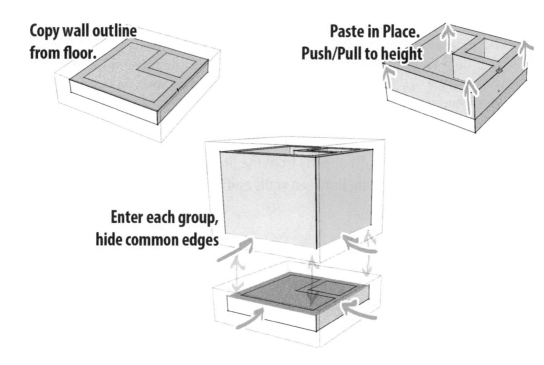

Hide the shared edges between the two groups so there is no visible seam between the two groups. (**Figure 5-23**)

Figure 5-23
No seam is visible, even though they are two separate groups.

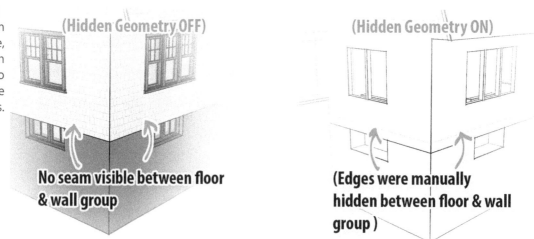

Walls Level of Detail

When determining how to represent your walls, you need to decide what will ultimately be dimensioned in the construction documents, and what details need to be included to accurately portray the design of the building. You want to aim for the lowest level of detail in order to keep the model simple and easy to make changes, while not sacrificing visual details that are critical to the overall design.

The thickness of your walls in SketchUp should be equal to the actual rough framing dimensions. You are not going to include the thickness of any wall coverings, such as gypsum board, insulation, sheathing or siding. Modeling to the framing dimensions will make it easier to generate your floor plan in LayOut and provide the framing crew the dimensions they need to build the structure. (**Figure 5-24**)

Since the foundation and frame are the first construction tasks, their dimensions are critical. Finishes are applied to that frame, so the finish dimension is less critical. You do need to be aware and understand the finishes and their thickness, especially if you are looking for a clear dimension.

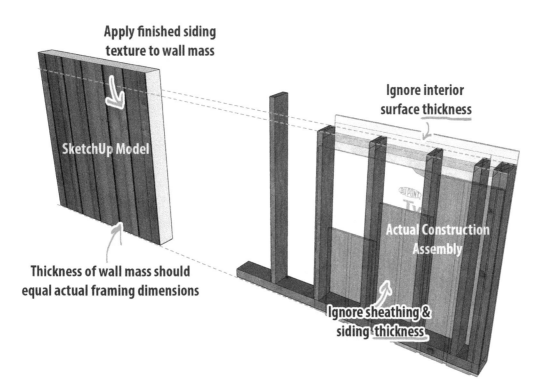

Apply finished siding texture to wall mass

Ignore interior surface thickness

SketchUp Model

Actual Construction Assembly

Thickness of wall mass should equal actual framing dimensions

Ignore sheathing & siding thickness

Figure 5-24
The level of detail of a wall compared to the actual construction assembly.

At this phase, you want to focus on the structural assemblies that need to be dimensioned in the construction documents. If there are other visual details you would like to include in the model, you will wait until the next phase to add them. You may have a wall with a stone veneer, for example, where you would like to model the thickness of the veneer, but for now you can simply use a texture to represent the stone.

Once your rooms are divided on their respective floors, you can use the **Offset tool** (**F**) to quickly define the wall framing space dividing up the floor area.

Tips for using the Offset tool:

Figure 5-25
You can offset a selection of connected edges.

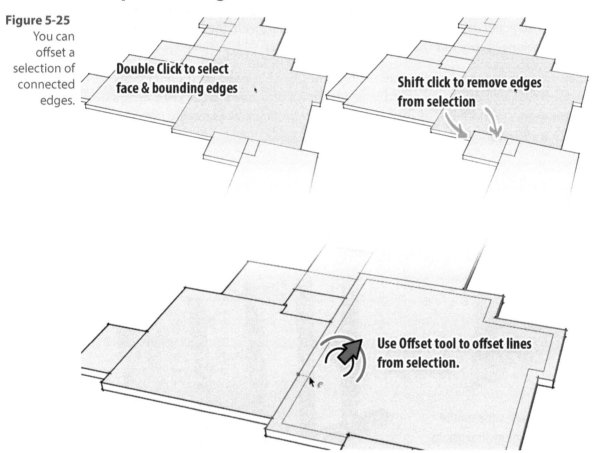

Double Click to select face & bounding edges

Shift click to remove edges from selection

Use Offset tool to offset lines from selection.

✓ **Quickly select all but a small selection of walls to offset**: You can use a subtractive selection method. First, **double-click** the surface within the area you would like to offset. Then, hold down the **SHIFT** key and click on selected entities that you would like the offset action to ignore. (**Figure 5-25**)

Double-Click Offset tool on selection

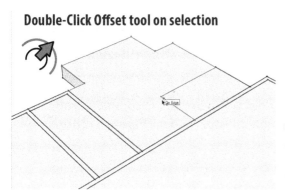

Offset same distance as previous offset

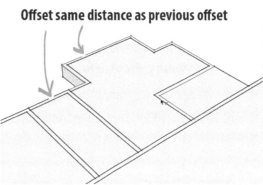

Figure 5-26
The Offset tool remembers the last distance offset.

✓ **Quickly offset the same distance.** - After using the **Offset tool** (F) once, you can offset other edges the same distance without having to type in the distance by simply **double-clicking** the **Offset tool** (F). (**Figure 5-26**)

✓ **Inference System** - Do not forget, the **Offset tool** (F) also works with the inference system. Instead of typing in the offset distance, it is possible to snap to other points in your model to specify the offset distance.

After creating your wall thicknesses, you will need to go around the model with the **Eraser tool** (E) and clean up any extra lines left on the floor surface, as well as erasing any lines that subdivide the wall areas (**Figure 5-27**). You will want all of the walls to be selected as one.

Figure 5-27
Erase any dividing lines between walls.

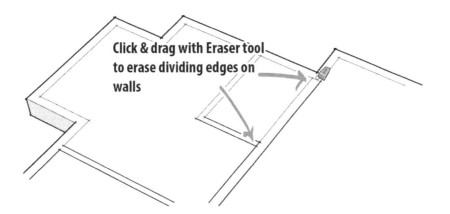

Click & drag with Eraser tool to erase dividing edges on walls

Use the **Push/Pull tool** (**P**) to extrude the walls up to the rafter or joist bearing height. Ignore gable end walls and any other type of angled wall condition at this point. You want all full height walls to be at the same level right now. You will refine them further once you begin to define the roof.

Repeat this process for each level of your project. When you are complete, you should have the following organizational structure in your model: (**Figure 5-28**)

Figure 5-28
Each level is in its own group, and is extruded to a common height at this time.

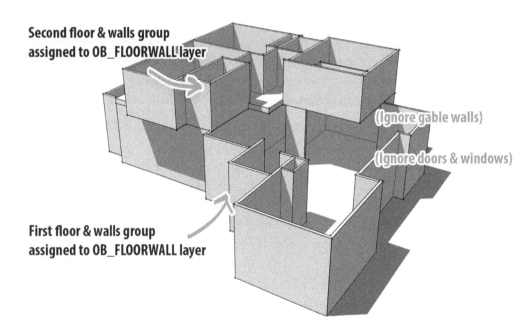

Second floor & walls group assigned to OB_FLOORWALL layer

(Ignore gable walls)

(Ignore doors & windows)

First floor & walls group assigned to OB_FLOORWALL layer

If you modeled the floors separately from the walls, you will have four groups instead of two in this example; two floor groups and two wall groups.

Stairs

Although stairs can be complicated, in the schematic model, you want to keep them as simple as possible. The goal is not to create detailed shop drawings from this model. You need to model the design intent of the stairs and that is it.

Figure 5-29
Even complex stairs can be designed in SketchUp.

Stairs Level of Detail

If you remember when you defined the floor level of detail, you modeled the dimensions to the rough framing dimensions. You included the floor joist dimension and the plywood subfloor dimension to calculate the total floor height. You then applied a finish floor material in order to fake the appearance of the finish floor on top of the subfloor. This expanded the utility of the model so you could provide framing dimensions in the drawings, while also communicating finishes within the same model. You are going to follow the same concept when modeling the stairs. (**Figure 5-30**)

Figure 5-30
Stairs level
of detail
compared
to an actual
construction
assembly.

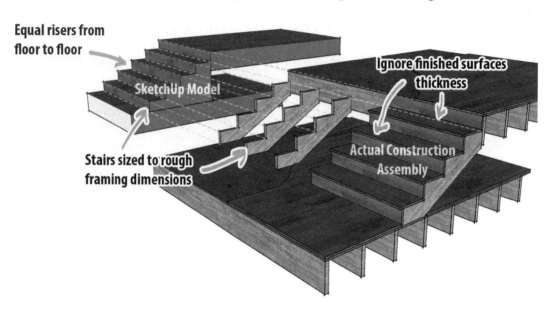

Equal risers from floor to floor

Ignore finished surfaces thickness

SketchUp Model

Actual Construction Assembly

Stairs sized to rough framing dimensions

Stairs can be constructed numerous ways. Sometimes stringers have a plywood substrate on top of them, under the finish tread. Other times, the treads are applied directly to the stringer. Then there are countless custom and creative ways of designing and constructing stairs. What is important to understand is that the model is not detailed enough to generate shop drawings. If you need to generate shop drawings, you will need to build a dedicated model for that.

Stair riser heights are calculated by measuring the total distance between the lower finished floor and the upper finished floor, then dividing that distance into equal riser heights. Depending upon how the stairs are constructed, the stringers need to account for tread thickness in order to end up at an equal riser height throughout.

In the model, you are simply going to measure the distance between the top of each floor, and model the riser height to be equally distributed between them. This will provide you with an accurate overall riser height (assuming the finish floor thickness is equal on both landings), and it will look visually correct in the model even though the stairs may not accurately depict a rough framing dimension or a finish dimension. The carpenters will need to do their own calculations in the field, or you will need to provide a more detailed shop drawing to provide that information.

Straight Stairs

Straight stairs are the easiest to model since you only need to know your overall rise and run. Actually, you do not even need to know the run, you can figure that out as you model. Start with the ideal step size, see where that gets you, then adjust accordingly.

To model a straight stair, follow these steps: (Figure 5-31)

1. Let's say you want to shoot for a step that has an 11" tread, and a 6-1/2" riser. Start by creating a rectangle at those dimensions, then **triple-click > Make Component**. (You are using a component so you can have identical copies of each step.) Place the component in the building at the top of where your stair will begin. (You will adjust this tread later since the top of the stair is actually the floor landing.)

2. Select the tread component, then with the **Move tool** (M), click on the top, back corner of the tread, tap CTRL (**Option** on Mac) to make a copy, then move that copy to the lower front corner of the riser.

3. Type in the number of copies you think you need and press ENTER.

Examine the stairs and determine whether you need to shorten or lengthen the riser height of each step in order to make each riser identical from the first floor to the second floor. Once you have determined that, you can use the **Scale tool** (S) to adjust the tread components.

4. Select all of the tread components, **right-click > Make Group**. **Double-click** to enter the group. While inside the stair group, select all of the tread components again, then activate the **Scale tool** (S). Grab the bottom scale handle and scale the treads along the blue axis to lengthen or shorten them equally along your total rise.

Figure 5-31
Model a set of stairs by creating a component for the treads and copying them.

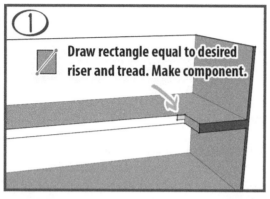
① Draw rectangle equal to desired riser and tread. Make component.

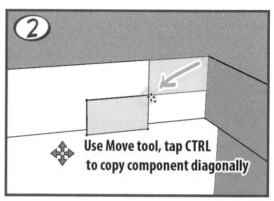
② Use Move tool, tap CTRL to copy component diagonally

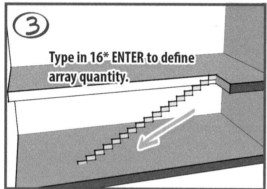
③ Type in 16* ENTER to define array quantity.

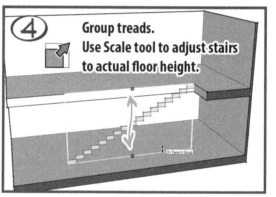
④ Group treads. Use Scale tool to adjust stairs to actual floor height.

Double-click on one of your tread components, use the **Push/Pull tool** (P) to extrude to the width of your stair. You may also need to adjust the position of your stairs and delete the top tread component, since the top of the stairs is actually the upper floor landing. (**Figure 5-32**)

The individual stair treads can remain on Layer0, but you should assign the parent group to the OB_STAIR layer.

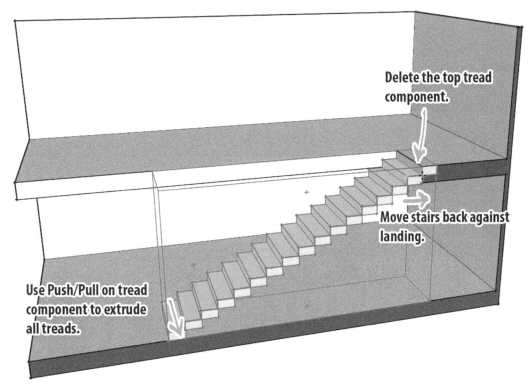

Figure 5-32
Extrude
the tread
component
and delete
the top
tread.

Right now, this simple stair is all that is needed for the Schematic Design phase. Once you get into the next phase of design, you can refine the stairs further and incorporate more detail into them.

Stair with Mid-Landing

In the example project model, there is a U-shaped stair that includes a mid-landing. You can use the same workflow to build this type of stair too. The most important thing to do is establish the correct riser height. Once you do that, you can decide at what height you want the landing, and where you want the stair to reverse direction.

To model a U-shaped stair, follow these steps: (Figure 5-33)

1. Follow steps 1-4 of building a straight stair until you have calculated the correct rise for each step. (It is ok if your stairs run through a wall right now, since you are only worrying about the height in this step. You will figure out the stair run in the next steps.)

2. Use the **Tape Measure tool** (T) to help you analyze the space available and determine which tread you will be turning into the landing, and which treads will reverse direction after the landing. Using the **Rotate tool** (Q), rotate the treads 180° so they are running the opposite direction.

3. Move the lower treads to the opposite side of the stairwell.

4. Open one of the tread components, then use the **Push/Pull tool** (P) to extrude it to the correct width. Then, **right-click** on the landing tread and **Make Unique**. Resize that component to fill the landing area.

Figure 5-33
Stairs that change direction can be created by rotating some of the tread components.

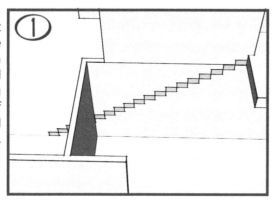

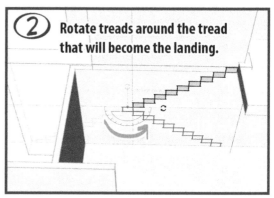

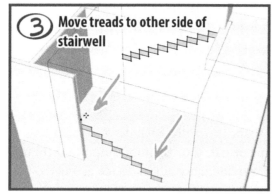

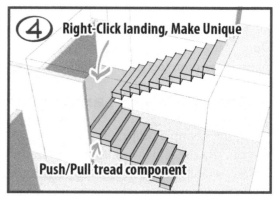

Roofing

When modeling roofs in SketchUp, you want to follow these three simple rules to determine how to represent them in your model.

1. Model the roof to the size that needs to be dimensioned in LayOut. (Typically the structural members.)

2. Add details and materials to enhance the look & design of the building.

3. Model as simple as possible, without sacrificing rule 1 & 2.

Roofing Level of Detail

You are basically approaching it the same way you have approached other parts of the building. Think about what needs to be dimensioned in LayOut, and what you need communicated visually in the design. In most situations, you can ignore the thickness of interior surfaces and exterior roofing coverings. However, since the roof covering is an important visual element, you will apply a roofing material to the surface of the roof object to simulate the appearance of the roof. (**Figure 5-34**)

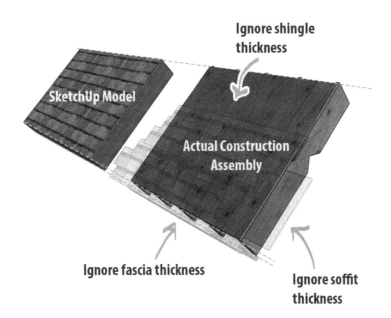

Ignore shingle thickness

SketchUp Model

Actual Construction Assembly

Ignore fascia thickness

Ignore soffit thickness

Figure 5-34
A roof level of detail compared to an actual construction assembly.

If you have a complex roof, with multiple dormers, complex valleys, or multiple pitches, try to isolate each part of the roof into separate groups. You do not need to try to model the entire roof as a single assembly. It is much easier to make changes to your building and experiment with different roof projections when each roof is isolated from the rest.

Do not worry about intersecting the roof planes with each other. Just let them run through the intersecting roofs and walls, even if they end up extending into the interior of your building.

In the Schematic Design phase, it is all about flexibility, and no one will see these temporary conflicts in your drawings anyway. You are only going to be producing floor plans and exterior elevations from this phase, so most of the roof cleanup can be held off until the next phase.

Gable Roof

To model a gable roof, the first thing you will need to do is create a pair of guides from the spring point of the walls it will bear on. (**Figure 5-35**)

 TIP Using the **Protractor tool**, you can provide a decimal degree for pitch, but you can also provide a pitch ratio, such as 3:12.

Then, draw a triangle, using the intersecting guides as reference. **Triple-click** the rectangle to select all, then **right-click > Make Group**. **Double-click** to enter the group.

Figure 5-35
Model a gable roof by starting with a triangle and offsetting it.

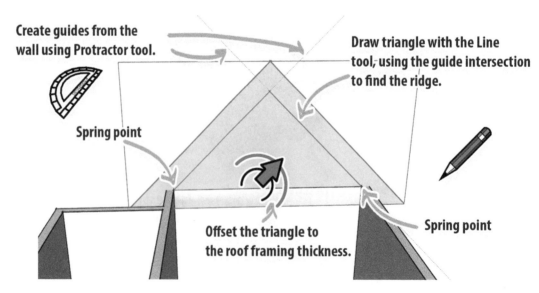

Create guides from the wall using Protractor tool.

Draw triangle with the Line tool, using the guide intersection to find the ridge.

Spring point

Offset the triangle to the roof framing thickness.

Spring point

Inside the triangle group, use the **Offset tool** (F) to offset the triangle outwards to create the rafter thickness. Remember, you always want to dimension to the framing members, so ignore sheathing thickness, roofing materials, etc.

Now, using the **Tape measure tool** (T) and the **Line tool** (L), model the profile of your roof eaves. Clean up the remaining geometry with the **Eraser tool** (E). (**Figure 5-36**)

Figure 5-36
Delete entities until you are left with the roof profile.

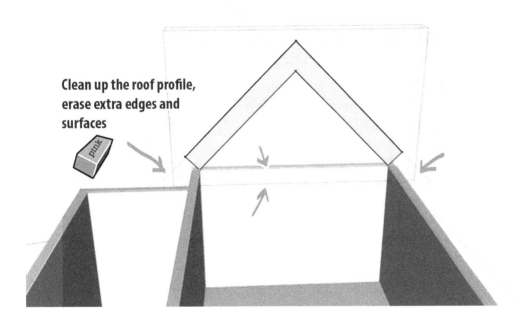

Clean up the roof profile, erase extra edges and surfaces

Finally, extrude your roof along the building using the **Push/Pull tool** (P). (**Figure 5-37**)

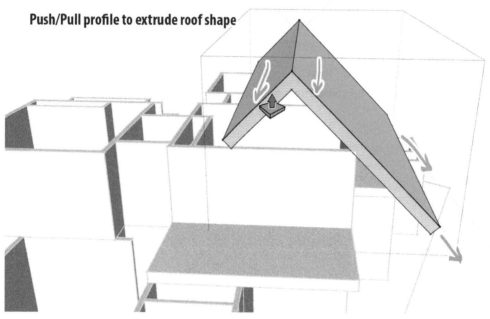

Push/Pull profile to extrude roof shape

Tips for roof modeling:

✓ **Double-clicking** on an edge with the **Tape Measure tool** (T) will create a guide projecting along the length of the edge. This is useful for lengthening roof eaves perpendicularly to the rafter when the eaves are not perpendicular to the rafter, preventing you from being able to use the **Push/Pull tool** (P). (**Figure 5-38**)

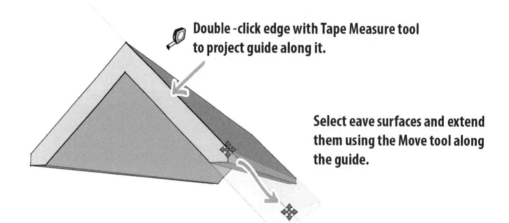

Double-click edge with Tape Measure tool to project guide along it.

Select eave surfaces and extend them using the Move tool along the guide.

✓ Once you have created one roof profile, you can reuse it on other roof planes. Just copy the original group using the **Move tool** (M) while tapping CTRL (Option on Mac) to make a copy. Use the arrow keys to lock axis while moving, then rotate the new copy to the correct orientation. (**Figure 5-39**)

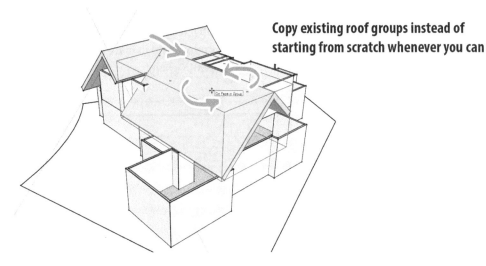

Copy existing roof groups instead of starting from scratch whenever you can

Figure 5-39
If possible, copy roof groups to other areas of the building, then customize.

✓ If you identify symmetry in your design, it may make more sense to only model one side of the roof as a component, then mirror it to the other side of the building. This will become handy once you start modeling all the trim details, saving you time. If there are small differences in the roofs, you can always make the components unique once you identify a deviation.

Hip Roof

A hip roof is easiest to model using the **Follow Me tool**. First, you want to find the part of the roof that will have the longest rafters, and create your flat profile of that part of the roof. With a hip roof, you only want to model half of the roof, because you will be extruding that profile around the perimeter of the building to create the hip roof.

Once your profile is modeled, you need to create a path inside the profile group for the **Follow Me tool** to follow. You can draw it manually by tracing the top of the wall with the **Line tool** (L), or you can copy the path from your floor group.

Figure 5-40
The Follow
Me tool can
be used for
hip roofs.

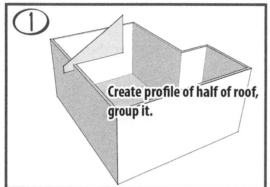

Create profile of half of roof, group it.

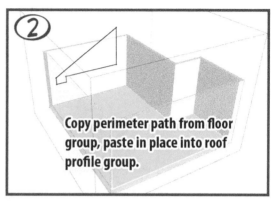

Copy perimeter path from floor group, paste in place into roof profile group.

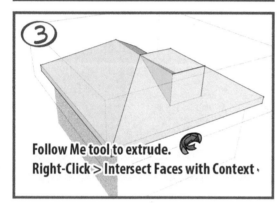

Follow Me tool to extrude.
Right-Click > Intersect Faces with Context

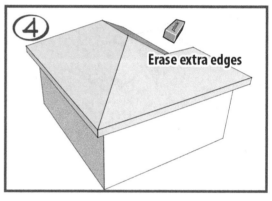

Erase extra edges

To model a hip roof, follow these steps: (Figure 5-40)

1. Determine which span of the building is the longest, and draw a profile of half of the roof. Make it a group.

2. **Double-click** on your floor group to open it. Orbit to the underneath of the floor (You may need to "Hide rest of model" to be able to see it.) Select the bottom of the floor. Copy it. Open your roof profile group and go to **Edit > Paste in Place**.

3. Grab the **Follow Me tool** and click on the roof profile surface to extrude the roof around the building. (The floor you pasted in place should still be selected when you do this. The **Follow Me tool** is best used when you preselect the path you would like to follow.) Once the roof is extruded, you may need to select the entire roof, **Right-click > Intersect Faces > With Context.** This will establish edges where surfaces intersect with each other, allowing you to delete extra surfaces produced from the **Follow Me tool. (Figure 5-41)**

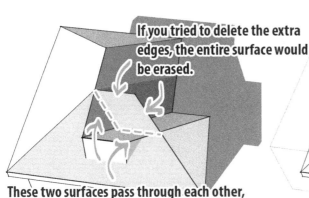

Figure 5-41
Intersect faces in order to clean up geometry after using Follow Me.

If you tried to delete the extra edges, the entire surface would be erased.

These two surfaces pass through each other, but there is no intersecting edge at the ridge.

After Intersecting faces, ridge lines are defined and you're able to select surfaces to delete.

4. Navigate around the roof group deleting extra faces and edges produced by the **Follow Me tool**. It is helpful to turn on X-Ray mode to see edges left inside the group. It is also helpful to enable **View > Component Edit > Hide Rest of Model** to limit your visibility to the active roof group.

An important thing to notice is that a profile does not need to be connected to a path in order to use the **Follow Me tool**. This makes it really easy to erase the floor surface from the roof group once you are done extruding it.

Tips for creating hip roofs:

✓ This method works for all kinds of roofs that have hips and valleys.

✓ If you need to make a change to an existing hip roof profile, sometimes it is easier to start over with a new profile. Other times, you can add a profile to the edge of a roof and use the **Follow Me tool** again to extrude it around the existing roof. Some manual cleanup may be required.

Gable Walls

Once you have established your roof lines, you can go around your model and edit your gable walls to meet up to the roof.

The fastest way to do this is to enter the wall group, draw a line at each spring point, then draw another line at the midpoint of the wall. Select the midpoint line, then use the **Move tool** (M) to move the line vertically and snap to the roof. (**Figure 5-42**)

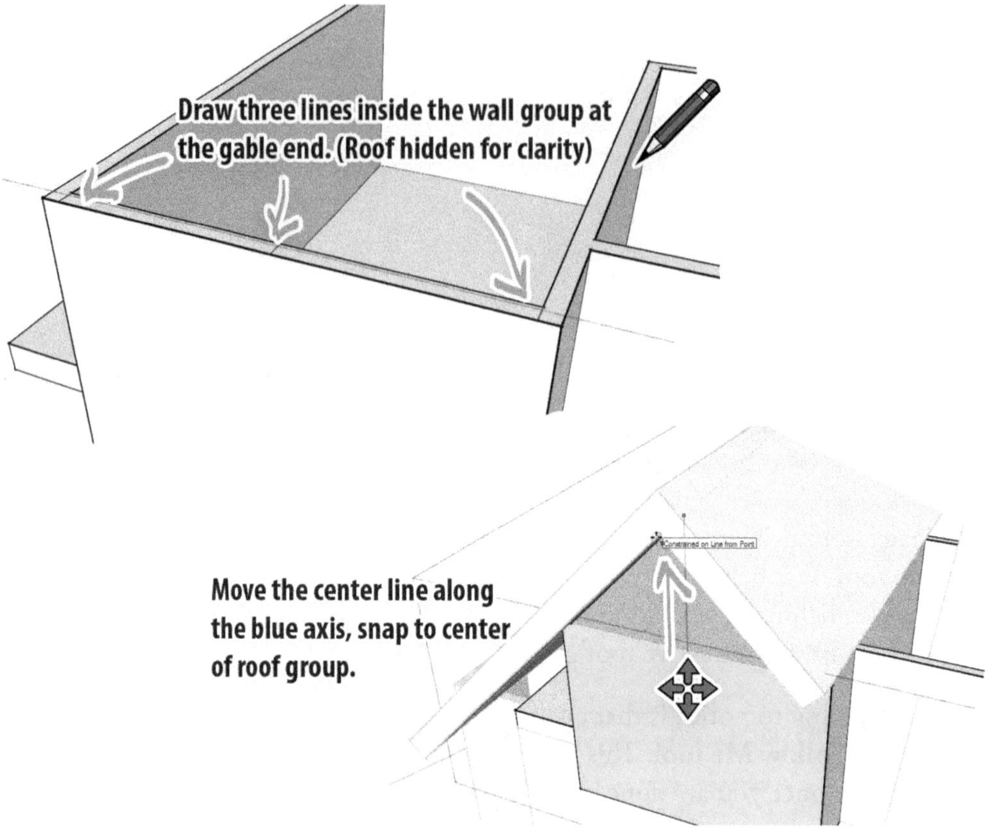

Figure 5-42
Gable walls
are extended
up to meet
with the roof.

Draw three lines inside the wall group at
the gable end. (Roof hidden for clarity)

Move the center line along
the blue axis, snap to center
of roof group.

Other Roof tips

At first, concentrate on creating roof profiles and extruding them to their rough
location. Do not try to intersect or clean up anything at this stage. By leaving each roof
profile contained within its own group, you give yourself the ability to look at the entire
model as a whole, then make small adjustments to each roof group until you are happy
with the result. Only at that point should you go through and perform some minor clean
up and intersection tasks. (**Figure 5-43**)

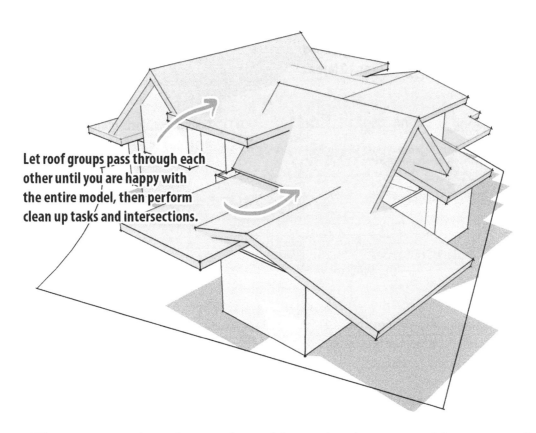

Let roof groups pass through each other until you are happy with the entire model, then perform clean up tasks and intersections.

When you are ready to clean up the model, it is ok to leave some of the interior walls unresolved. Since you are only going to be creating exterior elevations and floor plans from top view in the Schematic Design phase, no one will know if an interior wall is extruded through the ceiling or not. Leave that for later because you might be making changes to the layout and do not want to do more work than necessary if you are just going to end up changing it.

Once you have an assortment of objects in your model, you will want to pause from modeling and spend a little time organizing your model. All objects should be contained within a group according to which level of the building they are on, then assigned to a location layer (LO) so you can shut off different levels of the building. You should also group together common objects within each level of the building and assign them to their corresponding object layer (OB).

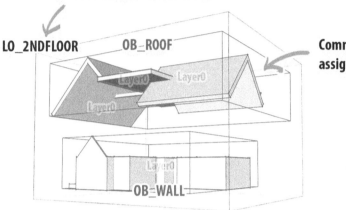

All objects located on a
specific building level are grouped
together, assigned to an LO layer.

LO_2NDFLOOR   OB_ROOF

Common objects grouped together,
assigned to an OB layer.

OB_WALL

In the image above (**Figure 5-44**), you will see the walls and roof of the second floor, contained inside a group assigned to the LO_2NDFLOOR layer. The first floor is organized in a similar manner.

Foundation

If your building includes a basement, you will have already modeled it as part of your initial floor space planning. If not, you can add your foundation now. The foundation is not modeled until now because its layout depends upon the design of the floor plan. The floor plan needs to be worked out first before modeling the foundation.

The level of detail depends upon whether or not you will be coordinating structural elements in your drawings. If you have a structural engineer who will be providing structural plans, that means you will not be creating the foundation plan from your model. You can simplify your model significantly by just modeling the perimeter footings, ignoring intermediate footings.

Perimeter Foundation

To quickly create a foundation with footings around the perimeter of your building, you can copy the bottom of the existing floor to use as a path, then draw the profile of your foundation and extrude it using the **Follow Me tool.**

To model a foundation, follow these steps: (Figure 5-45)

Step by Step

1. Enter the group assigned to the OB_FLOOR (or OB_FLOOR/WALL) layer, then copy the bottom surface.

2. Exit the floor group, but remain inside of the group assigned to LO_1ST FLOOR layer. Go to **Edit > Paste in Place** to paste the surface. **Right-click > Make Group**. **Double-click** to enter that group.

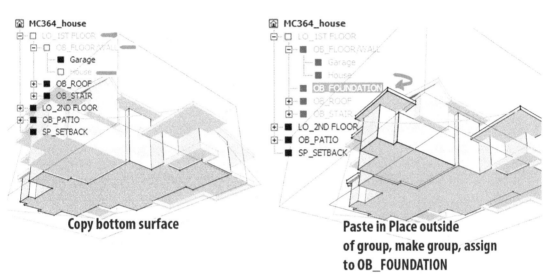

Copy bottom surface

Paste in Place outside of group, make group, assign to OB_FOUNDATION

Figure 5-45
Copy the bottom of the floor to use as a path for the foundation.

TIP This surface should represent the perimeter path of the foundation you want to create. If you have different foundation requirements at different parts of the building, now is the time to subdivide the face and create separate groups for each foundation section if necessary.

3. Draw the profile of the foundation wall, starting on the edge of the floor path. You may find it easier to use the **Line tool** (L) and lock one axis at a time using the arrow keys. If you try and draw a rectangle in "mid air" it is sometimes hard for SketchUp to know which orientation you are trying to achieve. The **Rotated Rectangle tool** is a helpful alternative as well. (**Figure 5-46**)

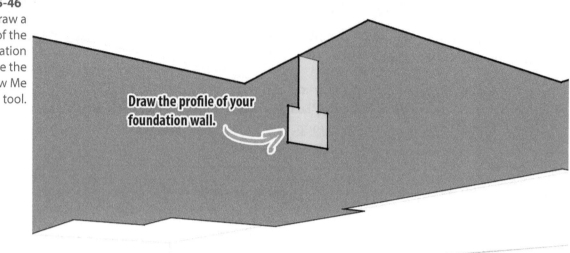

Draw the profile of your foundation wall.

4. Delete the floor surface, leaving only its perimeter path. (If you leave the surface, it will confuse SketchUp when you use the **Follow Me tool**, leaving the top of your foundation "open".)

5. **Triple-click** the path to select it. (You will need to deselect the foundation profile by holding **SHIFT** and **double-clicking** its face. You only want the path selected right now.) (**Figure 5-47**)

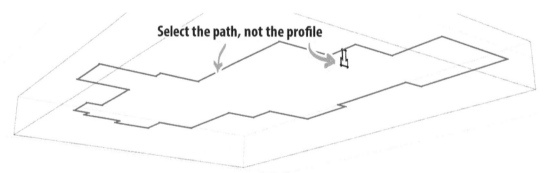

Select the path, not the profile

6. Grab the **Follow Me tool** and click on the foundation profile to extrude the foundation around the path. (**Figure 5-48**)

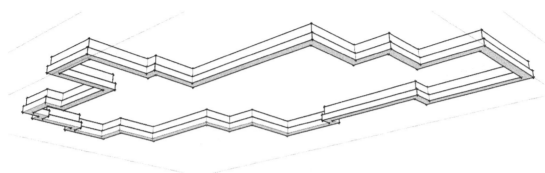

Figure 5-48
The Follow Me tool extrudes the profile around the path.

Some manual cleanup may be required as you go around your model, especially if you have two different foundation types intersecting. Again, if you will be producing foundation plans from your model, you will be required to coordinate and model all of the foundation walls. If you are outsourcing the structural drawings, you will only need to model the perimeter of the building. (**Figure 5-49**)

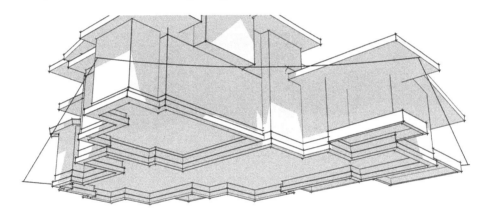

Figure 5-49
The completed foundation under the building.

Windows & Doors

In a perfect world, you would have access to a library of window and door components at your disposal to insert into your models. They would be modeled exactly how you like them, they would be at a perfect level of detail, and they would be easily customized to your specific job.

In reality, this ideal library of components does not exist. Especially when it comes to custom windows and doors. While you can find models on the 3D warehouse, or through subscription services such as Form Fonts, it is not likely that you will find components that meet your requirements every time. Instead, you will have to build your own personal library of components over time. Each project you create is an opportunity to extract and save components for future use.

If you do not have access to premade components, you do not need to spend a lot of time on windows and doors in Schematic Design. When you create the perspective views and Schematic Design documents, you are going to use a sketchy style, giving the building a very conceptual look. For this phase, using simple edges to represent the divided lights of windows is all that is needed. (**Figure 5-50**)

Remember, the Schematic Design phase is all about communicating the design while retaining the ability for fast and easy changes. Keeping your windows and doors conceptual at this stage helps you do that.

Figure 5-50
Windows are very simple in the Schematic Design phase.

Rough Openings

The first step is to knock out a hole where you want your windows and doors to go in your walls. To do that, enter your wall group and use the **Tape Measure tool** (**T**) and the **Rectangle tool** (**R**) to draw the rough opening of the door or window on the wall. Then, use the **Push/Pull tool** (**P**) to punch out a hole in the wall.

Actual or estimated rough openings?

Should you model your rough openings to the actual dimensions required, or should you estimate based on the door or window size you want installed at the location?

In order to model the actual rough openings, you would need to know the window or door manufacturer's required rough opening for each unit. That information will be hard to come by this early in the design process. Even if you have the rough opening sizes, it is better to refer to the manufacturer's documentation instead of copying the information into your drawings.

If you go back to the fundamental rules for determining the model level of detail, you can confirm that you should estimate the rough opening sizes.

1. **Provide dimensions for construction** - The rough opening dimensions are provided by the door/window manufacturer's documentation. Dimensions for window and door placement along the wall should refer to the center point of the unit.

2. **Model details to communicate design intent** - The door slab will be modeled to the intended unit size; the rough opening will add 1" all around to provide room for the door jamb. With windows, you can simply model the rough opening to the unit size.

✓ Use the **Tape measure tool** (T) to create an intersection at one corner of your door or window. Then use the **Rectangle tool** (R) from that first corner and type in the overall dimension of the door or window. With doors, you only need a single guide to pin one of the bottom corners of the door. For windows, you will need one guide at the header height, and another guide to intersect it to pin one of the top corners. (**Figure 5-51**)

Figure 5-51
Use guides to help create rough openings.

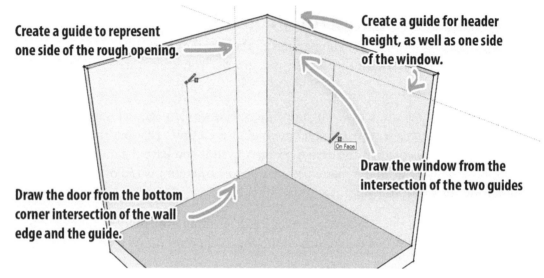

Create a guide to represent one side of the rough opening. ➡

Create a guide for header height, as well as one side of the window.

Draw the window from the intersection of the two guides

Draw the door from the bottom corner intersection of the wall edge and the guide.

✓ If you modeled your floors and walls all together inside the same group, keep in mind that the exterior bottom edge of the group represents the bottom of the floor assembly, not the bottom of the wall assembly. Doors will need to be located at a height equal to the top of floor. An easy way to insure this is to simply draw your doors from the interior side of you model. (**Figure 5-52**)

Figure 5-52
Make sure doors are modeled at top of floor height, not bottom of floor.

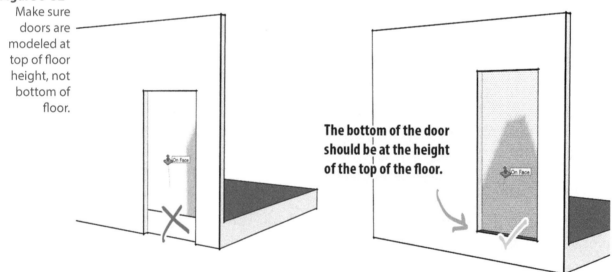

The bottom of the door should be at the height of the top of the floor.

✓ When using the **Push/Pull tool** (**P**) to punch out a hole, you do not need to orbit to the other side of the wall to get a surface inference point. Just reference the top edge of the wall, or any other point in plane with the other side of the wall. (Depending upon the camera orientation, it is sometimes difficult to push straight through to the other side of the wall. Instead, find an edge that is in plane with the back side of the wall for reference.)

✓ If you have multiple identical openings, do not push/pull them right away. Once you have drawn your first rectangle, select it, and copy it with the **Move tool** (M) to your other locations. Then, push/pull them to punch the holes. (**Figure 5-53**)

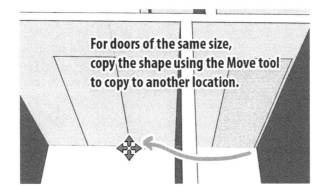

For doors of the same size, copy the shape using the Move tool to copy to another location.

Figure 5-53
Copy door shapes to other walls before push/pulling them.

✓ If you need to copy an opening onto a perpendicular wall, SketchUp can automatically orient the surface to be in plane with the wall. Use the **Move tool** (M) and tap **CTRL** (**Option** on Mac) to create a copy of an opening. Hover over the wall you want it on and click to place it. Now that it is copied and oriented, move it again into its final position. (Sometimes SketchUp will not get the orientation correct if you try to reference an edge or guide while copying. By doing it in two steps, you can force the correct orientation.) (**Figure 5-54**)

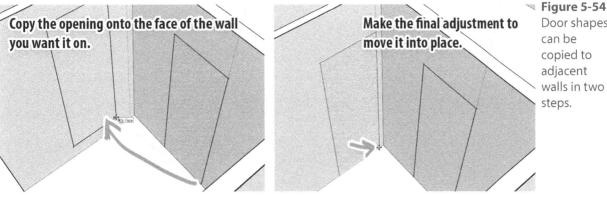

Copy the opening onto the face of the wall you want it on.

Make the final adjustment to move it into place.

Figure 5-54
Door shapes can be copied to adjacent walls in two steps.

✓ The **Push/Pull tool** (P) remembers the last distance you push/pulled. **Double-click** on the next surface to push/pull it the same distance as the last one. (**Figure 5-55**)

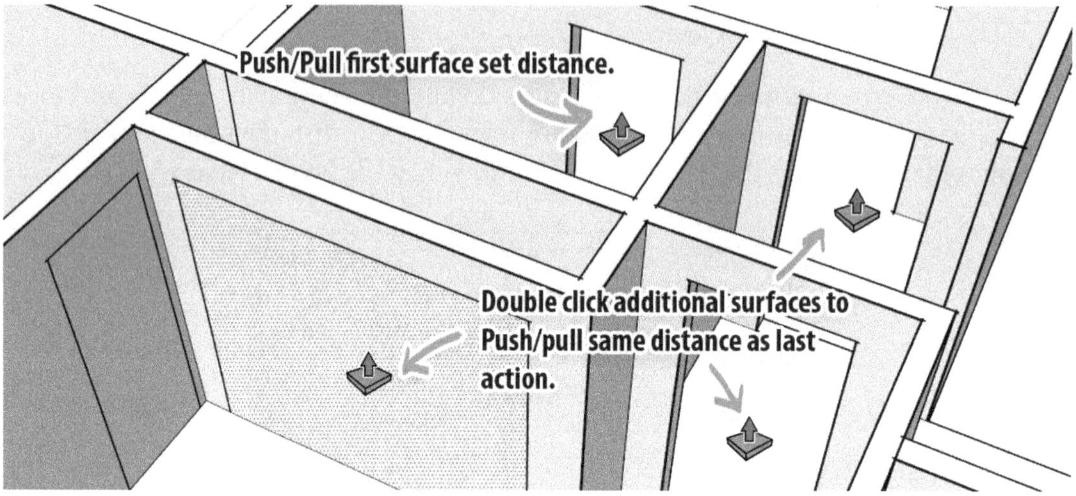

Figure 5-55
The Push/
Pull tool
remembers
its last
distance
by double-
clicking.

> Push/Pull first surface set distance.
>
> Double click additional surfaces to Push/pull same distance as last action.

Windows

After creating all the rough openings, exit the wall group. The next step is to create a component for each window unit, and place it in the window opening. You want each window and door to be its own component, because you will be replacing them later with more detailed components.

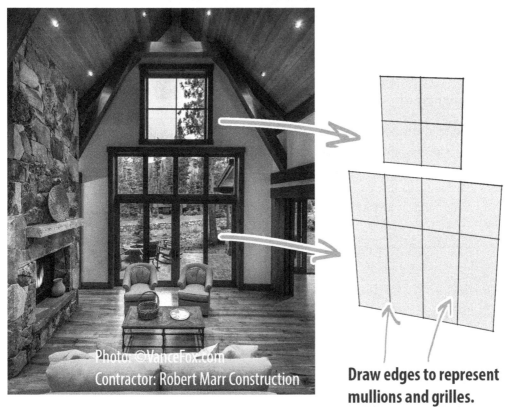

Windows and doors can be represented by simple rectangles in the Schematic Design phase if no premade component exists.

Photo: ©VanceFox.com
Contractor: Robert Marr Construction

Draw edges to represent mullions and grilles.

Figure 5-56
Simple rectangles are used to represent windows in Schematic Design.

A window in the schematic model is a flat, rectangular surface, subdivided by the number of lights (**Figure 5-56**). Use a semi-transparent material on the window surface to make it look like glass. (You can edit the opacity of any material in the **Materials dialog** under the **Edit** tab.)

If you have access to a more detailed window component that matches what you need for your project, by all means, use it. If not, wait until you get into the Design Development phase before modeling custom windows for the project.

Group all the windows together and assign to the OB_WINDOW layer for each level of the building.

Doors

You will treat doors a little differently than windows because you want to show the door swing in the schematic floor plans. In order to do that, the door component needs to be a little more complicated than the windows.

Since doors tend to be built to standard sizes, you may be able to grab door components from a previous project of yours, like Nick did in this example project. If you do not have an existing library of doors that match your project, you can just model a simple slab door for the schematic model.

A door unit is a component that consists of three main groups: The door frame group, door slab group, and the door swing group. The door slab should be dimensioned to the actual door size. For example, if you are modeling a 30" wide door that is 6'-8" high, model the door to those dimensions. The door frame will be 1" thick, and the door swing group will contain a simple arc and edge representing the door swing. (**Figure 5-57**)

Figure 5-57
Door components should include a frame group, door slab group, and door swing group.

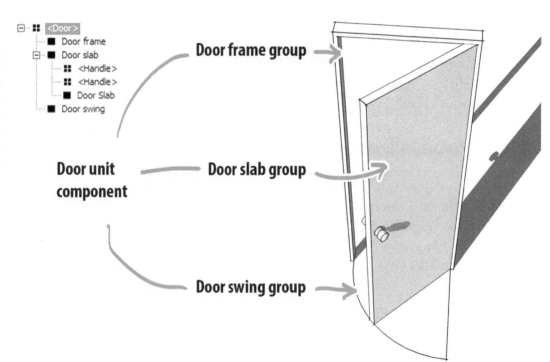

To model a simple door unit, follow these steps:

1. Model the door frame as a single solid object. The interior dimensions should be equal to the door slab dimensions, the exterior dimensions should be equal to the door unit rough opening. The width of the jamb should match the wall framing thickness. (In other words, ignore the gaps between the door jamb and the door/ rough opening.) Make group.

2. Model the door slab within the door jamb opening. If you are short on time or have not decided on the door style yet, just model a flat door slab for now. You can update the component in the next phase. You can add door knobs, but hinges are not necessary at this level of detail. Make Group. Rotate the door 45° from the frame so it is "half open".

3. To create a door swing, just create a group that contains an arc and an edge. Assign the door swing group to SP_2D layer, and assign the door slab and door frame to SP_3D layer.

4. Select the door frame group, door slab group, and door swing group, **right-click > Make Component**. You may want to name the component according to its size. For example, "3080 Interior door 2x6", or "3080 Interior door 2x4".

Group all the door components together and assign to the OB_DOOR layer for each level of the building.

As you copy doors throughout your model, there are a few things you should do:

✓ When you get to a door that is a different size, you will need to make the component unique (**right-click > Make Unique**), before you edit the component to resize it to the opening. The next time you come across a door opening of that size, find another door in your model that you have already resized to copy from.

✓ If you need to alternate the door swing direction, **right-click** the door **> Flip along**. You can also use the **Scale tool** (S) to flip a door by grabbing the center grip and typing in -1.

✓ Use the **Move tool** (M) to rotate the door component by grabbing one of the red  handles.

Decks & Patios

Decks and patios should be modeled within the building model, as they have a direct relationship to the floors in the building. Model them in the appropriate LO layer they step off onto, and place them inside their own group on the OB_PATIO layer. (**Figure 5-58**)

Figure 5-58
Use simple shapes to model decks and patios.

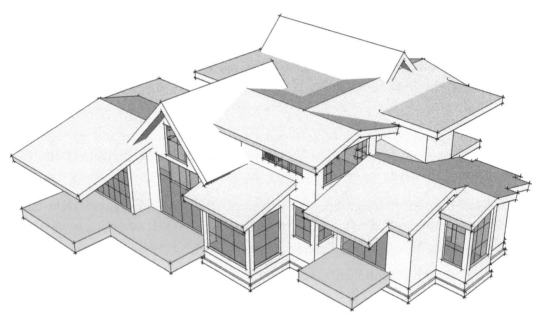

If you have a deck that includes a railing, you may decide to model a representation of that railing in Schematic Design. Even though it is not typically recommended to model stair railings on the interior of the building in the Schematic Design phase, deck railings have a large visual impact on the exterior perspective shots, which are included in the Schematic Design drawings.

Use basic rectangular components for the posts and balusters. You can change them or add more detail to them as you refine the design.

Do not forget to reload your building model back into your site model to review the relationship between the terrain and your patio/deck and guard rails. You will be able to determine where grading will be needed, or if you will need to include stairs. (**Figure 5-59**)

Figure 5-59
Compare patios with terrain height after reloading the building model into the site model.

Materials/Textures

One of the most noticeable differences between SketchUp & LayOut documents and traditional CAD drawings are the vibrant materials that are applied to the surfaces. In SketchUp, there are two types of materials:

✓ **Colors** - These are solid colors that can be defined in numerous ways. (RGB, Color Wheel, screen sample, etc.)

✓ **Textures** - Images that are tiled over a surface.

By applying texture materials on the surfaces, you can provide an accurate depiction of the various building materials being used on the project such as flooring, paint, siding, roofing, wood, stone, concrete, etc.

SketchUp includes a number of textures in the default materials library (**Figure 5-60**). You can access those materials from the **Materials panel** by clicking on the drop-down menu to select a folder. Within each folder is a collection of colors or textures. (You also have the ability to create your own colors, or your own textures from an image. For now, just explore the default library to paint the objects in your model.

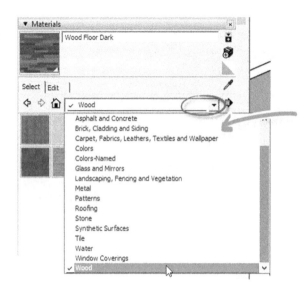

Figure 5-60
Many
materials are
included with
SketchUp.

SketchUp includes a library of materials to choose from.

Flooring

To identify the flooring type for each room or space, you will apply a texture. In order to do that, the floor surface will need to be subdivided for each space, or else the texture will be applied to the entire surface (**Figure 5-61**). **Remember, dimensionally, you have modeled to the top of the subfloor, but you are applying the finished floor material to the surface for visual identification only.** You should not model the finished floor surface above the subfloor. That level of detail is not necessary.

Figure 5-61
Use edges to
divide floor
surfaces
in order
to apply
different
materials to
rooms.

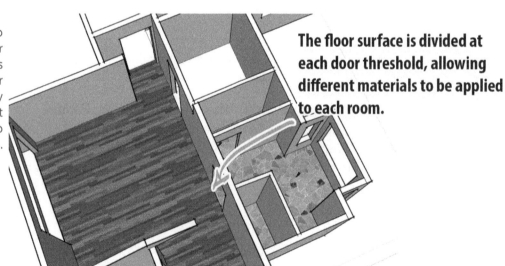

The floor surface is divided at each door threshold, allowing different materials to be applied to each room.

Group/component materials vs. surface materials

Whenever surfaces are created in SketchUp, they are assigned a default material to their front and back face. There are two ways to change the appearance of the surface material.

1. **Assign material to a group** - When you apply the **Paint Bucket tool** (B) to a group or component, all surfaces within that group that still have the default material applied to them will change to the new material. If any surfaces within the group have a material applied directly to them, they will not change appearance.

2. **Assign material to a surface** - When the **Paint Bucket tool** (B) is applied directly to a surface, that surface will not inherit the material assigned to its parent group. You also gain the ability to fine-tune the position and scale of the texture on the surface, useful for orienting directional materials such as wood flooring or siding.

When working with certain flooring materials, you will sometimes need to rotate the floor material to reflect the correct orientation. For example, you can rotate a wood flooring material to indicate the direction of the boards. In order to do this, you need to make sure you have applied the material directly to the surface, not to the parent group.

To rotate a material applied to a surface, follow these steps: (Figure 5-62)

1. **Right-click** a surface with a material applied to it. **Texture > Position**. (You will only see the Texture menu if a texture material is applied directly to a surface, and if nothing else is selected.)

2. Click and drag the green handle to rotate the material.

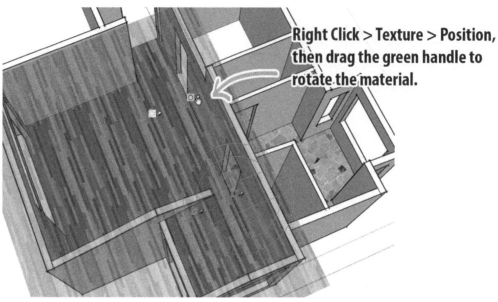

Right Click > Texture > Position,
then drag the green handle to
rotate the material.

Tiling Textures

When you apply a texture to a surface in SketchUp, the texture's image is tiled across the entire surface. All of the textures included in the default library use seamless images, meaning there is no discernible edge where the tiles meet. The image blends seamlessly from one tile to the next, creating the illusion of one continuous texture. If you zoom out far enough, you will start to see the repetition of the texture across large surfaces. (**Figure 5-63**)

Figure 5-63
Seamless
textures
show no
discernible
seam when
tiled.

**Seamless texture
image**

No visible seam when tiled.

Seamless textures offer numerous advantages. They allow you to use a much smaller image size, making your file smaller, and increasing your performance. They are also very easy to use, since you typically do not have to worry about scaling the texture to fit the surface. You can just apply the texture and it will tile endlessly to fill the surface.

You do not have to restrict yourself to only using seamless tileable textures. If your texture image is larger than the surface you are applying it to, you can apply it to the surface and position it so the edges of the texture do not fall within the surface. The model will look better, but it takes a lot more work to prepare and apply non-tiling textures. You will also sacrifice file size and performance.

Matching Textures

Sometimes you will have a situation where there are two surfaces in separate groups that you would like to blend together so they appear to be continuous. This happens when you have multiple levels on a building and have each floor in separate groups. From the exterior, you will see edges where the two groups meet, and the siding materials will not align properly. (**Figure 5-64**)

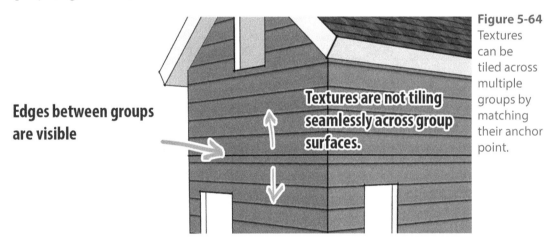

Edges between groups are visible

Textures are not tiling seamlessly across group surfaces.

Figure 5-64
Textures can be tiled across multiple groups by matching their anchor point.

The groups are separated for organizational purposes, but you want them to appear as though they are one continuous surface. To achieve this, you need to hide the common edges between the two groups, and anchor each texture to the same point.

To match textures along two surfaces follow these steps: (Figure 5-65)

1. Enter each group and hide the common edges using the **Eraser tool** (E) while holding the **SHIFT** key.

Step by Step

2. Inside one of the groups, paint one of the surfaces with the **Paint Bucket tool (B)**, then **right-click** on the surface, **Texture > Position**. Align the texture to the surface. (You must at least move the texture so it differs from the default position, or else you will not be able to sample the position for the other surfaces.)

3. Exit the group, enter the next group. Sample the first surface by clicking on it while holding the **ALT** (**Command** on Mac) key. This not only samples the texture, but it also captures the anchor point of the texture since you have altered it from the default position. Paint the second surface, and notice how the material tiles perfectly across both groups, creating the illusion of a seamless surface.

Figure 5-65
Match texture anchor points by using the Paint Bucket tool in sample mode.

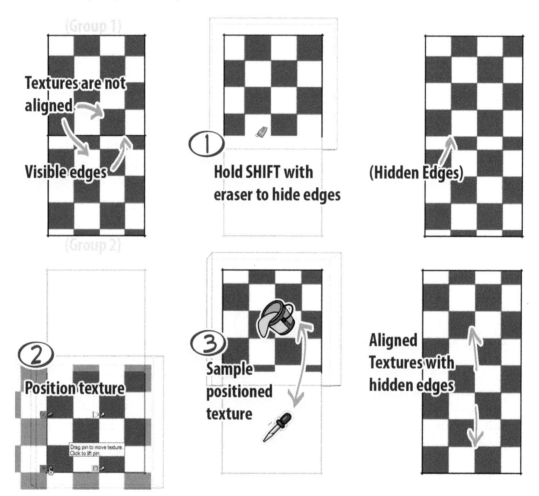

Texture Resources

If you want to explore beyond the materials included with SketchUp, you can download more, or create your own from an image.

The **SketchUp 3D warehouse** is a good place to start. Access it from the File menu inside SketchUp. By searching for terms such as "textures" or "materials", you can discover palettes of materials that you can import directly into your model to sample.

Eneroth Texture Positioning Tools (Free)

 Orienting textures is very fast and easy when you use this plugin. Instead of having to right-click a surface to access the Position Texture feature, then fuss around with the rotation handles, this plugin gives you a quick access toolbar with buttons that can rotate your texture with one click. It can also orient a texture to a selected edge. (Very useful when you need to align a texture off axis!)

www.sketchupbook.com/textureposition

Optional PLUGIN

Furniture/Other

Once you have your initial schematic model completed, you can add various components to the model to provide context to the spaces.

Kitchen/Bath

In the Schematic Design phase, you do not need to spend too much time modeling the kitchen. The objective is to create a basic layout to illustrate the design intent, without investing too much time modeling. You want to be able to make fast changes as you discuss the design with your client.

If you have already been using SketchUp to model kitchens, you are probably aware that there are many different types of cabinets available on the 3D warehouse. There are also a few plugins for SketchUp to help automate the process of modeling kitchens.

You could use one of these plugins, or import cabinet components from the 3D warehouse, but it really is not necessary to spend the time to do so in the Schematic

Design phase. Use simple boxes to represent kitchen cabinets, vanities, and other cabinetry throughout the building. You do not need to model the cabinet doors or hardware, just show a solid box wherever there is a cabinet. (**Figure 5-66**)

Figure 5-66
Simple boxes are modeled to represent kitchen cabinets in Schematic Design.

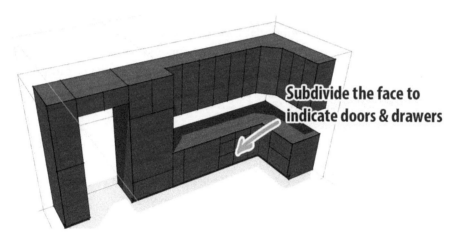

Subdivide the face to indicate doors & drawers

✓ Model cabinet runs as a continuous box, instead of individual cabinet components. You can include the toe kick if you would like. A single vertical edge on the front face of the cabinet run can illustrate the edge of each cabinet. Use horizontal edges to divide a cabinet face into drawer faces.

✓ Model the countertops separately in their own groups.

✓ Add components such as the appliances, stools, sinks, etc. Many times you can find the exact appliance on the 3D warehouse, provided by the manufacturer. Be mindful of the polygon count of the components you import into your model. (**Figure 5-67**)

Figure 5-67
Appliances can be imported to add detail to your model without much additional work.

Remember, the Schematic Design phase enables you to make quick, easy changes. By keeping everything simple right now, you keep the design very flexible.

Furniture

Continue to import components into your model such as; couches, chairs, tables, beds, rugs, plumbing fixtures, TVs, etc. It is important to include these things in the model in order to demonstrate the flow of the space and the intended layout of furniture.

These items should not be things that you are modeling manually. Again, search the 3D warehouse, or subscribe to a model service such as Form Fonts to get excellent 3D models that are low poly.

Schematic Site Model

With the building model completed for now, you can turn your attention back to the site model. Reload the building model back into the site model so it is up to date. With the building positioned properly inside the site model, you can now focus on modeling the driveway.

Driveway

The process of modeling a driveway is easiest when started in 2D. You want to begin by creating a flat profile of the driveway below the terrain, then you will create its sloping surfaces separately and you will combine the two to create the final driveway. You will finish by cutting out and stitching up the terrain to meet up with the driveway edge. (**Figure 5-68**)

Figure 5-68
A finished driveway modeled in the site model.

Before you begin, you should analyze your 3D terrain and come up with a plan in your head for how you want to design the driveway. Your driveway might be pretty straightforward, or you might have a steep site which requires a switchback. The **Tape Measure tool** (T) can be used to compare the elevation of any two points on your terrain. Just tap the **up arrow** on your keyboard to lock the blue axis.

Driveway Profile

Why do you want to draw your driveway as a flat profile first? It is easier, and more precise. You are going to be modeling a complex 3D mesh. By approaching it from two separate perspectives, you will have more control over the shape, and you will be able to take advantage of some automated tools for generating the driveway mesh.

By drawing the flat driveway profile from top view, you are isolating all drawing to a single plane, making it much easier. If your driveway will be meeting up to a garage or entrance, you will need to create a reference surface that you can place on the ground plane to connect to the driveway profile. (**Figure 5-69**)

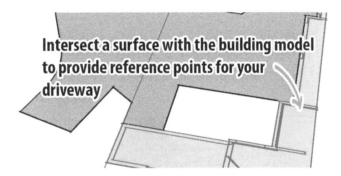

Figure 5-69
A temporary group is created by intersecting a rectangle with the building.

To create a reference surface, follow these steps:

1. Use the **Rotated Rectangle tool** to create a large surface cutting through your building model along the green and red axis. Make it a group. (You may need to turn off your OB_TERRAIN layer to hide the 3D terrain.) Move the rectangle along the blue axis until it is intersecting through important elements that you will need to reference for the driveway. (For example, raise it so the rectangle intersects the garage doors.) (**Figure 5-70**)

2. **Right-click** on the rectangle > **Intersect Faces** > **With Model.** If you need to move the surface up or down to intersect with other parts of the building model, simply repeat the process.

Step by Step

Figure 5-70
Intersect
Faces with
the building
to create the
temporary
guide
surface.

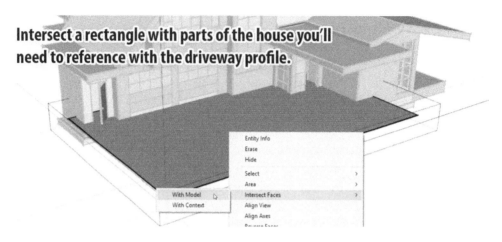

3. Exit the group, then move the group down the blue axis to the ground plane. Clean up the group by deleting perimeter edges of the rectangle you do not need. (**Figure 5-71**)

Figure 5-71
Move the
temporary
guide surface
down to
the ground
plane.

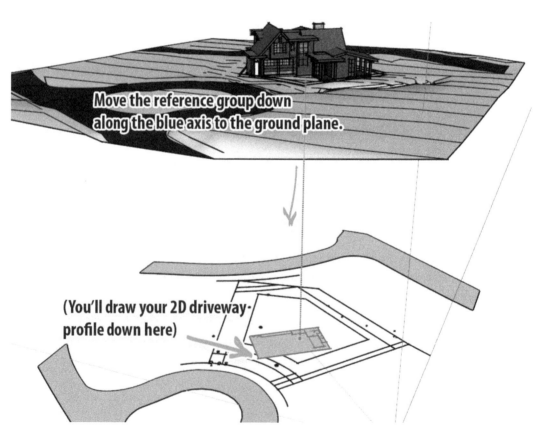

Since the road profile has already been imported from the site survey, you will be able to reference it on the ground plane as you draw the driveway profile. Before you start drawing the driveway, you will want to make sure to have the following entities visible on the ground plane:

✓ **Existing site contour lines** - The contour lines will give you a reference to the existing slope, so you can decide the best path of your driveway in regards to its slope. You will probably toggle these on and off as you work, as they can add clutter to the workspace.

✓ **Roads/sidewalks** - The driveway will meet up to the existing roadway, so it is important to have the road visible so you can match up to it precisely.

✓ **Trees/obstructions** - If there are any objects on the site that need to be avoided by the driveway, you should have those visible as well.

You will also want to turn off the LO_BUILDING layer and the OB_TERRAIN layer. Many of the site survey layers are unnecessary as well. Go to **Camera > Top**, and **Camera > Parallel Perspective** to align the camera to a top view. Your model should look like the image below: (**Figure 5-72**)

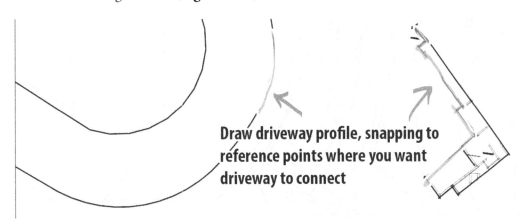

Figure 5-72
Draw the driveway by snapping to reference points that connect the driveway to the street and building.

Start drawing the driveway profile, making sure it is contained within its own group. While creating the driveway profile, you can use many of the drawing tools, such as the **Line tool (L)**, **Circle tool (C)**, **Arc tool (A)**, and **Rectangle tool (R)**, with assistance from the **Tape Measure tool (T)** and **Protractor tool** to create precise guides at the angles you want to create.

The best approach when modeling your driveway is to begin with basic shapes, such as rectangles and circles, intersecting them as needed, then going back to add arcs to round the corners and to erase any unnecessary edges.

For example, you might start by placing a set of guides perpendicular to the garage. You then create another set of guides perpendicular to the road. You could also take advantage of the parallel and perpendicular inference to help with alignment.

You can also copy existing edges from complex objects such as the road edge. Just jump inside of the road group and copy the edges that will be shared by the driveway. Then, go back into the driveway group and go to **Edit > Paste in Place** to paste the shared edges. (**Figure 5-73**) (You will learn more about this in the next section.)

Figure 5-73
Copy edges
that will be
shared with
the driveway.

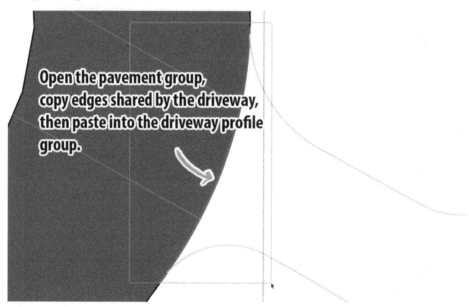

Open the pavement group, copy edges shared by the driveway, then paste into the driveway profile group.

With the **Arc tool** (**A**), you can find the tangent inference to draw arcs tangent to edges. Finish drawing the driveway profile so that you have a connected set of edges bounding a surface. (**Figure 5-74**)

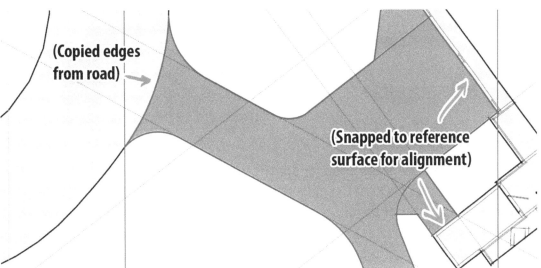

(Copied edges from road)

(Snapped to reference surface for alignment)

Figure 5-74
Draw the driveway profile on the ground plane.

When you are happy with your driveway profile, use the **Drape tool** to drape it onto your terrain, and double-check the placement of everything before continuing. If you need to make changes, undo the drape, and go back and change the driveway. (**Figure 5-75**)

Terrain Backup

If you ever make a mistake, or need to make a change to your terrain, you can easily copy parts of the existing terrain and "bandage" it back together. Since you saved a copy of the existing site model before you began to make changes, you will always have a source to copy parts of the terrain from the existing site model, and Paste In Place in your current site model.

Figure 5-75
Drape the
driveway
onto the
terrain.

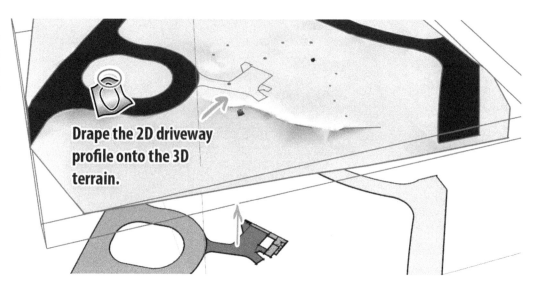

Figure 5-75
Drape the
driveway
onto the
terrain.

If you do not plan on grading the driveway or surrounding terrain, and simply want to have the profile draped onto the terrain, you are done. Just use the **Paint Bucket tool** (**B**) to apply a material to the surface. The 3D terrain will not be represented accurately, but you may decide that it is not important to you for your project. (**Figure 5-76**)

Figure 5-76
If you do
not want to
model the
driveway
slope, you
can simply
paint the
surface.

If you are going to grade the driveway to its actual elevation, you will need to do some more modeling. To begin that process, enter the terrain group and delete the face where the driveway was draped. You will continue in the next step to create the driveway mesh. (**Figure 5-77**)

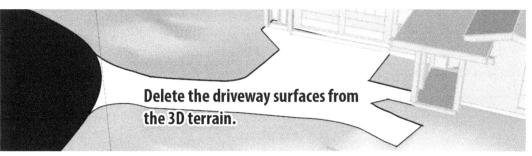

Driveway Slope

The driveway mesh will be created by drawing a series of calculated line segments that are pitched to define the driveway surface slope. You will then use the **From Contours tool** to generate a mesh from those lines. After draping the driveway profile back onto the mesh, you will do some cleanup and be left with your driveway. You will then cut back the terrain and do a little grading to connect the driveway to the existing terrain. (**Figure 5-78**)

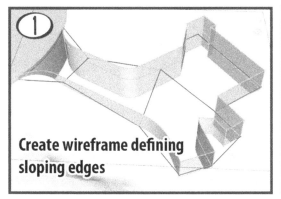

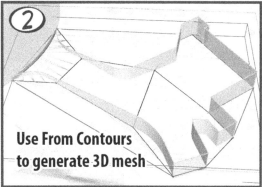

Figure 5-78
An overview of the process of modeling the 3D driveway and stitching it into the existing terrain.

To help create the driveway slope lines, you will extrude the driveway profile through the terrain as a temporary group to help you reference while you draw. (**Figure 5-79**)

Figure 5-79
Extrude
driveway
profile
through
terrain for
temporary
guide.

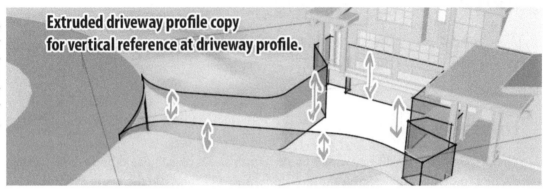

Extruded driveway profile copy
for vertical reference at driveway profile.

To create the driveway reference group, follow these steps:

1. Make a copy of the driveway profile group along the blue axis, and place it just above your 3D terrain.

2. **Double-click** to enter the group, and push/pull the profile down, through the terrain. Delete the top and bottom face so you only see the sides of the driveway profile extruded and intersecting with the 3D terrain.

You are going to use this extruded profile as reference to decide how to slope the driveway. (If you want, you can apply a transparent material to this group so you can see through it as you work.)

Terrain Intersections

Identify any areas on the terrain where the driveway will need to meet grade. (**Figure 5-80**). For example, where the road meets the driveway. Essentially, any part of the terrain that will not be graded differently from its existing position will need to share edges with the driveway so they can merge together.

You will need to copy these edges and make them part of the collection of edges that you use to generate the driveway mesh from.

To extract terrain intersections, follow these steps: (Figure 5-81)

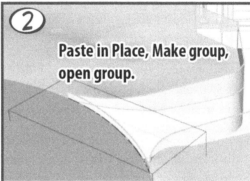

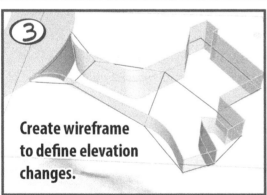

Figure 5-81
Copy shared
edges with
the terrain
into the
driveway
group.

1. Enter the terrain group and select all of the common edges between the driveway and terrain. Click and drag with the **Select tool** (SPACE) while holding CTRL (Option on Mac) to add to or CTRL+SHIFT (Option+SHIFT on Mac) to subtract from your selection. It is helpful to orient your camera so the selection box covers only the edges you want. Press **CTRL+C** (**Command+C** on Mac) to copy. Exit the terrain group.

2. **Edit > Paste in Place**. Then, with the edges still selected, you need to make them into a group. It can sometimes be hard to right-click on edges that are shared between groups, so if you do not have a keyboard shortcut assigned to Make Group, you might want to go to **Edit > Make Group**.

3. This group will be where you draw all of your lines defining the pitch of the driveway surfaces. Until you have more edges in the group to select, you might find it easier to open the group from the **Outliner dialog**.

Since you have already created the profile of the driveway in the first step, you can now focus on the pitch of the driveway surfaces. Create a wireframe around the driveway area, using sloping edges. These edges will then be used with the **From Contours tool** to create the driveway surface.

Do not worry about following the driveway profile exactly, you will intersect the driveway profile back onto the driveway mesh after it is generated. There are a number of tools at your disposal to help you create accurate lines to slope your driveway.

✓ **Protractor tool** - The **Protractor tool** can create guide lines at any angle, pivoting around any axis. You can align the protractor axis in numerous ways. Hover over one of the driveway profile wall surfaces, then hold **SHIFT** to lock that orientation. Alternatively, click and drag to orient the protractor axis to any point or axis in the model.

✓ **Tape Measure tool** - Use the **Tape Measure tool** (**T**) to measure elevation changes between two points by locking the blue axis. Create precise guides parallel to edges in your model. Create guide points.

✓ **Line tool** - The **Line tool** (**L**) can also be used to create temporary edges for the purposes of calculating an elevation change. For instance, you may project a line perpendicular to another line in order to get a length established. Then, you can draw another line straight down along the blue axis to establish the drop. You will then connect back to the original (creating a triangle), but then erase the other two lines you do not need.

If you have a complex driveway shape, do not worry about trying to follow the exact

perimeter of the driveway. You can draw edges beyond the boundaries of the driveway. See image (**Figure 5-82**) for a top view of what the wireframe group looks like compared to the driveway profile. There are many edges that cut across the outside of the driveway profile. Once the driveway mesh is created, you will drape the profile back onto the mesh to extract the final driveway shape.

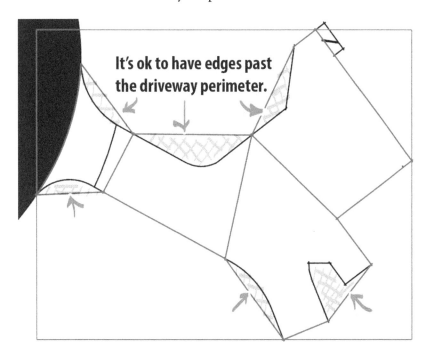

Figure 5-82
Edges used to define the sloping paths of the driveway can extend beyond the driveway profile.

Continue to adjust the pitch of the edges, keeping in mind how much grading will need to be done by looking at the distance between the height of the terrain and the height of the edges you are creating.

Generating Driveway Surfaces

When you are satisfied with the edges you have created, you can generate the mesh and intersect it with the driveway profile to create your final driveway surface.

To generate the final driveway, follow these steps: (Figure 5-83)

1. Select all of the edges and click **From Contours**. A new mesh will be created and placed in a group.

2. Delete the edges you created previously, then explode the mesh into that group.

3. Exit the driveway mesh group, then select the driveway profile below the terrain. Click the **Drape tool** then click on the mesh to drape the driveway profile onto the mesh.

4. **Double-click** on the driveway mesh to open it once again. You should see the profile of the driveway intersected with the surfaces. Clean up the mesh so only the driveway surface remains.

Figure 5-83
Use From Contours to generate a mesh from the edges you created.

① Select the sloped edges, run From Contours

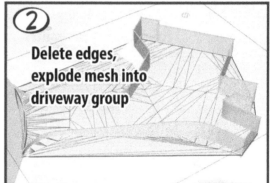

② Delete edges, explode mesh into driveway group

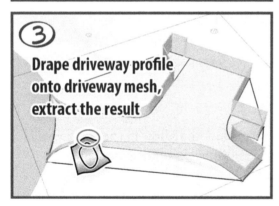

③ Drape driveway profile onto driveway mesh, extract the result

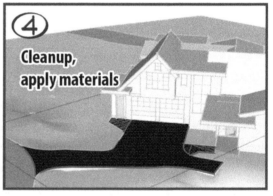

④ Cleanup, apply materials

TIP Instead of manually erasing all the extra lines, it may be faster to simply select the surfaces you want to keep, copying them, delete the entire mesh, then Paste in Place.

Drape and Intersect Problems

Whenever you drape or intersect, it might not always go according to plan. The most common problem that can occur is that a draped surface has a missing or softened edge on the mesh, preventing you from being able to select the surface. (**Figure 5-84**)

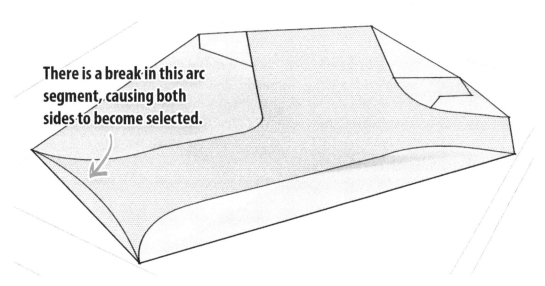

There is a break in this arc segment, causing both sides to become selected.

Figure 5-84
Sometimes SketchUp does not always work as expected.

If this occurs in your model, you are going to have to manually investigate and repair the broken or hidden edges with the **Line tool (L)**. Turn on **Hidden Geometry** by going to **View > Hidden Geometry**, then enter the driveway mesh group so you can see what needs to be repaired with the **Line tool (L)**. (**Figure 5-85**)

Problems like this typically occur when working with highly segmented curves. The more simple your model is, the better SketchUp will be at generating surfaces.

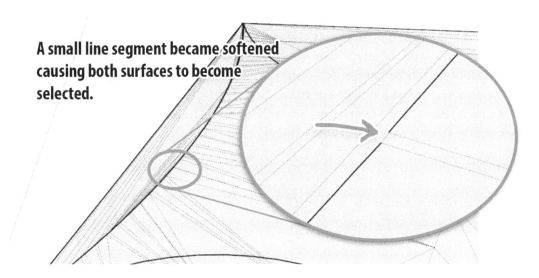

A small line segment became softened causing both surfaces to become selected.

Figure 5-85
Upon close inspection, one of the edges was softened, causing both surfaces to become selected.

Edge Tools² (Free)

This suite of tools is very helpful for finding small gaps in line segments. Installing the plugin adds a menu to the Tools menu, or you can add the optional toolbar to your workspace. Selecting the "Find Edge Gaps" action will identify parts of your model that have gaps in them.

www.sketchupbook.com/edgetools

Grading Terrain

In Schematic Design, do not worry about making any grading changes around the building. Save that for Design Development once the building design is more final. For now, you just need to concentrate on getting the driveway graded to the existing terrain.

For subtle grading differences, you can get away with cutting back the terrain a little bit, then using the **From Contours tool** to generate a mesh between the terrain and the driveway.

Cutting Back

Look at your existing terrain and decide where you want to cut it back. Use the **Tape Measure tool** (T) to examine distances and elevations to help you decide. Grab the **Line tool** (L) and create a line segment (outside of the terrain group) around the driveway where you want to cut the terrain. You need to start and end the line segment at a point where the driveway shares a point with the terrain (**Figure 5-86**). Do not worry about following each face on the terrain, you can easily use the **Drape tool** to drape the line segment onto the terrain once you are finished.

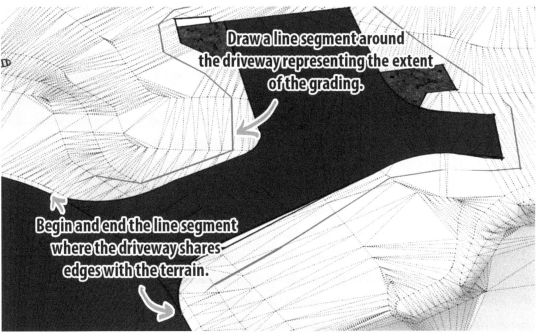

Figure 5-86
Draw a line segment around the driveway to define where the terrain will be cut back.

Once you've draped the line segment onto the terrain, enter the terrain group, select and delete the new face you have created. Then, delete the edges you want to cut back. (**Figure 5-87**)

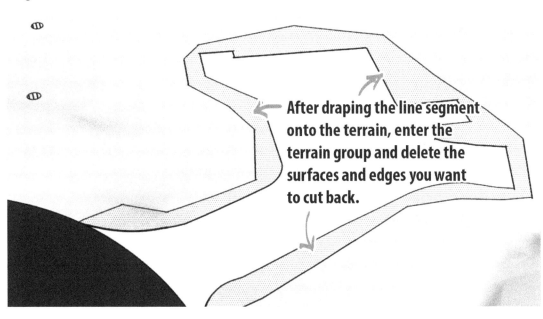

Figure 5-87
Drape the line segment onto the terrain, then delete it.

A quick way to delete the inner edges is to first delete the surface. Then, erase the two edges that connect to the shared point between the driveway and the terrain. This will disconnect the inner line segment from the rest of the terrain, allowing you to **triple-click** it and delete it in one fell swoop. (**Figure 5-88**)

Figure 5-88
Delete the surface first, then disconnect the line segment from the terrain so you can triple-click it.

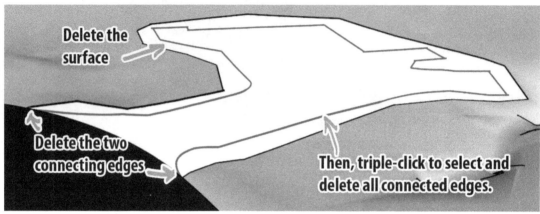

Delete the surface

Delete the two connecting edges

Then, triple-click to select and delete all connected edges.

Creating Graded Terrain

Carefully select the edges in the terrain that will define the edge of the new grade to the driveway. Click and drag a selection box while holding **CTRL** (**Option** on Mac) to add to your selection. To remove individual entities and faces from your selection, hold **CTRL+SHIFT** (**Option+SHIFT** on Mac) while clicking them. Then, press **CTRL+C** (**Command+C** on Mac) to copy the lines.

Since you currently have those edges selected, now is a good time to hide them. Since you are going to be generating a mesh to grade the driveway to the terrain, you do not want a visible edge here. **Right-click > Hide**. (**Figure 5-89**)

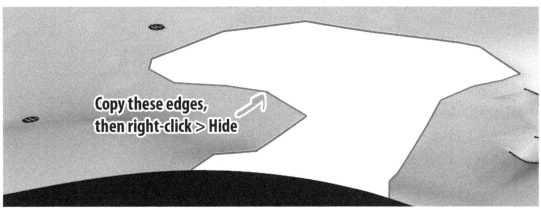

Figure 5-89
Copy the edges from the terrain, then hide them while they are still selected.

Enter your driveway group and **Edit > Paste in Place**. While the edges are still selected, add the perimeter edges of the driveway that will be part of your graded terrain to your selection (**Figure 5-90**). Copy all of the edges to your clipboard before generating the terrain using **From Contours**.

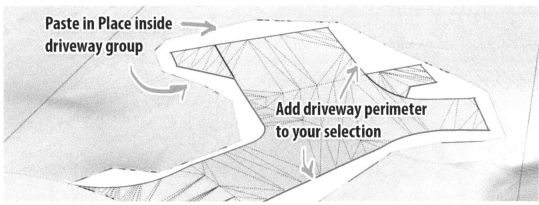

Figure 5-90
Paste in Place inside the driveway group, then add the driveway perimeter to your selection.

The **From Contours tool** will generate a "skirt" around the driveway (in a new group), grading it to the terrain. However, there will be a lot of extra edges and surfaces that will need to be cleaned up.

Enter the new group created by the **From Contours tool**. Notice how the original edges have been soften/smoothed, making it hard to clean up the extra surfaces? Since you still have the perimeter edges on your clipboard, just **Edit > Paste in Place**, and all the original edges will intersect with the mesh to define the boundaries of the mesh so you can easily clean it up. (**Figure 5-91**)

Figure 5-91
After using
From
Contours,
Paste in Place
the edges
once more
to redefine
the surfaces.
Delete the
extra entities.

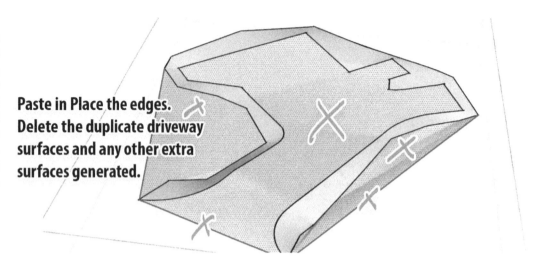

**Paste in Place the edges.
Delete the duplicate driveway
surfaces and any other extra
surfaces generated.**

You will want to hide the edges in the skirt group, so you do not see the transition from the skirt to the terrain. **Triple-click** to select everything, then **SHIFT+click** the surface to remove it from the selection. **Right-click > Hide**.

Exit the skirt group and the driveway group. You now have a sloped driveway mesh, with a graded skirt leading to the existing terrain. (**Figure 5-92**)

Figure 5-92
You should
end up with
the terrain
group, skirt
group, and
driveway
group.

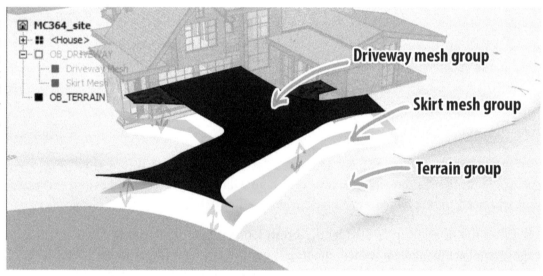

Driveway mesh group

Skirt mesh group

Terrain group

Tips & Tricks

✓ **Soften/Smooth** - When working with terrain, you will often find yourself wanting to soften and smooth subdivided surfaces of the mesh. You can use the **Eraser tool** (**E**) while holding down **CTRL** (**Option** on Mac) to soften/smooth a few edges, but a faster way to soften/smooth is to select an entire group, **right-click > Soften/Smooth**. When you are outside of the group, it will still affect all edges within the group. Just be careful of doing this when you have edges that need to be visible to define borders, such as roads or tree placements.

✓ **Hidden Geometry** - Toggling Hidden Geometry, (**View > Hidden Geometry**), is important when selecting parts of a mesh. If you want to manipulate the individual subdivided faces of the mesh, Hidden Geometry needs to be on. If you want to select the entire surface at once, make sure it is off.

✓ **Erasing edges** - When trimming back terrain, you will find yourself faced with a lot of cleanup. The best way to approach this is to first delete the mesh (make sure Hidden Geometry is off so you can delete the entire mesh in one easy step.) Then, find the two edges at each end that connect to the terrain. Delete those so now the remaining edges are completely disconnected from the main terrain. Now you can simply **triple-click** on a segment and the rest of the edges will become highlighted. Tap **DELETE** to erase.

✓ **Small edges** - It is very easy to snap to the wrong point when working with terrain. Make sure you zoom in far enough to confirm you are snapping to the correct point.

✓ **Explode terrain to intersect path** - When using **From Contours**, the original boundaries of the edges become softened/smoothed, making it harder to clean up the extra geometry that is generated. A simple trick you can do is explode the mesh group right after it is created, and it will intersect with your original lines. This makes it easier to identify and select extra surfaces that need to be deleted. This only works when all of the edges in the group were used to create the mesh.

✓ **Repairs** - You should always have a copy of the original site terrain. If you ever need to make a change to the site and need to return the terrain back to its existing state, you can copy parts of the terrain and paste in place to make a repair.

Section Cuts

As you get ready to prepare your building model for LayOut, one of the biggest challenges you will face will be creating section cuts of your model. You will need to create some sort of section cut whenever you want to create a floor plan or a vertical section through your building. (**Figure 5-93**)

You will create section cuts directly inside the building model, (not the site model), to produce your floor plan scenes.

Figure 5-93
Section cuts were used to create the viewports you see here.

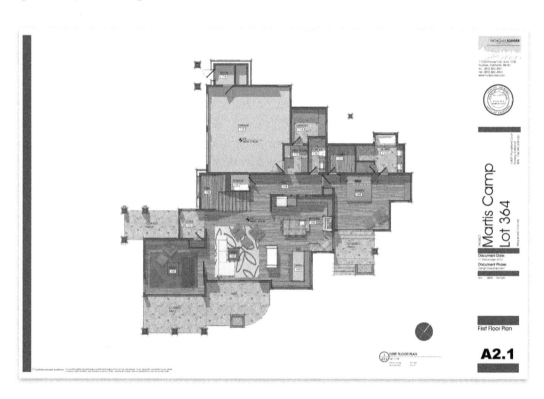

SketchUp does have a **Section Plane tool** that is easy to use, so the challenges may not be immediately obvious. What it really boils down to is how to make section cuts of your model that **look good and communicate clearly**. If you simply add a section plane to your model, you will see that it just exposes the back surfaces of your model, which quite frankly looks terrible. (**Figure 5-94**)

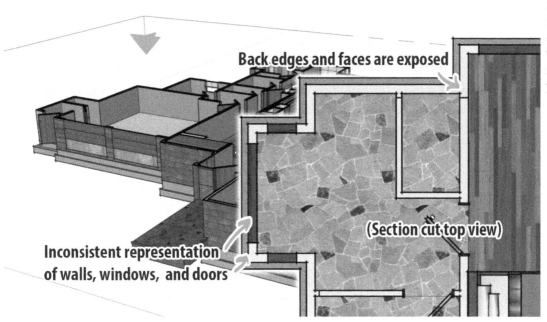

Figure 5-94
Section cuts expose the inner surfaces of your model.

There are numerous methods, tricks, and workarounds to address this issue, but not all of them work in every situation. Some of the methods only work when the sectioned objects are perfectly perpendicular to the camera. Other methods work in any situation, but require a ton of manual work to produce and create a disconnect between your model and LayOut. Some methods require the use of a plugin.

While we would like to be able to teach you a single method using native SketchUp tools that is universally fast, reliable, and remains dynamically linked to the model, it is impossible to do. Instead, we are going to show you multiple approaches in how to deal with section cuts, so you will have a few options at your disposal depending upon the project you are working on.

The Look

No matter which method you use to create section cuts, it is important to first understand the look and feel you want to achieve. The best floor plans are clear, easy to read, and clearly communicate the design.

While traditional CAD drawings are in black & white, SketchUp has the advantage of being able to show colorful materials to enhance the design and the depth of the illustration. However, if you are not careful, you will end up with a cluttered mess that causes confusion to whomever tries to read your drawings.

While you explore the various methods for creating section cuts of your model, there are three things we recommend doing no matter which method you choose.

1. Separate important elements - Instead of preparing a single viewport, create two. Isolate important elements such as walls, windows, and doors onto their own viewport that you can vector render in LayOut. Put everything else on a colorful raster viewport and place it underneath the vector viewport. This separation makes it easier to snap dimensions to important elements in LayOut. (**Figure 5-95**)

Figure 5-95
Stack two viewports on top of each other in order to create a clean-looking section.

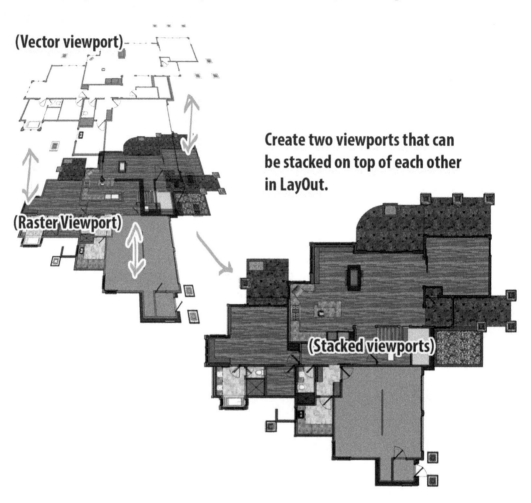

(Vector viewport)

Create two viewports that can be stacked on top of each other in LayOut.

(Raster Viewport)

(Stacked viewports)

2. Use Fog to create depth - Fog is a simple way to give a sense of depth perception. Elements that are farther away in the model will fade out into the distance. Fog is also an important tool to lighten the color of the materials so they do not overwhelm the viewport in LayOut. (**Figure 5-96**)

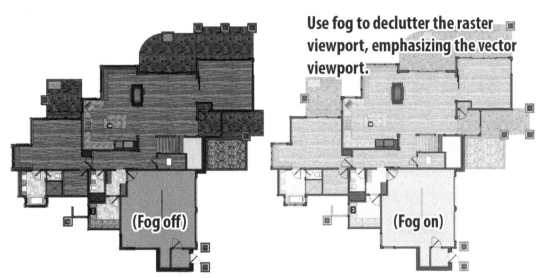

Use fog to declutter the raster viewport, emphasizing the vector viewport.

(Fog off)   (Fog on)

Figure 5-96 Using Fog on the Raster viewport makes the walls contrast more sharply on the page.

3. Use Shadows to enhance depth - Shadows are another great way to add depth to the model, making it easier to comprehend the height of objects in a scene. (**Figure 5-97**)

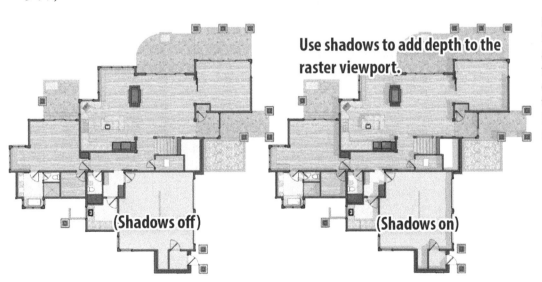

Use shadows to add depth to the raster viewport.

(Shadows off)   (Shadows on)

Figure 5-97 Shadows add depth to the section, enhancing the overall look of the section.

There are certainly methods that will give you a floor plan using a single scene and a single viewport, but we do not feel that it gives you enough control over the look and feel in order to communicate clearly.

No matter which method you choose to produce your section cuts, you should always create two scenes for each view you would like to create, and stack them in two viewports inside LayOut.

Two Scenes Per View

This method is fairly easy to implement, **as long as you have a reasonably well organized model, and you model the floors and walls in separate groups.** Insert a section plane cutting through the walls, create two scenes from the same camera perspective, but have different sets of objects visible in each scene.

You then stack two viewports in LayOut and assign one scene to each viewport (**Figure 5-98**). This creates a composite viewport showing a colorful raster rendered viewport underneath, and a vector viewport on top only showing sectioned elements.

Figure 5-98
With a well organized model, you can stack viewports to achieve the desired look.

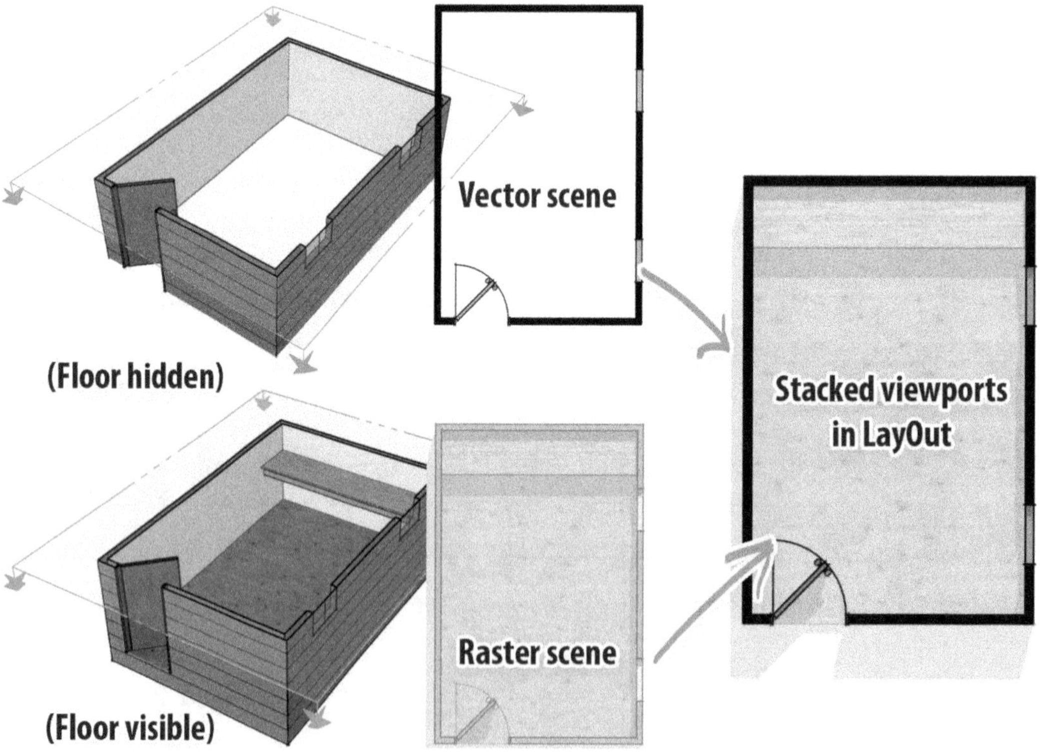

Vector scene

(Floor hidden)

Raster scene

(Floor visible)

Stacked viewports in LayOut

Raster Scene

✓ All layers are visible.

✓ Have a colorful style selected so you can show off all the beautiful materials you have applied to your model.

✓ Turn on fog.

✓ Turn on shadows to create depth and distance.

Vector Scene

✓ Only have the objects intersecting the section plane visible. In a floor plan, that would be the walls, windows, and doors.

✓ Since the section cut is exposing the inside surfaces of these objects, you need to paint the inside faces of these objects black.

The problem with this approach is it only works when the objects intersected by the section plane are perpendicular to the section plane. When they are perpendicular, it creates the illusion that you are looking at flat linework at the intersection of the section plane. If you have walls at anything other than 90°, the illusion does not work because you see those walls beyond the section plane. (**Figure 5-99**)

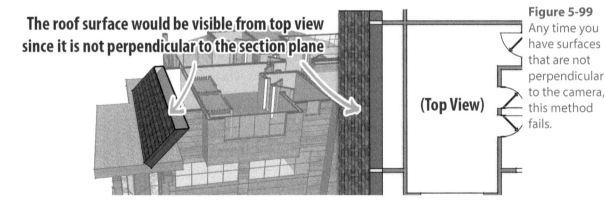

Figure 5-99 Any time you have surfaces that are not perpendicular to the camera, this method fails.

The advantage of this method is that it remains dynamic to the model. If you make any changes to the model, they are easily updated in LayOut. This method also uses 100% native SketchUp tools, so you do not need any special plugins.

✓ If you desire even more control over the look of your model in LayOut, you can create 3 or more scenes to illustrate isolated objects. This will allow you to apply different styles to each scene, but requires many more scenes and viewports and can quickly become overwhelming to keep organized.

✓ You can create floor plans using a single viewport by coloring all the back faces black. The black color blends with the edge color, creating a poche effect. Unfortunately, you sacrifice a lot of control over the look of your model, so this method is not recommended.

✓ You may decide to use this method in Schematic Design, but then use a different method once you get into Design Development. The advantage of this method is it is very quick to set up and update.

Creating Linework

To overcome the limitations of the previous method, which creates the illusion of section cut linework, you could actually create linework from the section plane manually. You would still create two scenes in SketchUp and two viewports in LayOut. The raster viewport would be created the same way as before, but the vector viewport would be created from a scene displaying flat linework of the model where the section cut occurs.

SketchUp has a built-in feature called **Create Group From Slice** which helps automate some of the process. There is also a free plugin called SectionCutFace that not only creates linework, but fills in the surfaces as well.

In either method, start by adding a section cut to your model. Position it at an optimal height where it will slice through most windows/doors and walls. (There may be objects that are above or below the section cut which will need to be added manually.)

Step by Step

To create linework in your model, follow these steps: (Figure 5-100)

1. **Right-click** on the section cut, select **Create Group From Slice**.

2. Go to **View > Section Cuts** and **View > Section Planes** to turn off both. You should see the newly created linework group selected. Assign it to the SP_2D layer. **Double-click** on it to open, go to **View > Component Edit > Hide Rest of Model** to hide the rest of the model.

3. Inside the linework group will be multiple components organized in the same way as your model. Enter each component and retrace over a single edge to produce

a face.

4. Add a material to the linework group to apply a color to all of the surfaces inside the group. If you want to apply a different color to some of the surfaces, apply the material to those surfaces from directly inside the group.

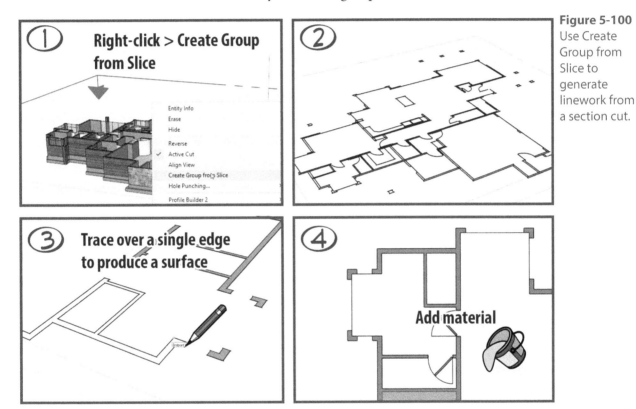

Figure 5-100
Use Create Group from Slice to generate linework from a section cut.

Although this method is very forgiving and flexible to any type of model, it is a time-consuming process. It also requires you to make updates to the linework whenever you make a change to the model.

There is a free plugin that can save you a ton of time, which you would use in place of the Create Group From Slice feature. It is called **SectionCutFace**, and it will automatically explode the linework groups and fill in faces for you. It has an option to auto update, but you will find that it slows down your model quite a bit while you model.

SectionCutFace (Free)

This section linework tool is not hosted in the SketchUp Extension Warehouse. Instead, you will need to create a free account on **Sketchucation.com** in order to download it. Follow the link below to create an account.

www.sketchupbook.com/sectioncutface

To use SectionCutFace, follow these steps: (Figure 5-101)

1. After installing the SectionCutFace plugin, **right-click** on a section cut, select **Add SectionCutFace**.

Figure 5-101
SectionCutFace generates linework much faster and fills in faces automatically.

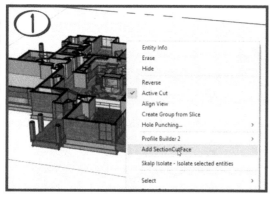

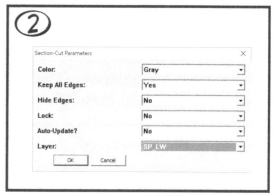

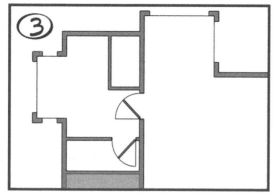

2. Select a color (you can change it later.) Set "Keep all Edges" to Yes, "Hide Edges" to No, "Lock" to No, "Auto-Update?" to No, and assign the layer to SP_2D.

3. Inspect the resulting group for anomalies, edit materials if needed.

The SectionCutFace plugin is a lot faster than manually doing it with Create Group From Slice, and you can reduce nearly all manual updating by choosing "Update on Demand".

Below, you'll see another example of a floor plan generated using the techniques described in this chapter. (**Figure 5-102**)

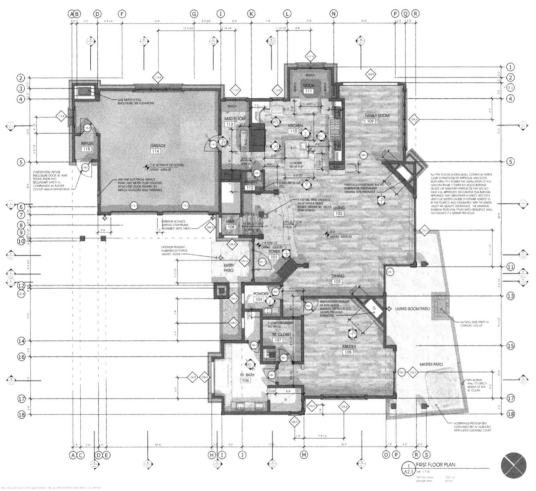

Figure 5-102
Sample floor plan generated using a raster viewport and a vector viewport.

In the next chapter, we will review what the schematic documents should look like, then analyze how the template scenes should be updated and prepared for LayOut.

Schematic Documents

With the schematic site model and the schematic building model completed, you can begin to prepare SketchUp scenes for LayOut. Scenes allow you to take a snapshot of your model, saving camera settings, style, fog, shadows, etc. You will use these scenes by assigning them to viewports in LayOut.

Template Scene Adjustments

In the building template you are using, there are numerous scenes preset for the purpose of creating viewports in LayOut. There are also a pair of section planes placed in the model of which you will need to adjust the position in order to properly slice your building according to the section cut method you chose to use in the previous chapter. The template assumes a two-story building, so you will have to add more if your building is higher than that.

Using a template like the one provided with this book can save you a lot of time with your projects, but due to the unique nature of each project, you will still need to make some adjustments and additions to the preset scenes.

New Layers

Any time you add a layer to your SketchUp model, that layer will be visible in all pre-existing scenes by default. You will have to manually update all of your scenes and hide any new layers that you do not want visible in that scene.

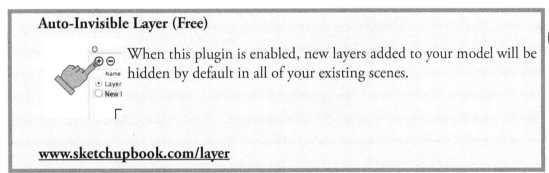

Auto-Invisible Layer (Free)

When this plugin is enabled, new layers added to your model will be hidden by default in all of your existing scenes.

www.sketchupbook.com/layer

Optional
PLUGIN

Camera Position

The camera positions are preset for each scene. Since each project is different, you will likely find that the camera position does not fully capture your entire model. While it is possible to reposition the boundaries of a viewport in LayOut, it is quite easy to reconfigure the camera positions for the scenes.

The traditional way to update a scene is to click on the **Update button**, select which properties you would like to update, then click ok. When you want multiple scenes to share some of the same scene settings, there is a faster way to update all of those scenes at once.

To reconfigure the floor plan scene camera perspective, follow these steps: (Figure 5-104)

Step by Step

1. **Double-click** on one of the floor plan scenes to quickly get to Top view, parallel projection. Press SHIFT+Z to zoom extents, or frame your model how you would like it to be seen from the viewport.

2. In the **Scene panel**, select all of the floor plan scenes by **SHIFT**+clicking them to select multiple.

3. Uncheck the Camera property checkbox so the scenes "forget" their camera position.

4. Check the camera property checkbox again, and the current camera position will be saved in all of the selected scenes.

Figure 5-104
Reset camera position for multiple scenes all at once.

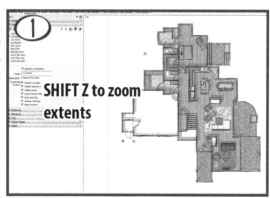
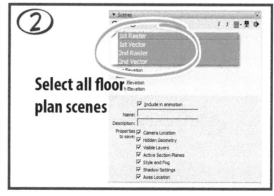
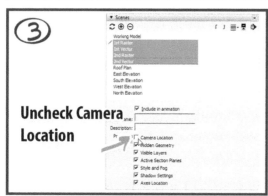
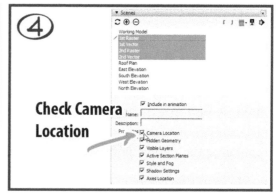

For the elevation scenes, you can follow the same process, but since the camera position is unique to each scene, you will have to update them one scene at a time.

Styles

The SketchUp template scenes also have specific styles applied to each scene. One of the most important properties to save in styles that are being used in scenes for LayOut is to disable section plane visibility. Section cut visibility should be controlled by activating or deactivating a section plane directly. (**Figure 5-105**) You do not want to see the section plane object in any of your viewports, so make sure that is disabled.

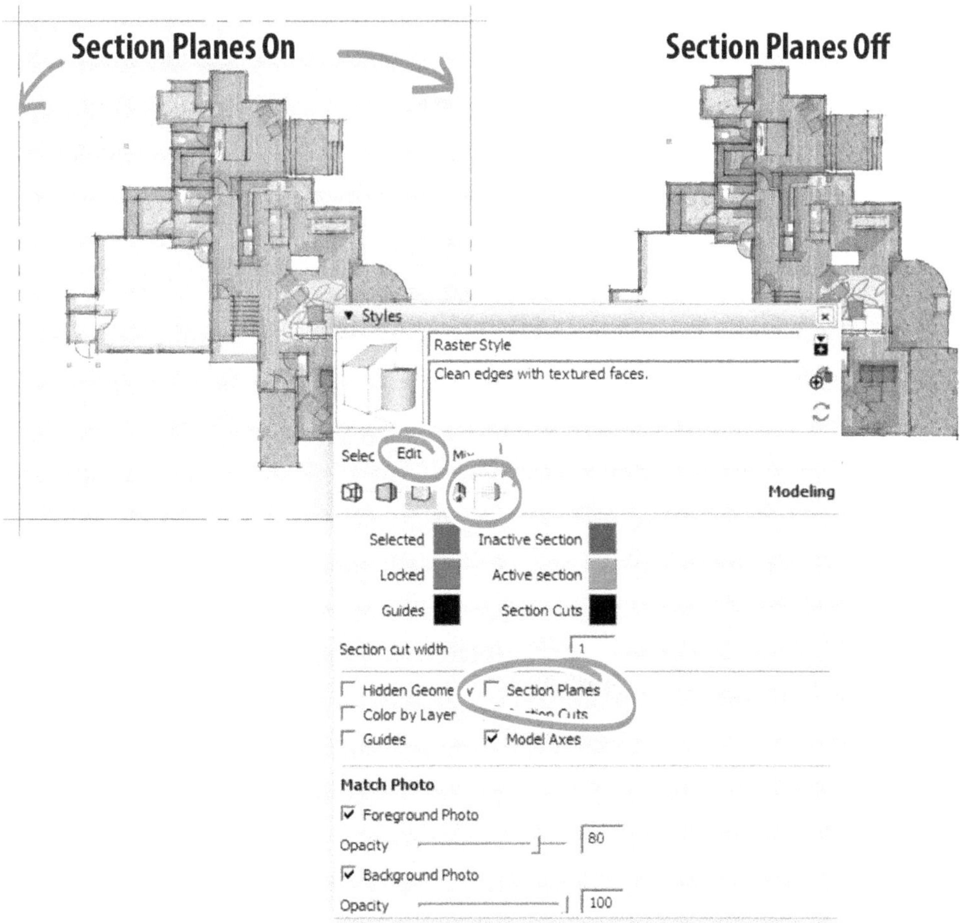

Figure 5-105
Make sure your styles do not have section planes visible.

As far as the template scene styles, you will want at least three styles. The template includes these by default: (**Figure 5-106**)

✓ **Raster Style -** This style is saved with all scenes that will be assigned to viewports rendered in raster mode in LayOut. This includes all of the raster floor plan scenes, as well as the exterior elevation scenes. By default, this style has very basic edge settings for better performance while modeling, but it is intended that you update the edge style to something more conceptual before sending the model to LayOut to produce your schematic documents.

✓ **Vector Style** - This style is saved with all scenes that will be assigned to viewports rendered in vector mode in LayOut. This includes the vector floor plan scenes which include the linework of the section cut. This style uses a thick edge, with Profiles set to a value of 2 to add emphasis.

✓ **Working Model Style** - There is a third style reserved for the utility scene "working model". It is a basic, fast style that gives you an opportunity to make overrides to it without worrying about affecting your other scenes.

Figure 5-106
An overview of style assignments to scenes.

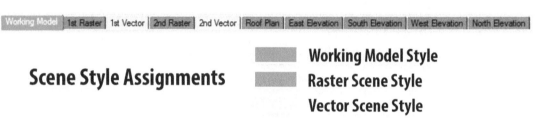

TIP Whenever you toggle section plane or section cut visibility, or turn on X-ray mode, or toggle countless other style properties, **you are overriding the saved settings of the current style.** If you activate a different scene which uses the same style as the one currently active, **those overrides do not reset.** The only way to clear the style overrides is to activate a different style.

The danger in this is if you save your model as-is and update it in LayOut, all scenes which are assigned to that style will update to show all of those temporary overrides you made to the style, **even though you did not explicitly update the style with the changes.**

Therefore, a simple solution to this potential problem is to get into the habit of activating the Working Model scene just before saving your model. Since the Working Model scene uses a unique style, you can be assured knowing that none of your viewport scenes will retain any temporary style changes you may have made. By switching to a different style, any temporary overrides will be forgotten.

Before inserting viewports of the model into LayOut, you should update the raster style used by the scenes to something with a more conceptual feel to it. Updating the existing style saved in the scenes is much faster than creating a new style and updating each scene with the new style. You can use the style Mix feature to quickly sample edge styles from other saved styles.

To edit the edge properties of the style saved by the scenes, follow these steps: (Figure 5-107)

1. Activate one of the raster floor plan scenes so that its saved style becomes active.

2. In the **Styles panel**, click on the **Mix** tab. Navigate through the drop-down menu and find a style from which you would like to borrow the edge properties. Click and drag the style onto the **Edge Settings** category to apply the settings.

3. Click on the **Update button** to save the changes.

Figure 5-107
Use the Mix tab to apply specific style properties to your current style.

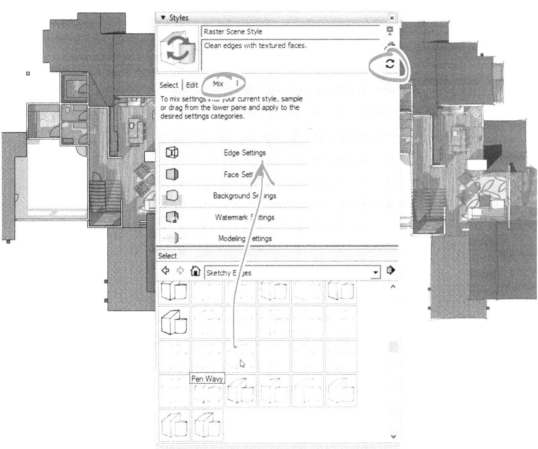

Now, all scenes using that style will be updated with the new changes you made. You can play around with other settings if you would like, or jump into the Edit tab and play around with settings manually.

Overview

Let's review each type of page you will be creating. You will learn how to configure the corresponding SketchUp scenes, and how to identify which elements need to be added inside LayOut.

Figure 5-108
An overview of the Schematic Design documents.

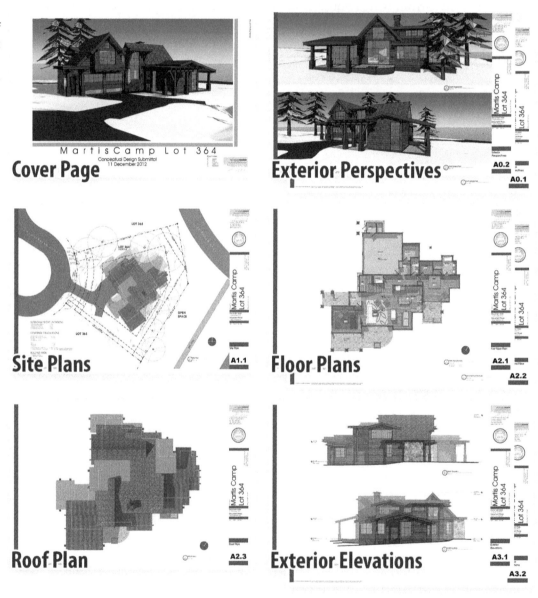

Cover Page

A single scene is needed from the **site model** for the cover page to give an overall view of the front of the building. (**Figure 5-109**)

Figure 5-109
The Schematic
Design cover
page.

MartisCamp Lot 364

Conceptual Design Submittal
11 December 2012

LayOut Template	0-Cover.layout
SketchUp Model	Site.skp viewport, placed on **Raster Viewport** layer.
Visible Objects	All layers on
Camera	Perspective Mode Front of building from entrance
Style	"Raster", Fog off, Shadows on

Since the cover page title block is different than the interior pages, you will need to manually update the project information on this page.

The layers on the cover page are very basic. The TITLE BLOCK layer holds all the project info. The Raster Viewport layer holds the one perspective viewport of the site model. (**Figure 5-110**)

Figure 5-110
Cover page
layers.

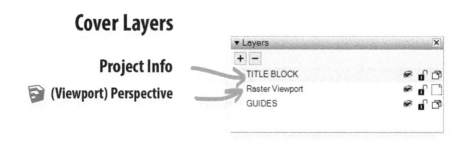

You can add your own creativity to the cover page. Experiment with different style properties to create a unique look for your projects. You might want to use a rendered image if you are familiar with rendering software. Maybe you would prefer having a parallel projection view of the project on the cover page. It's up to you how you'd like to present the project.

Exterior Perspectives

At least four scenes should be prepared inside the **site model**, one for each side of the building, to create the exterior perspectives. (**Figure 5-111**)

Figure 5-111
The Schematic Design exterior perspectives page.

LayOut Template	A0-Perspectives.layout
SketchUp Model	Site.skp viewport, placed on **Raster Viewport** layer.
Visible Objects	All layers on
Camera	Perspective Mode Various angles of the building
Style	"Raster", Fog off, Shadows on

The layer organization for the exterior perspective pages is very simple. The viewports go on the Raster Viewport layer, and the detail tags go on the Page Notes layer. (**Figure 5-112**)

Figure 5-112
The Schematic
Design
exterior
perspectives
template
layers.

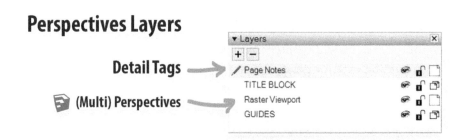

When creating scenes for viewports shown in perspective camera mode, you may need to adjust the **Field of View** in order to fit the model into the scene properly. Increasing the Field of View will create a wide angle view of the model. This can also be useful for interior shots in tight spaces. Go to **Camera > Field of View**, then type in a new angle and press **ENTER**. Alternatively, click and drag the mouse up or down to actively adjust the Field of View.

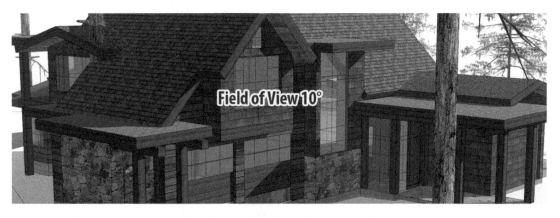

Site Plan

The site plan LayOut document should already exist from when you created the existing site plan. Since you have now imported the building and added the driveway to the site, this page will no longer reflect the existing site conditions. Rename the page to "Site Plan", and you will transform it into the Schematic Design site plan. (**Figure 5-113**)

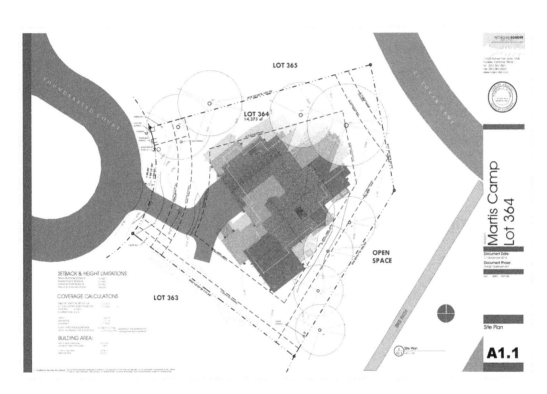

Figure 5-113
The Schematic Design site plan.

LayOut Template	A1-Site.layout
SketchUp Model	Site.skp viewport, placed on **Raster Viewport** layer.
Visible Objects	All layers on
Camera	Parallel Perspective Top View
Style	"Raster", Fog on, Shadows on

After updating the site model reference in LayOut, the survey boundary layers and tree layers should be visible. The footprint will be added to the FOOTPRINT layer, and general site notes are added to the Page Notes layer. (**Figure 5-114**)

Figure 5-114
The Schematic Design site plan template layers.

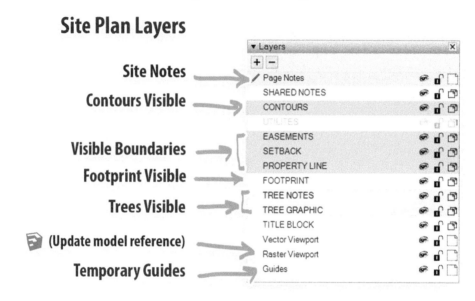

Building Footprint

For the schematic site plan, you will want to show a top view of the building sitting on the site, but you will also want to overlay an outline of the building footprint on top of the viewport. (**Figure 5-115**)

Figure 5-115
The footprint is an outline of the building overlaid on top of the roof.

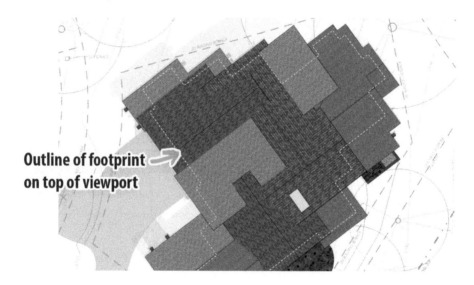

In order to create the building outline, you will need to trace over the floor plan in LayOut. Since you do not have a scene of the floor plan, open the site model and edit the template scene "1st Vector". You will want to configure the scene to have the same camera properties as the site scenes, but you want to isolate the first floor linework layers. This will allow you to trace over the floor plan walls from inside LayOut. Before you do this, make sure you reload the building model into the site model so it is up to date.

To update the 1st Vector scene, follow these steps: (Figure 5-116)

1. In the site model, activate the Site Plan scene. This will set the camera to the settings you want to copy to the 1st Vector scene.

2. In the **Layers panel**, hide all except layer0, LO_1st FLOOR, LO_BUILDING MODEL, and SP_2D. This will isolate the linework you prepared for the first floor section cut of the imported building model.

3. Configure your style settings, then in the **Scenes panel, single-click** on the 1st Vector scene, then click on the **Update button**.

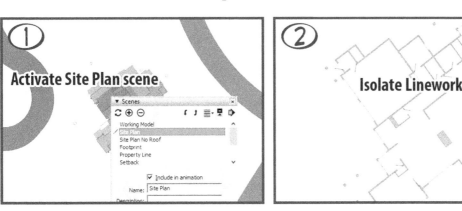

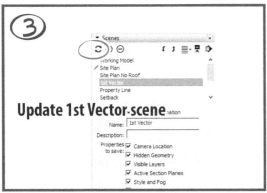

Figure 5-116
Update the 1st Vector scene to show the first floor linework.

Save the site model, then update it in the LayOut site plan document. Temporarily change the viewport scene to **1st Vector scene** to show the scene you just created. You can now trace over the floor plan to create your footprint shape.

To create the building footprint, follow these steps:

1.   In LayOut, **right-click** on the **site plan viewport > Scenes > 1st Vector**.

2.   In the **Scenes panel**, change the render mode to vector so you have sharp lines to snap to.

3.   **Right-click** somewhere in paper space, make sure **Object Snap** is turned on, **Grid Snap** is turned off.

4.   In the **Layers panel**, activate the Footprint layer.

5.   Grab the **Line tool** (L), then in the **Shape Style panel** click on the **Stroke** color swatch and change the color to white. Change the **Dashes** style to a dashed line.

6.   Zoom into a corner of the building, and draw a polygon around the building while snapping to each corner. When you are finished, switch the viewport back to the **Site Plan** scene.

Removing Trees

When you started modeling the building, you should have hidden any trees that need to be removed. On the site plan in LayOut, you want to indicate which trees need to be removed.

Activate the TREE NOTES layer and draw an X using two line segments. Group them together. Place an X over each tree location that needs to be removed. You will learn how to save this in a scrapbook in a later chapter so you do not have to draw it from scratch each time. (If you do not have tree locations in the LayOut file as vector linework, you may need to unhide the trees in the SketchUp model temporarily in order to identify their placement.) (**Figure 5-117**)

Grading

Wherever you have graded the terrain, you need to edit the existing contour lines to show where the terrain changes. Although it is possible to generate new contour lines from your newly graded terrain in SketchUp, It is faster to estimate contour line changes right in LayOut. (**Figure 5-118**)

Use the **Split tool** to break a contour line into segments where you estimate the grading change occurs. Select the part of the contour that will change, and edit the **Shape Style panel** color and dash style.

Use the **Line tool** (**L**) to draw a new line segment representing the new estimated contour path. (Click and drag as you anchor each point to create a curved line segment.)

Figure 5-118
Split existing
contour lines
and add a new
contour path.

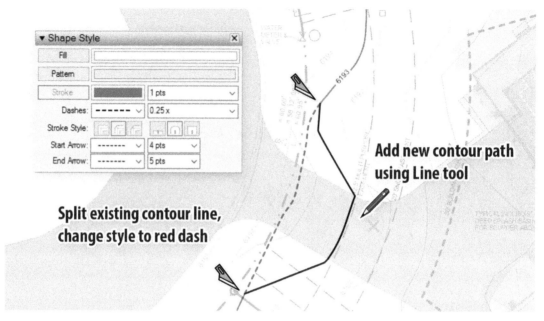

Sheet Notes

Add sheet notes like setback & height limitations, coverage calculations, and building area. These can be created from a single block of text, and you can edit the text style by highlighting the text and editing the **Text Style panel**. Alternatively, you can configure the **Text Style panel** before you begin typing. (**Figure 5-119**)

Figure 5-119
Sheet notes on
the Site plan.

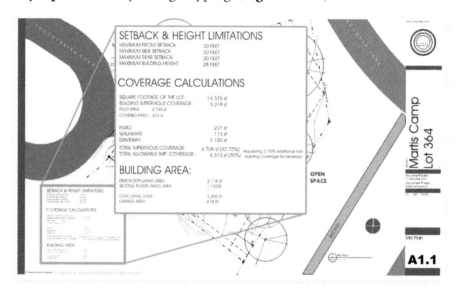

Floor Plans

To achieve the desired look and style for the floor plan drawings, you will need to create two scenes for each floor plan you intend to create using one of the section cut methods described in the previous chapter. Each of these scenes will be assigned to viewports that are stacked on top of each other in LayOut in order to create a composite drawing of the floor plan. (**Figure 5-120**)

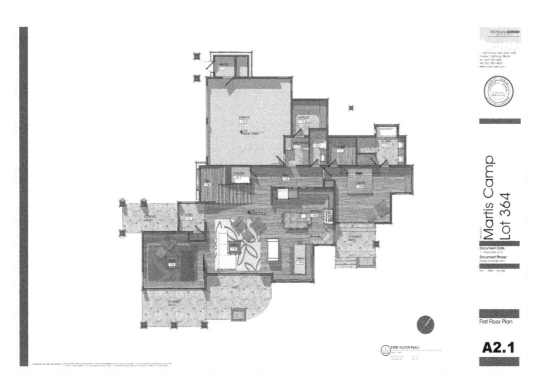

Figure 5-120
A Schematic Design floor plan.

Vector viewport

This is a top view of the floor plan. You only want important objects visible that will be dimensioned in LayOut, and anything else you want to pop on your drawings. Walls, windows, and doors are all that is needed for this scene.

LayOut Template	A2-Floor plans.layout
Model	Building.skp viewport, placed on **Vector Viewport** layer

Visible Objects	Linework only
Camera	Camera > Parallel Projection Mode
	Camera > Standard Views >Top View
	(Position should be identical to the raster scene.)
Style	"Vector", Fog off, Shadows off

Raster viewport

This is a top view of the floor plan with a colorful style applied, nearly all layers are turned on, including furniture, trim, walls, floors, etc. Shadows and fog are turned on to add depth to the scene. Create one scene for each level of the building.

LayOut Template	A2-Floor plans.layout
SketchUp Model	Building.skp viewport, placed on **Raster Viewport** layer.
Visible Objects	All layers on, section cut active
Camera	Camera > Parallel Projection Mode
	Camera > Standard Views >Top View
Style	"Raster", Fog on, Shadows on

This two-scene, two-viewport approach has become the preferred approach because it creates a beautiful floor plan that also displays crisp vector lines for the important wall elements (**Figure 5-122**). Repeat this process on a new page for each level of the building.

Figure 5-121
Floor plan
LayOut layers.

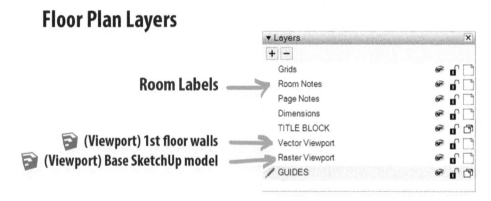

Floor Plan Layers

Room Labels

(Viewport) 1st floor walls

(Viewport) Base SketchUp model

Layers:
- Grids
- Room Notes
- Page Notes
- Dimensions
- TITLE BLOCK
- Vector Viewport
- Raster Viewport
- GUIDES

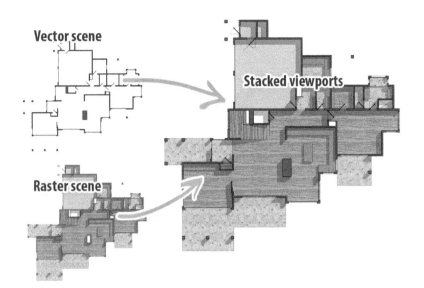

Figure 5-122
Two scenes
stacked to
create a single
view.

You do not need to add dimensions inside LayOut in Schematic Design phase, but you should add the following info.

Room Names and Tags

In each room on the floor plan, add a text room description, along with a room number. You can add a border and fill around the room number by selecting it and editing the **Shape Style panel**. (**Figure 5-123**)

Once you have one created, you can simply copy and paste it to each room, then edit the text boxes accordingly. (Hint hint, this is another great example of something that can be saved in a scrapbook to be used on future projects.)

Figure 5-123
Room names
and numbers
styled using
the Shape
Style panel.

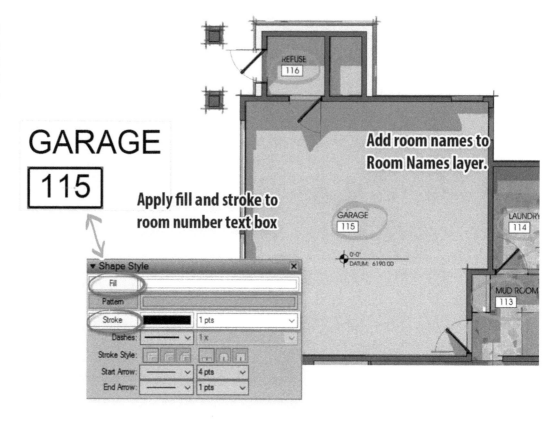

Other information such as floor datum elevation, north compass, and viewport tags are all things that should be inserted from a scrapbook, instead of created from scratch on every project. Some of these items are already included in the floor plan template and may need to be edited. Through the use of Auto-Text, some elements will automatically update as you insert them on the page.

Viewport Tags

The viewport tag, for example, can share the same name as the page, eliminating the need to manually type it in. In this situation, you can use the Auto-Text feature to populate the page name and the tag description. The tag's page reference is generated using Auto-Text as well, so it will always refer to the correct page, no matter which page it is on or in which template document it is placed.

The page reference is generated using a custom Auto-Text variable named <PageSet>, appended to one of the default <PageNumber> Auto-Text variables. In each of the template files, the <PageSet> variable has been created and configured, so you can drop this viewport tag from your scrapbook into any of the template files and it will display the correct page without any manual entry. (**Figure 5-124**)

Figure 5-124
Auto-Text is used in detail tags.

Roof Plan

Figure 5-125
A Schematic
Design phase
roof plan.

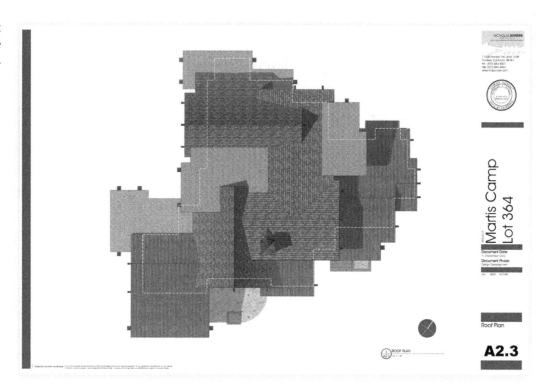

LayOut Template	A2-Floor plans.layout
Model	Building.skp viewport, placed on the **Raster Viewport** layer.
Visible Objects	All layers on, no section cuts active
Camera	Camera > Parallel Projection Mode Camera > Standard Views >Top View
Style	"Raster", Fog on, Shadows on

A top view of the building model will create your roof plan (**Figure 5-125**). Since there is no section cut, you can create this with a single viewport. Copy and paste the footprint line segment from the site plan, then rotate and scale it to size.

Exterior Elevations

The fastest way to create exterior elevations is to use the building model to show the exterior, then draw shapes inside LayOut on top of the viewport to represent the grade. There are no section cuts on these pages, so you can use a single raster-rendered viewport for each view. (**Figure 5-126**)

Figure 5-126
A Schematic Design phase exterior elevation page.

LayOut Template	A3-Elevations.layout
Model	Building.skp viewport, placed on the **Raster Viewport** layer.
Visible Objects	All layers on
Camera	Camera > Parallel Projection Mode Camera > Standard Views >Front, Left, Back, Right
Style	"Raster", Fog on, Shadows on

Figure 5-127
Exterior
elevation
LayOut layers.

Elevations Layers

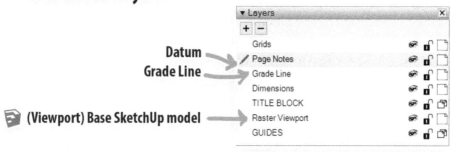

Datum → Page Notes
Grade Line → Grade Line

(Viewport) Base SketchUp model → Raster Viewport

Elevation Mask

Exterior elevations are created from the building model at aligned views of each side of the building.

✓   You can align the camera to any face in your model by **right-clicking** a surface > **Align View**. (You have to be inside the group/component so the face can be selected.)

✓   Use fog to show depth in your scene.

✓   Do not worry about the parts of the model that will appear below grade. You will mask those in LayOut.

Although it is possible to create a slice of your site terrain and bring that into LayOut, it is faster to estimate it and manually draw a grade line in LayOut. First, you need to draw a shape to mask out the area that will be below grade. Then, you will need to add some dark grade lines to emphasize the grade. (You could alternatively create a clipping mask with the viewport, which you will learn about in a later chapter.)

To create a mask over your viewport, follow these steps: (Figure 5-128)

1.   Activate the **Elevation Mask** layer.

2.   Activate the **Line tool** (L). In the **Shape Style panel**, enable fill and set it to white so it matches the page color. Disable stroke.

3.   Draw a polygon on top of the viewport where the ground plane is. Make sure you completely cover all parts of the viewport that will be below grade.

Figure 5-128
A solid polygon can be used to mask over a viewport.

After completing the mask, use the **Line tool** (L) again, this time with no fill, but with a stroke set to 3px. Draw lines to represent the top of grade, placed on the Grade Line layer. (**Figure 5-129**)

Figure 5-129
A series of solid line segments represent grade.

Add the following elements to the exterior elevations in LayOut:

✓ **Datum lines** - Find a datum symbol in the scrapbook. Make sure **Object Snap** is on, then snap the datum line to the top of the floor in your viewport. If you have trouble snapping to the desired points in the viewport, you can jump back to the SketchUp model and create some temporary guide objects that will appear in those scenes, then hide them once you have snapped the objects to them in LayOut.

✓ **Detail labels** - These are included in the template, but you may need to change their description depending upon how you set up your scenes.

Get ready to refine your design. The **Design Development phase** is all about moving from a conceptual model to a well coordinated, detailed model that you can bring into the Construction Documentation phase.

Objectives

By the end of the Design Development phase, your main building model should be 100% complete. When you leave this phase, there should not be any major design changes or details added to the model. Well, in the real world, there will always be changes made to the design, even well into construction. The goal is to minimize those changes whenever you can.

The next phase, Construction Documentation, focuses on generating the construction documents in LayOut. Very little time is spent in SketchUp during that phase, so you want to get your design as complete as possible now. This workflow is set up to allow big changes in Schematic Design, smaller changes in Design Development, and minor refinements in Construction Documentation.

The main objectives of this phase are as follows:

✓ Finalize major design decisions as you begin to add more detail to the model.

✓ Replace your simple window components with more detailed ones depicting the actual window shape and style.

✓ Add trim details to the interior and exterior of the building.

✓ Insert more detailed cabinets and millwork to the interior of the building in order to convey a more accurate vision of the selections made by the client.

Although you will likely be required to create or update some LayOut documents during the Design Development phase, we are going to focus solely on the modeling in this chapter, leaving the rest of the LayOut documentation for the last part of the book. Feel free to jump ahead to learn how to create specific types of documents as needed, once you have completed your Design Development modeling.

In the Design Development phase, you should be finalizing all design decisions. Since you modeled at a low level of detail in the Schematic Design phase, you have plenty of flexibility to make changes to your model. Once the design is finalized, you will work your way through the model, cleaning it up and adding detail to the model.

Figure 6-1
A photo of the exterior of the sample project.

Photo: ©VanceFox.com
Contractor: Robert Marr Construction

Adding Detail

Imagine standing about 40' away from your building. What details can you see from this distance? These are the details you should incorporate into your model in the Design Development phase, after finalizing design decisions. (**Figure 6-1**)

Although we are not going to review a step-by-step method for modeling at a higher level of detail, we will show examples of various objects so you can see the level of detail you should provide in this phase of design.

Windows/Doors

In the previous phase you created very simple surfaces to represent windows. In Design Development, you will want to convert those components into fully detailed windows. Notice how the window design has changed from the Schematic Design phase to the Design Development phase in the image below (**Figure 6-2**). The center picture window was changed to not have divided lites. By not wasting any time modeling a detailed window early on, there was no time wasted because of this design change.

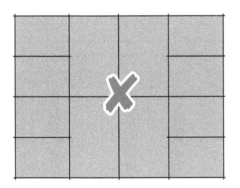

Schematic model window

Design Development Window

Figure 6-2 A comparison between the level of detail of a Schematic Design window and a Design Development window.

To model a window, you can start with the existing component you created in Schematic Design. Its surface will represent the window glass, and the dividing edges will serve as guides to help you align the sashes, jambs, and other window elements. **Figure 6-3)**

As you build the window, make each part of the window into its own group or component. This will make it easier for you to make changes to the window if needed.

FredoScale (Free)

The Fredo Scale plugin allows you to scale an object along a plane, in which the entire object does not stretch, but is extruded from the defined plane. This allows you to quickly scale windows without affecting lumber thicknesses.

www.sketchupbook.com/fredoscale

Figure 6-3
An overview of a Design Development window organization.

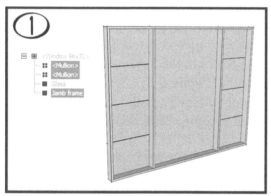

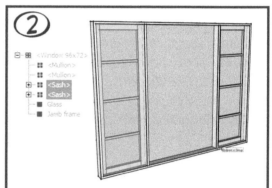

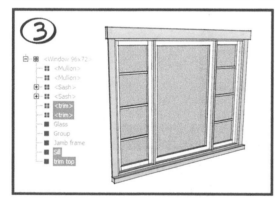

Model the interior trim as well, making sure it is within the window component. The main window component should be on the OB_WINDOW layer, and within it you should assign the trim groups to the OB_TRIM layer.

As you model other windows, copy objects from previous ones and resize them to fit, instead of modeling them from scratch.

Level of Detail

✓ **Installation flanges** - A lot of windows/doors these days have vinyl installation flanges that are nailed to the sheathing. Weatherproofing is then applied, and the siding or trim is run over the flange. In your main model, none of this information is needed. Since the walls represent the entire wall assembly, you should only model the parts of the window/door that are visible up to the siding.

✓ **Raised Panels** - Modeling the raised panels of a door is a purely visual enhancement you can choose to make to your model. It adds a lot of visual depth to the model, especially when shadows are turned on or if you are creating renderings of the model. It will also add bulk to your file size, so make sure to set your segments to a low number if the panel involves curved profiles. Alternatively, you could create a custom texture image to apply to the door to simulate the raised panels.

✓ **Wood Trim** - Take the time to apply wood textures directly to the face of the trim so you can orient the grain properly. **Right-click** on a textured face **> Texture > Position.**

✓ **Glass** - Use a single surface to represent the glass set to a gray color at about 50% opacity, and recess it in from the edge of the mullions and muntins to create depth.

✓ **Visual details vs. installation details** - In general, any details that enhance the visual appeal of a design or contribute to the overall look of a design are included in the model. Installation details which are hidden from view are omitted, and instead are communicated through a separate detail model. (**Figure 6-4**)

✓ **Forget the reveal** - For the sake of easy alignment, do not worry about adding a reveal around the window trim and the jambs. It will be too small to notice in your elevations, and it would make it harder to align your trim to the jambs.

✓ **Use edges to simulate joints** - An easy way to represent joints and corners on trim, is to simply draw a line. It takes less geometry than actually drawing two separate boards in separate groups, saving you some file space.

✓ **Rendering** - If you are using a rendering program, make sure you follow its recommendations regarding translucent textures. Single surfaces need to be oriented the correct way or they will not be rendered properly. (You can reverse a face by

right-clicking > Reverse face.)

Figure 6-4 An example of the level of detail of a Design Development door.

Baseboard/Trim

Adding baseboard and trim to your model can add a lot of detail to your model, especially when viewing the model with shadows on.

 The fastest way to draw trim and baseboard is with the **Follow Me tool**. Since you have the footprints of the walls in the models, you can copy the geometry from the floor to provide a path for the **Follow Me tool** to extrude the baseboard around the room.

 **To extrude baseboard around a room, follow these steps: (Figure 6-5)**

1. Enter the floor group, navigate to the room in which you will be creating the baseboard and copy the floor area.

2. Exit the floor group and **Edit > Paste In Place**. Move the entities down, below the building. Make it a group, and assign to the OB_TRIM layer. Enter the group.

3. Draw a baseboard profile in the room. Select the path below, activate the **Follow** **Me tool**, and click on the profile face.

4. Clean up the trim by deleting parts of the baseboard that pass through doorways and openings.

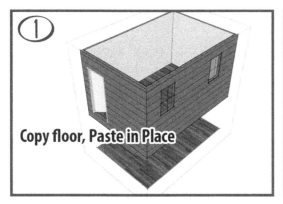

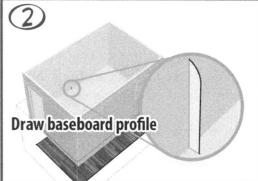

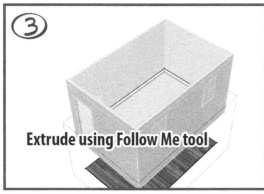

Figure 6-5
How to extrude baseboard around a room.

Notice how the path does not need to be connected to the profile in order to use the **Follow Me tool**. This is convenient because you can use the same path for multiple objects. For instance, maybe you have crown molding as well as baseboard you want to extrude. Once you are done you can just delete the path from the model, leaving just the trim you created.

Each set of baseboards and trim should be in their own group. Many times, you can copy baseboard from one room into another, then edit the group to fit the new room. This is much faster than starting from scratch with the **Follow Me tool** every time.

Roof Details

In Schematic Design, you were not too concerned about roof lines intersecting into rooms below, but now you want to review them and get them cleaned up. Before you do that, you should review the trim details and determine if you need to dimension the roof overhangs in LayOut before modeling the trim. Dimensioning the roof in LayOut before adding trim makes it easy to snap to the framing dimensions.

Trim

Before cleaning up your roof intersections, you should extrude any roof trim details you want to include in your model (**Figure 6-6**). It will be easier to do this now because when you do the roof cleanup in the next step, you will be able to intersect your roof trim elements at the same time.

Think back to the level of detail at which you modeled the floors and walls and you will remember that the walls are modeled to the rough framing dimensions even though the exterior of the walls have the siding material applied to them. Keeping in mind that the leading principle is to model accurately to the dimensions required in LayOut, while creating the illusion that you are looking at finished surfaces. Designing in this way allows you to use a single model for multiple purposes.

Figure 6-6
Roof trim
details added
to a roof
in Design
Development.

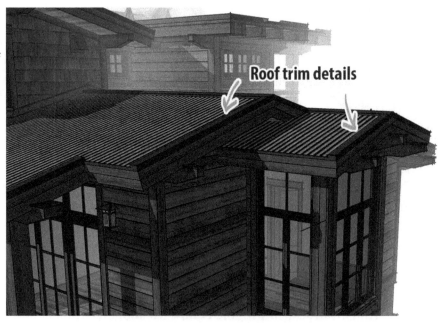

Roof trim details

With that said, you will want to add trim to your roof groups to represent rake board thickness and fascia thickness. There are a couple of challenges with roof trim:

✓ Adding rake boards or fascia boards as a separate group outside of the roof group creates a visible seam between the top of the roof and the top of the trim. In most real-world cases the trim boards are tucked underneath the roofing material so there is no gap.

✓ You need to snap dimensions to the roof framing in order to show overhang measurements. Adding trim thickness around the roof group will make it hard to measure the overhangs in LayOut.

There are two solutions to these problems. You could add the trim entities directly inside the roof groups, which would effectively extend the top roof surface, eliminating the problem of having a seam there. However, in order to dimension the roof accurately, you would have to create the dimensions inside LayOut first, before going back to the model to add the trim. Once you have reloaded the model into LayOut, the dimensions will remain unchanged, even though the roof has been extended. (**Figure 6-7**)

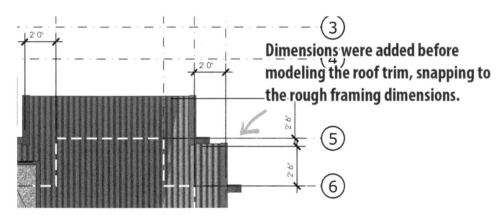

Dimensions were added before modeling the roof trim, snapping to the rough framing dimensions.

Figure 6-7
Roof dimensions need to be added in LayOut before extending trim or other details.

Alternatively, you could create separate groups for all of the trim, placing them on the OB_TRIM layer. You would have to hide the edges of the roof group and edge group wherever they intersect, and match the roof material texture to create the illusion of a seamless roof.

In this case, it ends up being faster and easier to just add the dimensions ahead of time in LayOut and extend the roof edges.

Roof Intersections

One of the more challenging tasks of roof cleanup is intersecting all of the various roof groups with each other, as well as with any intersecting walls. Most of the modeling you do in SketchUp is very straightforward, but when you have roofs intersecting at various angles, it is not as easy as using the **Push/Pull tool (P)** to extrude surfaces. You will need to use some other tools available to intersect complex objects.

Solid tools

SketchUp Pro includes Solid tools, which are a collection of tools that you can use to intersect two solid groups or components in various ways. The Solid tools include **Outer Shell, Intersect, Union, Subtract, Trim, and Split**.

In order to use the Solid tools, the two groups/components need to be solid, and they need to exist within the same context. For example, if you want to use the trim command to trim the roof where the wall intersects it, you will not be able to because the wall group is in a different group.

One way to take advantage of the Solid tools is to create a temporary solid shape that you can use as a sacrificial "trimming" group. Use the walls and other intersecting roofs as guides while creating the shape. Then you can use the **Subtract tool** to subtract the temporary shape from the roof group. (**Figure 6-8**)

Figure 6-8 The Subtract tool can subtract one group from the other.

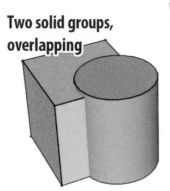

Two solid groups, overlapping

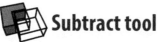 **Subtract tool**

Subtract first group from the second group

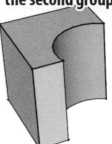

To use the Subtract tool with a temporary trimming group, follow these steps: (Figure 6-9)

Step by Step

1. Temporarily hide other roof groups so you can see how the target group intersects walls and other objects. (To unhide them later, go to the **Outliner panel**, select the groups in italics, **right-click > Unhide.**)

2. Orbit around to see which parts of the building you want to intersect with the roof group.

3. Draw a solid object, snapping to the various edges and points in the model to create a "trimming" group that you will subtract from the roof group. Make it a group.

4. Activate the **Subtract tool**, click on the "trimming" group first, then the roof group second.

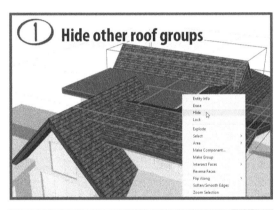

Figure 6-9
Temporary groups can be used with Solid tools.

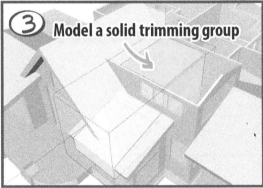

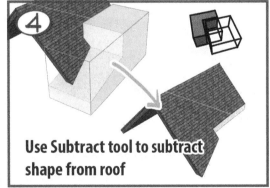

With subtractive Solid tools such as **Subtract** and **Trim**, it is sometimes hard to remember which order you should click on the groups in order to create the desired result. An easy way to remember is the second group you click is the one that will be trimmed by the action.

  ✓ **Subtract tool** - The second group will be subtracted by the first group. (The first group will be deleted.)

  ✓ **Trim tool** - The second group will be trimmed by the first group. (The first group is unaffected.)

The **Trim tool** is also useful for intersecting two roof groups with each other. In the example below, the main roof will be unaffected, and the second roof will be trimmed where it intersects with the main roof. (**Figure 6-10**)

Figure 6-10
The Trim tool is another Solid tool that can be used on roof groups.

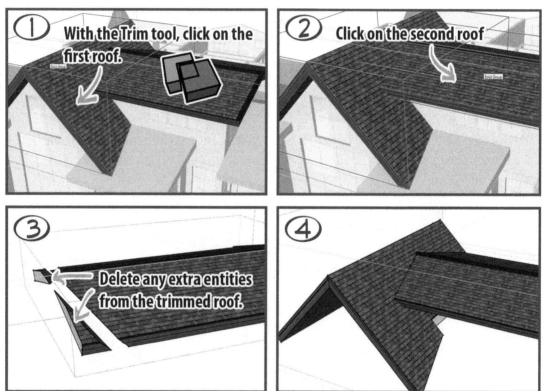

You can only use the Solid tools on groups or components that are solid. That is one of the reasons why it is important to model perfectly and make sure your groups are solid. It makes things much easier to work with as you progress through the model.

Notice how easy it was to miter the roof eave trim? You should always leave your intersection clean ups until after you have added all the roof eave details. It makes it much easier when you can simply use the Solid tools to miter and intersect.

Intersect with Faces

If you can not use the Solid tools for any particular reason (for instance, if you were not able to model solid groups), there is another tool you can use to help you trim and clean up entities. The **Intersect with Faces** command offers a few options that will generate edges on the selected faces wherever there are entities intersecting it. You have some control over which entities it intersects, which can sometimes give you greater control than with the Solid tools.

The **Intersect Faces > With Context** command will generate edges on the selected faces where they intersect with other entities that are inside the current group. If you want to generate edges with intersecting entities outside of the current group as well, you will need to use the **With Model** option. (**Figure 6-11**)

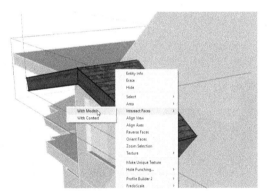

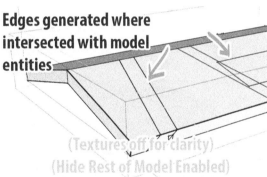

Edges generated where intersected with model entities

(Textures off for clarity)
(Hide Rest of Model Enabled)

Figure 6-11
Intersect faces can be used on complicated intersections but requires manual cleanup.

Once you have generated edges with Intersect faces, you will need to manually walk through and erase edges that are not needed, as well as creating new edges as needed in order to repair faces.

Manual Cleanup

When all else fails, you always have the option to tackle the geometry cleanup one edge at a time. Although it is the most time-consuming, it is sometimes the most straight-forward.

Perpendicular Intersections

Sometimes it is easy to forget about the **Push/Pull tool** (**P**). Whenever you have a situation where you can extrude a profile from a surface, that is typically the easiest solution. As you know, this only works when the surface is perpendicular to the direction you want to extrude. Just draw a line where the perpendicular surface intersects with the other roof, then push/pull to the other side. (**Figure 6-12**)

Figure 6-12
Use the Push/ Pull tool whenever possible.

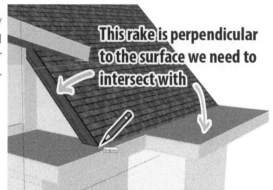
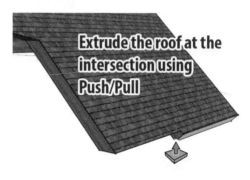

Figure 6-13
A completed roof after intersecting and cleanup.

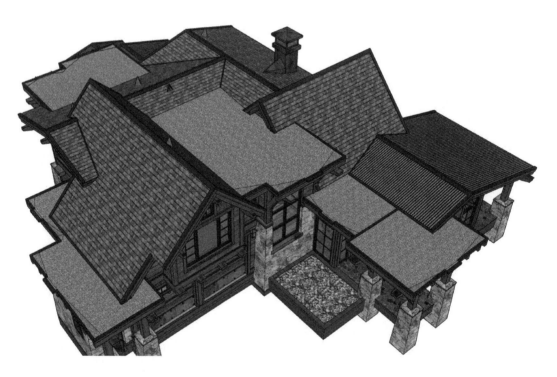

Kitchen/Bath

Kitchens and baths can vary in complexity depending upon the amount of detail you want to show in your model. In a set of construction documents you are typically not looking to produce a set of detailed shop drawings ready for manufacturing, so you do not need incredibly detailed cabinets. However, you do want to show enough visual detail in order to illustrate the design intent and style, so you will want to find a balance in between. (**Figure 6-14**)

Figure 6-14 A fully detailed kitchen in Design Development.

✓ **Pre-made components** - Cabinets are one of those things that are actually quite plentiful on the free 3D warehouse (**File > 3D Warehouse > Get Models**), and thankfully many are professionally modeled by the cabinet manufacturers. You can find libraries of good quality cabinets at your fingertips to load right into your model. However, it can be a challenge to search through their library to find the exact configuration you are looking for, although many of the components available are dynamic components, giving you an easy way to change the sizes of the cabinets.

✓ **Cabinet Plugins** - There have been a number of various cabinet plugins that have become available for SketchUp which aim to automate the process of inserting and configuring cabinets. While they provide you with a ton of customization, you pay for it in file size, (and money, since all of these plugins require a paid license). They tend to be more detailed than necessary.

✓ **Manually modeled** - If you can not find the right style of cabinets that you need, you can always model them yourself. This is the method that Nick prefers. Most cabinets can be a simple box with the toe kick modeled, then you model the cabinet doors and drawer fronts as components.

Use your Schematic Design cabinet runs as temporary guides, then delete them from your model once you have created the more detailed cabinets.

Appliances, showers, faucets, and other fixtures can all be found on the 3D warehouse, or through professional subscription services such as Form Fonts. Many manufacturers will provide SketchUp models of their products directly on their website, so even if you do not see it on the 3D warehouse, you still may be able to find it.

The most important criteria for selecting models to import is the file size and number of polygons in the component. For example, the faucet component below is 1.3mb and over 3,000 polygons (**Figure 6-15**). While the component may look amazing under a microscope, no one will ever notice when viewed at 1/4" scale in you drawings. It is typically not worth the performance sacrifice to use large components like this, but if your computer can handle it, it can be nice to see the exact product you intend to install in the project, instead of a generic representation.

Figure 6-15
Low polygon components will keep your file size down and will not bog down your model.

A similar faucet can be found on Form Fonts with 164 kilobytes, and only 961 polygons.

Lights

If you are planning to use rendering software with your model, you will need to insert special components into your model so that the lights will work in the render engine. Rendering software will apply light physics to your model in order to create a more photorealistic image or animation. Most allow you to insert lights in addition to the default sun position in SketchUp.

Some rendering software like LumenRT uses proxy components (**Figure 6-16**), which are SketchUp components that you insert into your model, but are automatically replaced when the model is imported into the rendering software. The strength in this is that you can populate a single light fixture that is used multiple times in one move. Other software requires that you insert lights directly from their interface, after you have imported the SketchUp model. Then there are more simple renderers like Visualizer that do not use lights at all, but only use the SketchUp sun position to calculate light and shadows.

Figure 6-16
Proxy light components are replaced automatically inside the rendering software.

Site grading

Just as you did with the driveway, go around the building in the site model and grade the terrain as needed for proper slope. (**Figure 6-17**)

Figure 6-17
Grade the terrain around the building.

Grade terrain around the house where needed in the site model.

Examples

On the following pages are examples of the level of detail you should aim for when completing your Design Development model. The top half of the page shows the SketchUp model or a LumenRT render. The bottom half of the page shows a photograph of the completed building.

See if you can identify some of the design changes made to the projects by comparing the two images.

SketchUp Model

Photo: ©VanceFox.com
Contractor: MD Construction & Consulting

SketchUp Model (LumenRT Render)

Photo: ©VanceFox.com
Contractor: Robert Marr Construction

SketchUp Model

Photo: ©VanceFox.com
Contractor: Robert Marr Construction

SketchUp Model

Photo: ©VanceFox.com
Contractor: Heslin Construction

Design Development Documents

As you work through the model, you will continue to refine the design until you reach the point where no further changes will be made.

When you need to prepare documents for city approvals, update your existing LayOut documents as needed by simply updating the model references. Add annotations to the drawings if needed. You will need to determine which types of documents you will need to prepare during this phase.

Since that varies so much by area and by project, we won't review specific Design Development documents here. Instead, the next section will dive into the Construction Documentation phase, where you'll learn how to create the rest of the documents you will need to complete your project.

So far, you have spent most of your time in SketchUp. From here on out you will be spending most of your time in LayOut.

Design Development Documents

Figure 6-18
You will need to determine which documents you will need during the Design Development phase.

During this last phase in the design process, you will be completing the documentation of your project, so that you can hand over a set of completed drawings to the governing authorities, planning department, building department, utility companies, special districts, and other building partners to start construction.

Objectives

In the previous phases, you have worked through the entire design, refining the model, and achieving a completed design. In the Construction Documentation phase, you will be spending most of your time in LayOut, updating existing documents or creating new ones.

The main objectives of the Construction Documentation Phase are as follows:

✓ Finish detailing existing LayOut documents.

✓ Produce additional documents, including General Notes, MPE drawings, Interior elevations, building sections, schedules, and construction details.

✓ Create custom schedules using basic LayOut tools.

✓ Use scrapbooks to develop a library of notes and symbols frequently used.

✓ Create additional detail SketchUp models to illustrate construction details.

In reality, you may be required to produce some of these documents during the Design Development phase, but for simplicity we have focused this last part of the book on LayOut, instead of splitting the information between the two sections. It is acceptable to jump ahead to this section in order to learn how to generate certain documents for Design Development.

Construction Documents

Figure 7-1 A sample set of Construction Document pages.

The final set of construction documents is compiled using much of the same techniques you already know. Since you are using many of the same documents you originally created in the Schematic Design phase, you are just adding more detail and updating the model references. The documents continue to evolve over the life of the project.

However, there are a handful of documents that you will be creating for the first time in this phase. Some require additional preparation in SketchUp, or a special workflow in LayOut, so we will be reviewing those techniques in this chapter.

We will review each document type, then review some additional LayOut tips towards the end of the chapter.

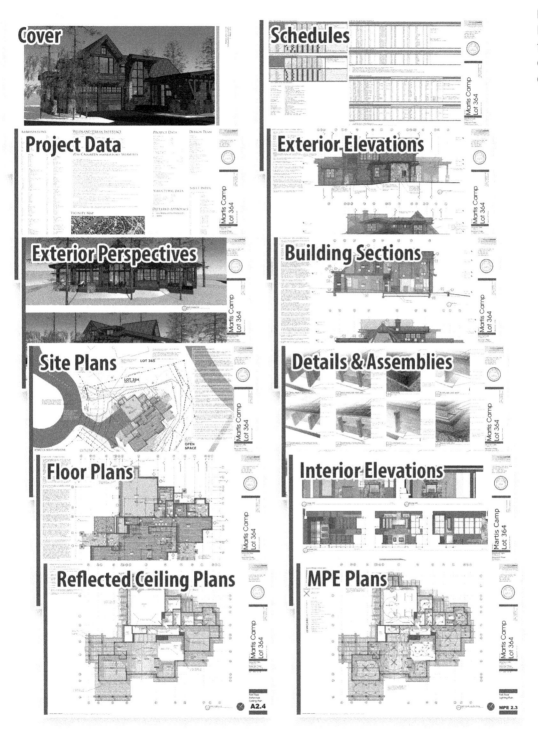

Figure 7-2
Different types of construction documents.

Project Data

The Project Data sheet includes important information such as abbreviations, project data, structural data, design team info, sheet index, etc (**Figure 7-3**). Much of the information on this page can be reused on future projects by saving it in a template, or even saving it as a scrapbook item. You can then edit just the project specific information in the template as it pertains to the project.

Figure 7-3 The Project Data page.

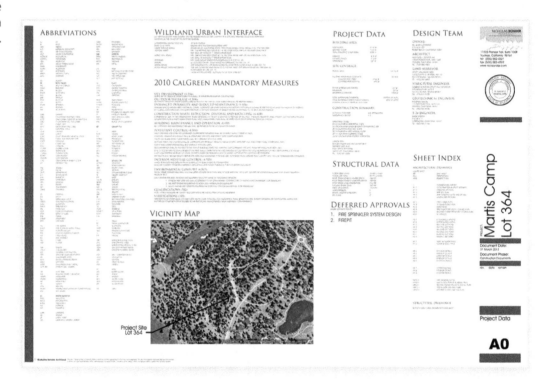

LayOut Template	A0-Data.layout
Model	N/A
LayOut Objects	General notes, conditions, specifications, contact info

There are a small number of layers in this document, since most of the notes will be placed on the Page Notes layer. The Vicinity Map layer is there for you to place an image from Google Maps of the job site vicinity. A single guide box is placed on the GUIDES layer to help you align the vicinity map, and can be hidden or deleted once you have placed it. (**Figure 7-4**)

Project Data Layers

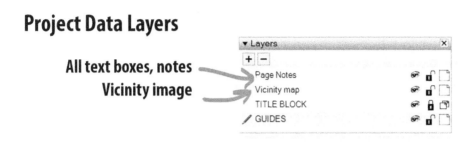

Figure 7-4
The Project Data template layers.

You can organize text blocks into columns by using the **tab** key as you write. It can be easier to organize text in this way instead of creating a separate text box for each column. (**Figure 7-5**)

Figure 7-5
The general notes are made up of blocks of text.

Construction & Utilities Site Plan

This page, which you have ignored up until now, exists inside the site plan template. Most of the work is already completed for preparing this page since you used shared layers in LayOut to display site plan elements on multiple pages.

The Construction & Utilities Site Plan provides information about the various utilities being delivered to the building. It also includes notes regarding general construction coordination on site, as well as defining work zones and boundaries for the site during construction. All of these various boundaries and notes are added to the page from inside LayOut. (**Figure 7-6**)

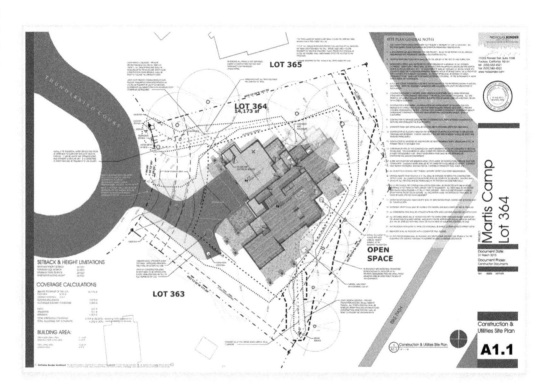

You already have a raster viewport of the site model on the first page, along with exploded viewports for all of the various boundaries. After updating the model reference to the latest model, you can copy the site plan viewport and paste it onto the Construction & Utilities Site plan page on the Raster Viewport layer.

Instead of showing the roof of the building, this page should show the floor plan, so you will want to change the viewport scene to "Site plan No Roof". In addition, you can stack a viewport onto the Vector Viewport layer, using the 1st Vector scene from the site model. (**Figure 7-7)**

Vector Viewport

LayOut Template	A1-Site.layout
Model	Site.skp **1st Vector** scene, placed on the **Vector Viewport** layer.
Visible Objects	First floor linework.
Camera	Camera > Parallel Projection Mode Camera > Standard Views >Top View
Style	"Vector", Fog off, Shadows off

Raster Viewport

LayOut Template	A1-Site.layout
Model	Site.skp **Site plan No Roof** scene, placed on the **Raster Viewport** layer.
Visible Objects	Terrain, Walls, Floors, Stairs, etc. Hide furniture.
Camera	Camera > Parallel Projection Mode Camera > Standard Views >Top View
Style	"Raster", Fog on, Shadows on

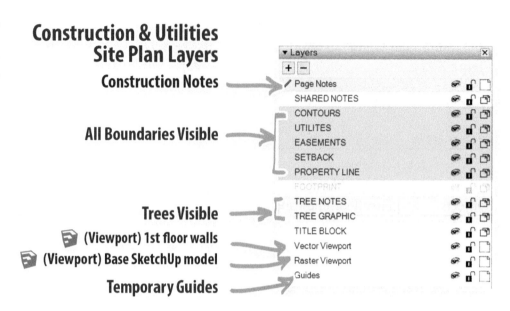

LayOut Shapes

Using the drawing tools and **Shape Style panel** in LayOut, you can draw any information that is not depicted in the SketchUp model. It is usually a good idea to draw things in LayOut when they do not require precise dimensions. For instance, The utility services are drawn directly on the LayOut page using the **Line tool** (L), set to a specific color and a dashed line type. (**Figure 7-8**)

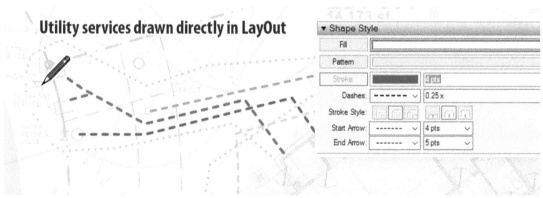

Other examples of areas that are not dimensionally critical are most construction areas such as snow removal area, silt fence locations, and construction boundaries. The **Line tool** (L) can create filled polygonal shapes by simply enabling Fill in the **Shape**

Style panel, and by finishing the shape back at its origin to close the shape. (**Figure 7-9**)

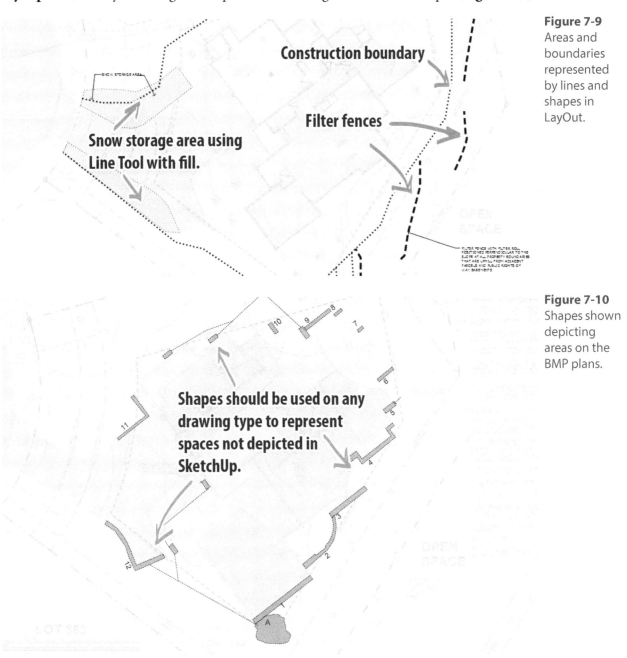

Construction boundary

Filter fences

Snow storage area using Line Tool with fill.

Figure 7-9
Areas and boundaries represented by lines and shapes in LayOut.

Shapes should be used on any drawing type to represent spaces not depicted in SketchUp.

Figure 7-10
Shapes shown depicting areas on the BMP plans.

Grading Plan

Although the contour lines are shown on most of the site plans, the grading plan will share additional grading information such as slopes and elevation heights pinned to specific parts of the building. (**Figure 7-11**)

Figure 7-11
The Grading plan.

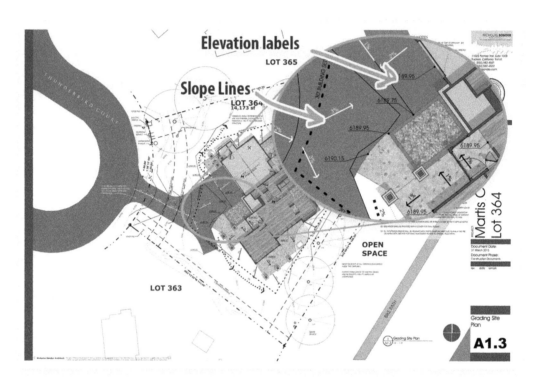

The grading plan will have the same viewport setup as the Construction & Utilities Plan, so you can simply copy and paste the viewports from that page. The UTILITIES layer and the FOOTPRINT layer should be hidden on this page since they are not needed. (**Figure 7-12**)

To add elevation labels around the building, you will use the **Tape Measure tool** (**T**) in SketchUp to measure the actual height of the terrain at different points in the site model. Type in the measurements manually using the **Label tool** in LayOut.

Vector Viewport

LayOut Template	A1-Site.layout
Model	Site.skp **1st Vector** scene, placed on the **Vector Viewport** layer.
Visible Objects	First floor linework.
Camera	Camera > Parallel Projection Mode Camera > Standard Views >Top View
Style	"Vector", Fog off, Shadows off

Raster Viewport

LayOut Template	A1-Site.layout
Model	Site.skp **Site plan No Roof** scene, placed on the **Raster Viewport** layer.
Visible Objects	Terrain, Walls, Floors, Stairs, etc. Hide furniture.
Camera	Camera > Parallel Projection Mode Camera > Standard Views >Top View
Style	"Raster", Fog on, Shadows on

Grading Plan Layers

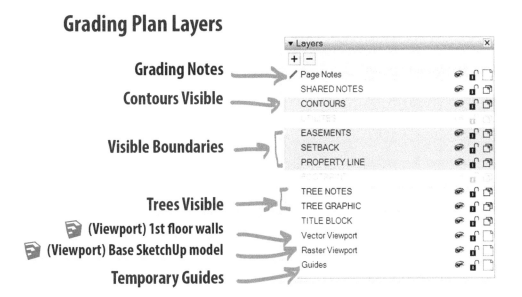

Figure 7-12
The grading plan layers.

BMP Site Plan

This is another page inside the site template you have already developed. BMP stands for Best Management Practices and is identical to the commonly used SWPP (Storm Water Prevention Plan.) This page is used for water retention planning on site. In addition to showing the shared site plan layers, you will use LayOut's drawing tools to define areas you would like to specify on this plan. (**Figure 7-13**)

You might want to include an infiltration schedule on this page, which you will learn how to do in the section ahead on schedules.

Figure 7-13
The BMP Site Plan.

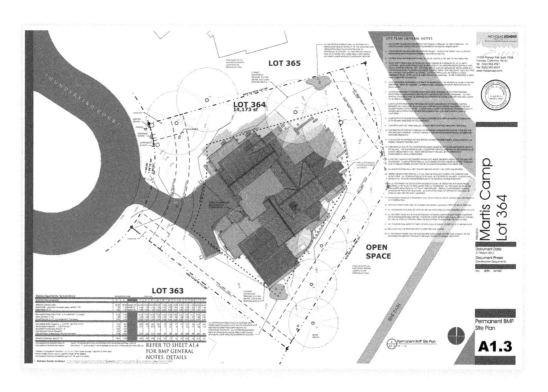

The viewport needed on this page is the same one you used to create the Schematic Design site plan. You will want a raster viewport of the site with the building roof visible. The FOOTPRINT layer will be visible on this page to show the building footprint overlaid on the roof. (**Figure 7-14**)

Raster Viewport

LayOut Template	A1-Site.layout
Model	Site.skp **Site Plan** scene, placed on the **Raster Viewport** layer.
Visible Objects	Terrain, Walls, Floors, Roof, Stairs, etc. Hide furniture. No Section Cuts.
Camera	Camera > Parallel Projection Mode Camera > Standard Views >Top View
Style	"Raster", Fog on, Shadows on

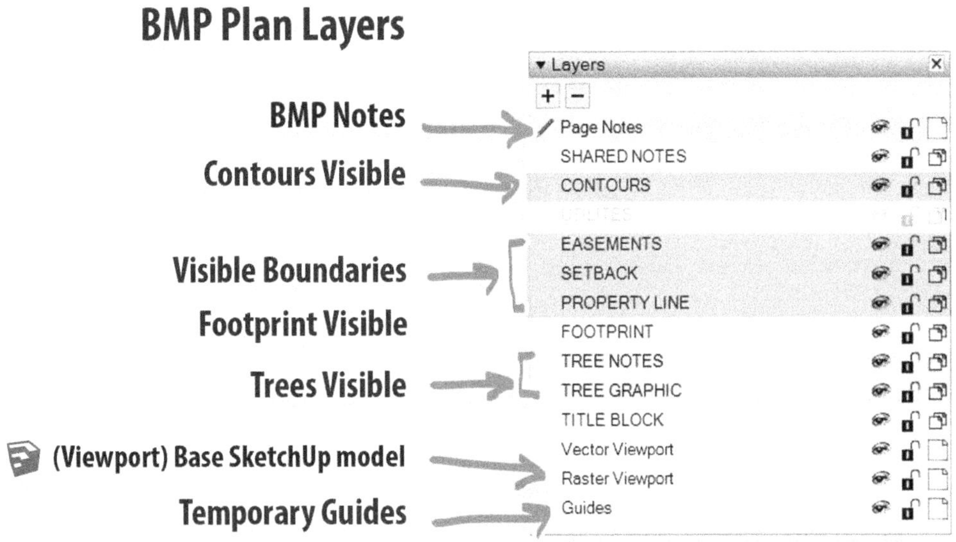

BMP Plan Layers

Figure 7-14
The BMP site plan layers.

BMP Notes → Page Notes

SHARED NOTES

Contours Visible → CONTOURS

UTILITIES

EASEMENTS

Visible Boundaries → SETBACK

PROPERTY LINE

Footprint Visible → FOOTPRINT

TREE NOTES

Trees Visible → TREE GRAPHIC

TITLE BLOCK

(Viewport) Base SketchUp model → Vector Viewport

Raster Viewport

Temporary Guides → Guides

BMP Details

The BMP details sheet will be the first time you will be creating a separate SketchUp model to represent various construction details in the project (**Figure 7-15**). For example, instead of modeling a construction fence in your site model, you can just create a new model showing a small section of a construction fence, and insert a viewport of that model on the BMP detail sheet. Then on the BMP site plan, you can use simple drawing tools to draw a boundary representing where the fence should be installed.

There are many uses for detail models, which we will go into later on in the section titled Construction Details.

Figure 7-15
The BMP
Details page.

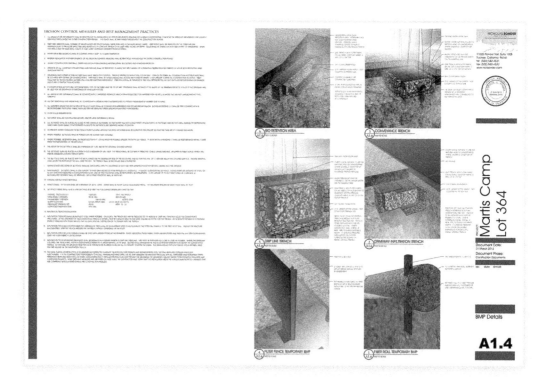

Since this page does not show a plan view of the site, it is the only page in the site plan document which hides all of the shared site plan entities. You will be inserting multiple detail models onto the Raster Viewport layer, and all of the page notes and annotations will be placed on the Page Notes layer. (**Figure 7-16**)

Raster Viewports (Multi)

LayOut Template	A1-Site.layout
Model	Multiple detail models as needed.
Visible Objects	All objects visible
Camera	Camera > Perspective
Style	"Raster", Fog on, Shadows on

BMP Details Layers

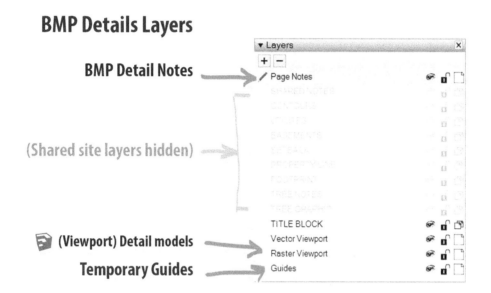

BMP Detail Notes

(Shared site layers hidden)

(Viewport) Detail models

Temporary Guides

Figure 7-16
The BMP details page layers.

Landscape Site Plan

The Landscape plan is where you show information regarding trees, shrubs, and groundcover (**Figure 7-17**). Depending upon how you chose to display trees, your trees may be displayed from your model, or you may have to insert tree symbols from within LayOut.

You will use the scrapbook to place plant symbols on this page, (if they are not included in your SketchUp model), and you will create a legend to describe what the symbols represent. LayOut's drawing tools can be used to define specific groundcover areas as well.

Figure 7-17
The Landscape Site plan.

The Contours layer and the Utilities layer are hidden on this page. All landscape symbols and labels are placed on the Page Notes layer. (**Figure 7-18**)

Vector Viewport

LayOut Template	A1-Site.layout
Model	Site.skp **1st Vector** scene, placed on the **Vector Viewport** layer.
Visible Objects	First floor linework.
Camera	Camera > Parallel Projection Mode Camera > Standard Views >Top View
Style	"Vector", Fog off, Shadows off

Raster Viewport

LayOut Template	A1-Site.layout
Model	Site.skp **Site plan No Roof** scene, placed on the **Raster Viewport** layer.
Visible Objects	Terrain, Walls, Floors, Stairs, etc. Hide furniture.
Camera	Camera > Parallel Projection Mode Camera > Standard Views >Top View
Style	"Raster", Fog on, Shadows on

Landscape Site Plan Layers

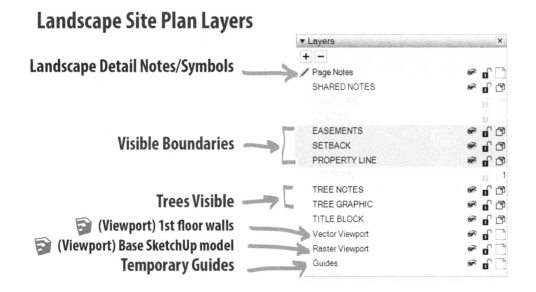

Landscape Detail Notes/Symbols

Visible Boundaries

Trees Visible

(Viewport) 1st floor walls
(Viewport) Base SketchUp model
Temporary Guides

Figure 7-18
The Landscape Site Plan layers.

Floor Plans

While your floor plans and roof plans were first created in Schematic Design, they have not been fully annotated for construction issue. In this phase, you will continue from where you left off by adding column grid lines, section cut tags, dimensions, window and door tags, and general notes (**Figure 7-19**). (You may actually need to produce these sheets during the Design Development process. The same principles apply here.)

We will review the best approach for fully annotating your floor plans in the next section.

Figure 7-19
The Floor
Plans.

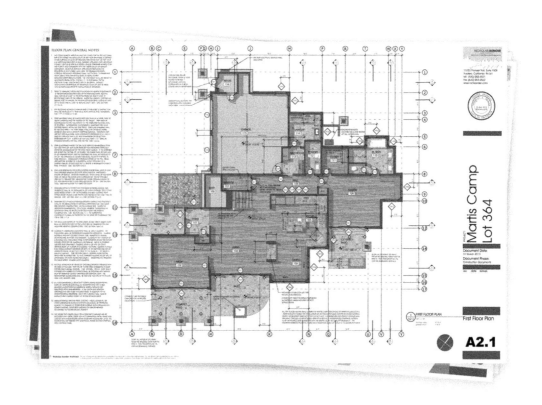

In addition to the layers that already have objects on them from the previous phase, you will be using the Grids layer, Page Notes layer, and Dimensions layer when adding objects to the page. (**Figure 7-20**)

Floor Plan Layers

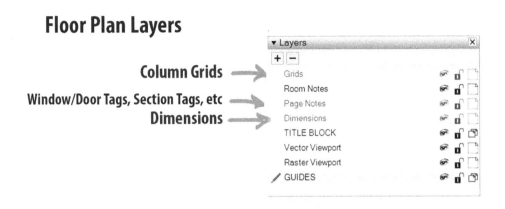

Figure 7-20
The Floor Plan layers.

Symbols

Explore the default scrapbooks to discover a variety of symbols and labels. Keep in mind, they are all created using a combination of basic LayOut shapes and text. Creating your own is very easy when you keep the following tips in mind:

✓ **Align text** - When creating symbols which include text that are intended to be edited, make sure you set the text box alignment so when the text is edited it does not have to be realigned. By default, text is aligned left, but for text that is centered inside a shape, make sure to set a center alignment on the text box. (**Figure 7-21**)

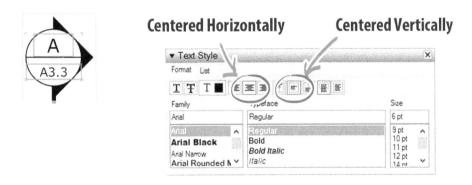

Figure 7-21
Align text according to the symbol it is used for.

✓ **Align shapes** - Most symbols have some sort of symmetry or other alignment. You can align multiple objects by selecting them, then **right-clicking > Align > (Left, Right, Top, Bottom, Vertically, Horizontally.)**

Grid Lines

Gridlines are used to mark important structural points on a building. Instead of manually creating them each time, prepare a set of gridlines ahead of time and save them in a scrapbook for future use.

When you are about to begin placing gridlines, lock all of the other layers to make it easier to select the gridlines and prevent accidental movement of other elements on the page. Keeping gridlines within a group helps prevent accidental selection of objects, but locking layers is also a good habit to get into to prevent accidents. It is also helpful to hide the raster viewport layer and only have the vector layer visible to provide a more positive snapping point for alignment.

Figure 7-22
Grid lines are contained within multiple groups meant to be exploded as you align them on the page.

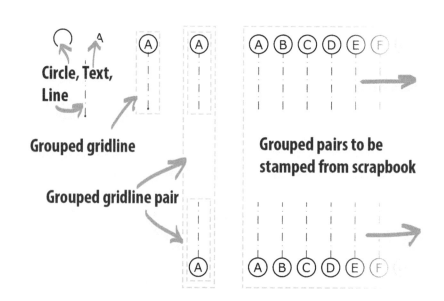

The trick to being able to set your gridlines quickly is to organize them in a series of groups that you can ungroup as needed as you start to align them on the document (**Figure 7-22**). For example, let's look at the vertical gridlines labeled A-Z. You will want the default number of grid line pairs grouped together so you can stamp them into your document in one shot right from the scrapbook. Inside that group, each pair of gridlines will be grouped together (upper grid line A will be grouped with lower grid line A) so you can move them into alignment with the floor plan in one step.

Once you have snapped the grid line pair to the floor plan, you will want to **right-click > Align > Top** so all of the labels are aligned with each other. Then, you will need to ungroup the upper from the lower so you can position the top and the bottom labels vertically on the page, independently from one another. (The reason why you want to explode the groups at this point is so you can select all of the lower labels at once and move them together on the page. If you kept them in their groups, you would be forced to enter each group one by one and manually move them into alignment.)

Once all of the labels are aligned, the last step is to extend the lines down to the reference point on the floor plan. By exploding the groups one more time, you will be able to drag the line directly to extend its length, instead of having to enter each group to edit the line. Let's look at this again, step by step.

To insert gridlines over a floor plan, follow these steps: (Figure 7-23)

1. Place the grouped gridlines on your page, on the Gridlines layer. **You will keep this parent group intact to make it easier to select gridlines**. **Double-click** on this group to edit its contents.

2. Move each grid line onto the floor plan, snapping the midpoint to a point on the floor plan. Do not worry about vertical alignment right now, you just want to make sure the horizontal alignment is correct. Delete the other gridlines you do not need.

3. **Right-click** on the Gridlines layer **> Select Entities** to select all of the gridlines. Then, **right-click** on one of the gridlines **> Align > Top**. All of the gridlines will be aligned vertically now. If you need to raise or lower them, just hold the SHIFT key while you move them in order to maintain their vertical alignment. Alternatively, use the arrow keys to nudge them. Do not worry about the lower gridlines labels right now; you are just aligning and positioning the upper labels in this step.

4. With all of the gridlines still selected, go to **Edit > Ungroup**. (Unfortunately, ungroup is unavailable in the context menu when multiple objects are selected.) Ungrouping will allow you to select the bottom grid labels separately from the top ones.

Figure 7-23
Grid lines are aligned to the viewport in a certain order to maximize efficiency.

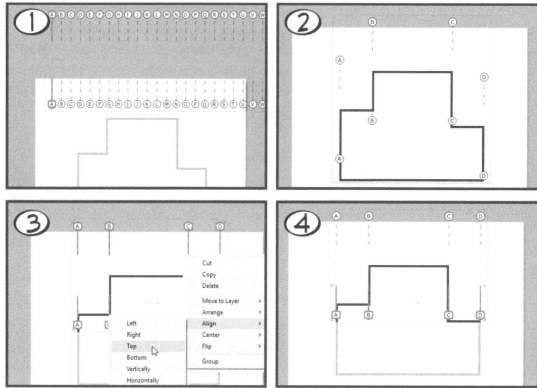

5. Drag a selection box around all of the lower grid labels. Move the lower labels to the bottom of the page while holding **SHIFT** to maintain alignment.

6. Right-click on the **Gridlines layer > Select Entities** to select all, then go to **Edit > Ungroup** to ungroup for a final time. This time, you have ungrouped the circle label from the dashed line, allowing you to manipulate the line length without affecting the circle label.

7. Extend the dashed line for each grid label to snap to the floor plan reference point.

8. Repeat this process for the horizontal grid lines. Your vertical gridlines should be in one group, and your horizontal gridlines should be in another group. They should both be assigned to the GRIDLINES layer. Once you are done, you can copy your completed gridlines to other pages and documents that need to show them. (**Figure 7-24**)

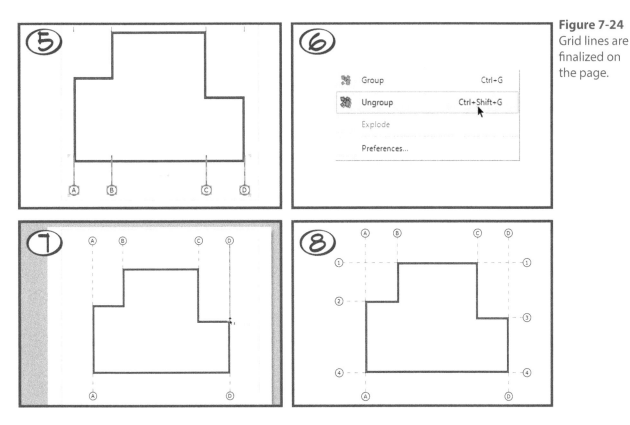

Figure 7-24
Grid lines are finalized on the page.

If you are having trouble finding the correct object to snap to, you can go back into your SketchUp model and create a set of edges aligned where you need to have gridlines, placed on a special layer. Create a scene with the same camera perspective as your floor plan scenes, and set your viewport to that scene temporarily in order for you to snap the gridlines to the edges you just created. When you are done, switch the viewport scene back to the floor plan.

This technique is also useful when adding datum elevation tags. Many times you do not have anything to snap to, so having a scene with temporary edges placed for reference can help you snap to and measure from them.

Reflected Ceiling Plans

You will use a separate template model to generate your reflected ceiling plan scenes (**Figure 7-25**). The RCP.skp SketchUp template is provided so you can import your main building model into it.

In LayOut, the viewports are set up in the same way you created the floor plans, using a raster viewport showing the building and a vector viewport showing the walls of the building.

The gridlines and room names shown on this page are easily copied from your floor plans, eliminating duplicate work.

Figure 7-25
The Reflected
Ceiling Plans.

The layers in LayOut are identical to the layers used in the Floor Plan templates. Reflected ceiling plan notes are added to the Page Notes layer. (**Figure 7-26**)

Vector viewport

LayOut Template	A2-Reflected ceiling plans.layout
Model	RCP.skp **RCP Vector** viewport, placed on **Vector Viewport** layer
Visible Objects	Linework only
Camera	Camera > Parallel Projection Mode Camera > Standard Views >Top View (Position should be identical to the raster scene.)
Style	"Vector", Fog off, Shadows off

Raster viewport

LayOut Template	A2-Reflected ceiling plans.layout
SketchUp Model	RCP.skp **RCP Raster** viewport, placed on **Raster Viewport** layer.
Visible Objects	All layers on, section cut active
Camera	Camera > Parallel Projection Mode Camera > Standard Views >Top View
Style	"Raster", Fog on, Shadows on

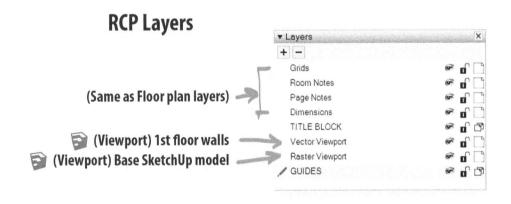

RCP Layers

(Same as Floor plan layers)

(Viewport) 1st floor walls

(Viewport) Base SketchUp model

Figure 7-26
The Reflected
Ceiling Plan
layers.

The reflected ceiling plan is similar to the floor plan, but instead of showing the floor, the perspective is looking upwards, towards the ceiling. Reflected ceiling plans (RCPs) are used to display lighting layouts, sprinklers, smoke detectors, and other objects located on the ceiling. (**Figure 7-27**)

Figure 7-27
Reflected
ceiling plans
used for
lighting plan.

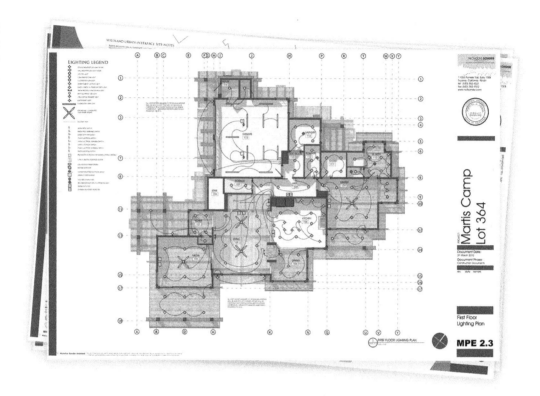

One of the challenges of generating scenes for an RCP is that the view is mirrored from the floor plan. It is not as simple as inserting a section cut into the model pointing upwards and aligning the camera to it. In order to get the viewport oriented properly, you would have to **right-click** on each viewport > **Flip Along**, then rotate the viewport to the proper orientation. Instead of having to do that, you can take care of the building orientation directly inside the SketchUp model.

The first step is to import the building model into the RCP template. The scenes and section planes are preconfigured to produce your RCP viewports. The trick to getting the scenes oriented properly is to **right-click** on the building model after you import it > **Flip Along > Blue axis**. This will invert the model upside down, so your section planes will be pointing downward towards the ceiling. (**Figure 7-28**)

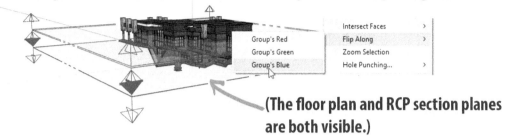

Import the house model into the RCP template, then flip along Blue axis.

Intersect Faces
Group's Red
Group's Green   Flip Along
Group's Blue   Zoom Selection
Hole Punching...

(The floor plan and RCP section planes are both visible.)

Figure 7-28
The building model is flipped along the blue axis to generate reflected views.

The section planes you place in the RCP model should be at the same relative position as the floor plan section planes, just pointing in the opposite direction. This is very easy to do since the floor plan section planes are imported with the building model and can be used as reference when placing the RCP section planes.

Since the linework from the building model is imported into the RCP model, you can update the vector scenes to show the isolated linework. As long as your RCP section planes are in the same location as the section planes used to generate the linework, everything should line up correctly. (**Figure 7-29**)

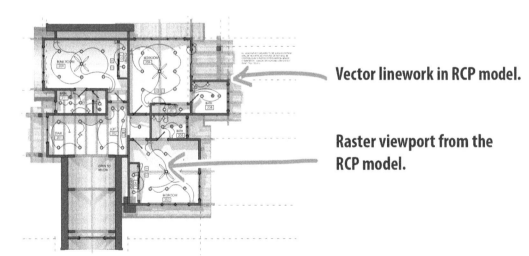

Vector linework in RCP model.

Raster viewport from the RCP model.

Figure 7-29
RCP plans use the same linework imported from the building model.

If you make changes to the building model, remember to open the RCP model and reload the building component into the model.

Door & Window Schedules

The door and window schedules sheet provides the information identifying each window and door type on the project (**Figure 7-30**). You have a lot of flexibility in how you create schedules in LayOut. We will show you a few examples in the chapter on schedules. Once you create them, you can save them in a scrapbook for quick access on other projects.

Figure 7-30
The Door & Window Schedules.

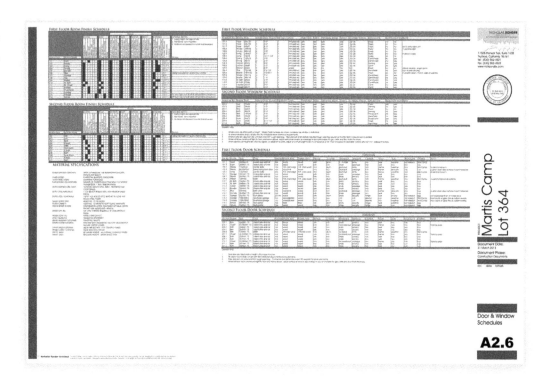

The layer organization is pretty simple, as all of the schedules are placed on the Page Notes layer. A standard Raster Viewport layer is also included in case you decide to include a viewport of window and door types used on the project. (**Figure 7-31**)

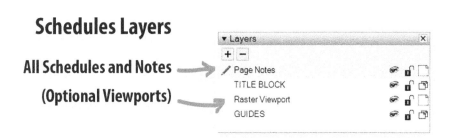

Figure 7-31
The Door & Window Schedules layers.

Although there are no specialized tools in LayOut for creating schedules, you can create your own customized schedules using the basic drawing and text tools (**Figure 7-32**). By being smart about how you lay out and style text boxes, you can create a number of different types of schedules.

FIRST FLOOR ROOM FINISH SCHEDULE

ROOM NO.	ROOM NAME	CEILING HEIGHT	GENERAL NOTES
101	Foyer	12'-1"	1. Ceiling heights are approximate
102	Media	10'-1"	2. Wall texture: Semi-Imperfect
103	Living	14'-1"	3. All stained and exposed concrete shall be sealed
104	Dining	10'-1"	
105	Kitchen	8'-1"	Ceiling measured from second floor landing
106	Stair	8'-0"	
107	Storage	10'-1"	
108	Hall	12'-1"	
109	Master	10'-1"	
110	M. Bath	10'-1"	
111	M. Closet	10'-1"	
112	Powder	10'-1"	
113	Mud Room	10'-1"	
114	Laundry	10'-1"	
115	Garage	12'-1"	
116	Refuse	12'-1"	

Column headings: FLOOR (HARDWOOD, CARPET, STONE TILE, CERAMIC TILE, CONCRETE/STAIN); BASE (1X6 WOOD, 4" STONE TILE, CONCRETE CURB, NONE); NORTH, EAST, SOUTH, WEST (GYP. BD. PAINTED, WOOD PANELING, WOOD WAINSCOTING, EXPOSED CONC.); CEILING (GYP. BD. PAINTED, 1X6 T&G WOOD, FALSE BEAMS, LOWERED CEILING, CEILING HEIGHT, "*" INDICATES VAULTED)

Figure 7-32 A sample finish schedule created in LayOut.

Use the grid

To create a schedule like this from scratch, turn on the grid for guidance. (**Right-click** on a blank spot > **Show Grid**), and turn on **Grid Snap** (**Right-click** on a blank spot > **Grid Snap**). Snapping to the grid will make it much easier to lay out your schedule and make sure everything is aligned. (You may want to turn **Object Snap** off in order to verify that you are indeed only snapping to the grid.)

It is sometimes helpful to display the grid as points, instead of lines, and to display the grid on top of the page elements. It makes it easier to see the grid as it relates to the page elements without being too distracting. You can change these features under **File > Document Setup > Grid. (Figure 7-33)**

The default grid spacing works well for 36"x24" paper, allowing you to use 10pt font size in the space of one grid cell, but if you want to change the spacing of the grid, you can do that from this menu as well.

Figure 7-33
Configure
the grid to
help you
align your
schedule.

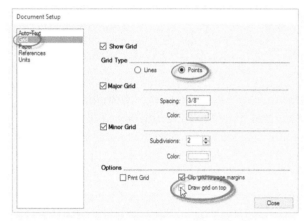

Text Boxes

Text boxes in LayOut are treated as LayOut shapes. In addition to being able to add text, you can also add a fill, pattern, or stroke to the text box using the **Shape Style panel** just like you can with any other shape. (**Figure 7-34**)

Figure 7-34
Use the Shape
Style panel
to apply a fill
and stroke
to your text
boxes.

Text boxes are affected by Shape Style panel

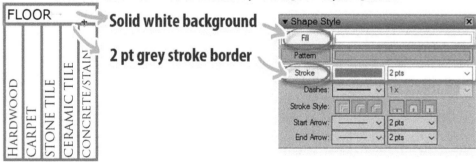

Use the **Grid Snap** feature to align the various elements of your schedule. With the **Text tool** (**T**), click and drag from one grid point to another to define a bounded text box. This will ensure that every text box is the same size, and will make it much easier to rearrange them as you create the schedule.

TIP The **Text tool** (T) can create both bounded, and unbounded text boxes. Unbounded text boxes are created with a single-click of the **Text tool** (T), allow you to type freely, and the text box will resize automatically depending upon the amount of text you type. A bounded text box constrains the text to a specified area, defined by you when you click and drag a text box. When creating a schedule, you want to use a bounded text box since the layout and alignment of the text elements is fixed.

LayOut also allows you to create an array copy, just like in SketchUp. Instead of creating each text box individually, just create one row, then copy it by using the **Select tool** (SPACE) to move it while holding CTRL (Option on Mac) to make a copy (**Figure 7-35**). After placing the initial copy, type in the number of copies you want, followed by an x, and press ENTER. Once you have got all the rows laid out, you can **double-click** on each individual text box to edit the text.

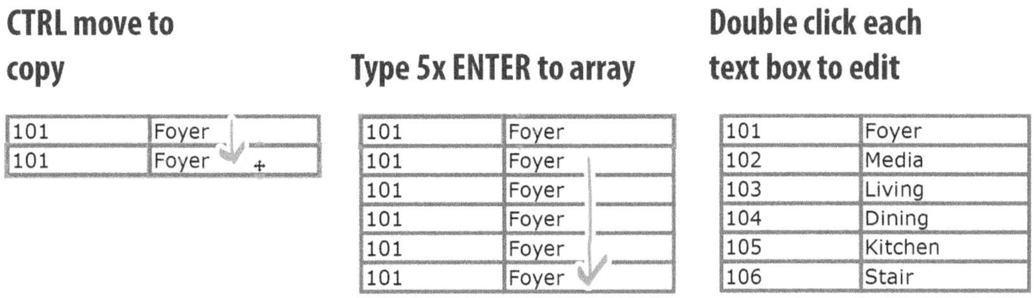

Figure 7-35
Create an array of text boxes to build your schedule rows.

CTRL move to copy

| 101 | Foyer |
| 101 | Foyer |

Type 5x ENTER to array

101	Foyer
101	Foyer
101	Foyer
101	Foyer
101	Foyer
101	Foyer

Double click each text box to edit

101	Foyer
102	Media
103	Living
104	Dining
105	Kitchen
106	Stair

When you insert a text box as part of a schedule template, there will be times when you want to insert a blank text box, to be filled out later. Unfortunately, LayOut does not allow you to have a blank text box. A simple workaround is to place a single space in the text box, then press ESC to exit, and the text box will remain, appearing empty.

Checkboxes

Checkboxes are commonly used in schedules to coordinate the relationship between rows and columns. In the example schedule, the **Rectangle tool (R)** was used to create a square the size of a single grid cell, then that square was copied as needed using the array copy shortcut mentioned previously to fill out the schedule. Again, the **Grid Snap** feature was used to align and space out all the boxes. (**Figure 7-36**)

Figure 7-36
Small squares can be used as check boxes in a schedule.

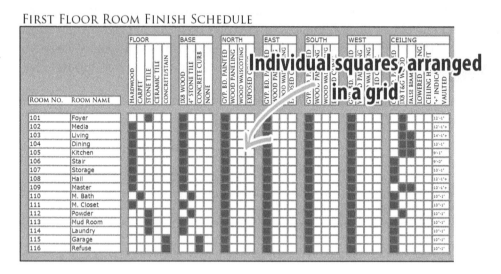

By default, the squares have a white fill, and a grey stroke. When it comes time to actually fill out the schedule with specifications, use the **Style tool (B)** to quickly change the fill of the appropriate checkboxes in order to indicate a relationship between the row and column.

There are numerous ways you can set up your sample source to color the squares. Although you can set up a custom scrapbook and sample properties directly from scrapbook items, another approach is to use your artboard space. (**Figure 7-37**)

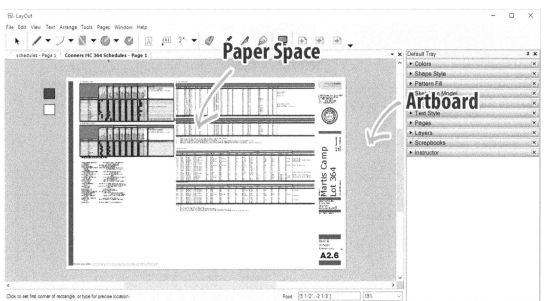

Figure 7-37
The Artboard can be used to place objects for sampling.

The artboard is the grey space around the page in LayOut. Elements can be placed here, but they will not appear on any prints or exports. In this case, you can place two squares on the artboard, and style them the way you want each checkbox condition to look.

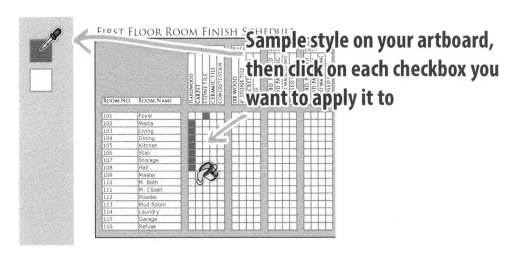

Figure 7-38
Use the Style tool to sample colors and apply them to your check boxes.

When you are ready to configure the schedule, you can grab the **Style tool** (B), click on the appropriate artboard square to grab its style properties, then click on each checkbox on the schedule you would like to change (**Figure 7-38**). Unfortunately, the

Style tool (B) does not work inside groups, so you will not be able to use this method if you are grouping your schedule elements together.

If you need to reset multiple checkboxes at once, remember you can always drag a selection box or SHIFT+click on individual shapes, then use the **Shape Style panel** to change them all at once. (**Figure 7-39**)

Figure 7-39
You can edit the fill on multiple boxes at once.

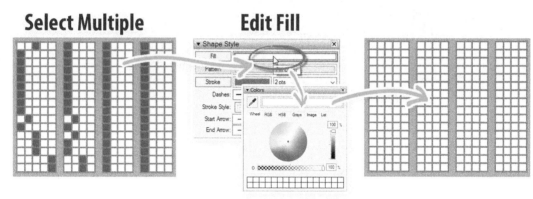

Exterior Elevations

Building on the existing exterior elevation sheets you have already created, you will add section tags, window and door swing annotations (if you did not include that in your window/door component), window/door tags, grid lines, and general notes. (**Figure 7-40**)

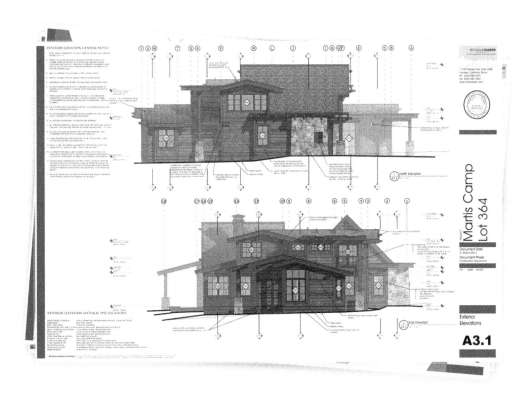

Figure 7-40
The Exterior Elevations pages.

The grid lines can be copied from the floor plans and placed on the Grids layer. All other annotations belong on the Page Notes layer. (**Figure 7-41**)

Raster viewports (Multi)

LayOut Template	A2-Elevations.layout
SketchUp Model	Building.skp viewports, placed on **Raster Viewport** layer.
Visible Objects	All layers on.

Camera	Camera > Parallel Projection Mode Align camera to each side of the building.
Style	"Raster", Fog on, Shadows on

Figure 7-41
The Exterior
Elevations
layers.

Elevations Layers

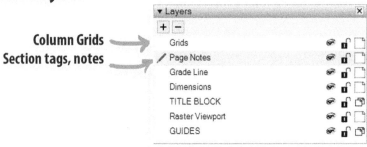

Column Grids
Section tags, notes

✓ **Transparency** - Instead of using a solid white fill on your window and door labels, set the opacity to about 65% so you can see the viewport behind it. It creates a nice effect by softening the label slightly. (**Figure 7-42**)

Figure 7-42 A slight opacity can soften the look of window and door tags.

Set opacity to 65% to make labels semi-transparent

Building Sections

A building sections template model will be used to prepare building sections by importing the building model and placing sections through the building (**Figure 7-43**). To create the sections you will use the same techniques that you used to create your floor plans. Using two viewports, you will create a composite view of your model with one raster viewport and one vector viewport.

The building sections will also include gridlines, datum tags, as well as various detail annotations referring to construction assemblies you will be preparing a little later on.

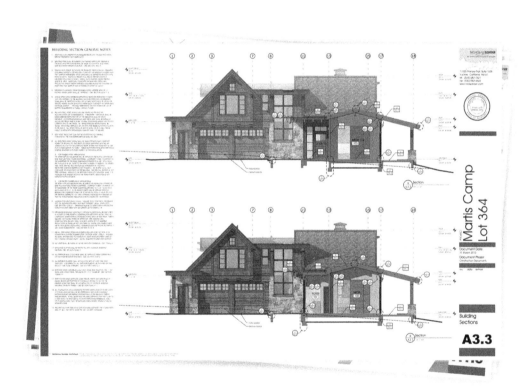

Figure 7-43
The Building Sections pages.

The raster viewport of the building goes on the Raster Viewport layer, and the section linework viewport goes on the Vector Viewport layer. Detail tags and other notes go on the Page Notes layer, and column grids copied from the elevations document go on the Grids layer. (**Figure 7-44**)

Vector viewports (Multi)

LayOut Template	A3-Sections.layout
Model	Sections.skp **A Vector** viewport, placed on **Vector Viewport** layer
Visible Objects	Section Linework only
Camera	Camera > Parallel Projection Mode Camera > Standard Views >Top View
Style	"Vector", Fog off, Shadows off

Raster viewports (Multi)

LayOut Template	A3-Sections.layout
SketchUp Model	Sections.skp **A Raster** viewport, placed on **Raster Viewport** layer.
Visible Objects	All layers on, section cut active
Camera	Camera > Parallel Projection Mode Camera > Standard Views >Top View
Style	"Raster", Fog on, Shadows on

Figure 7-44
The Building Sections layers.

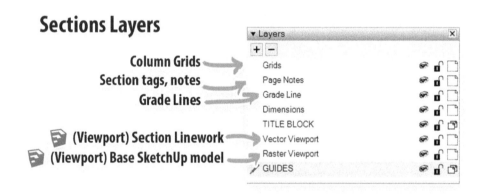

Similar to how you created a raster and vector scene for the floor plan section cuts, you will need to do the same thing for the vertical building sections. However, in order to keep the number of section planes and scenes in the building model down to a minimum, you will import the building model into a separate "sections" template model, and use section planes in that model to create your sections and scenes. (**Figure 7-45**)

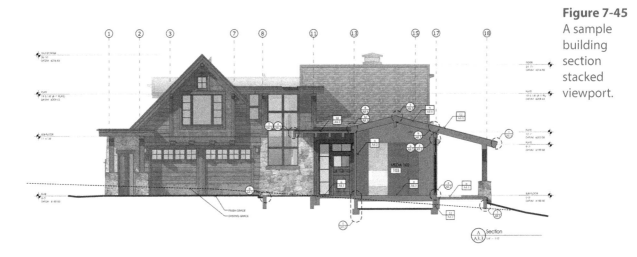

Figure 7-45
A sample
building
section
stacked
viewport.

Whenever you import a model into another, the scenes do not import with it. This is great because you will have a blank slate for creating building section scenes without having to worry about any of the building scenes that exist in the building model.

The sections template includes a number of section planes and preconfigured scenes. All you need to do is import your building model, move the section planes to the correct positions, then double-check the scene settings and camera positions. If you need to add more section cuts or scenes to the model, you can do so manually.

When you create your sections documents in LayOut, you will import the sections model instead of the building model.

Figure 7-46
The building model is imported into a separate sections model to prepare scenes for LayOut.

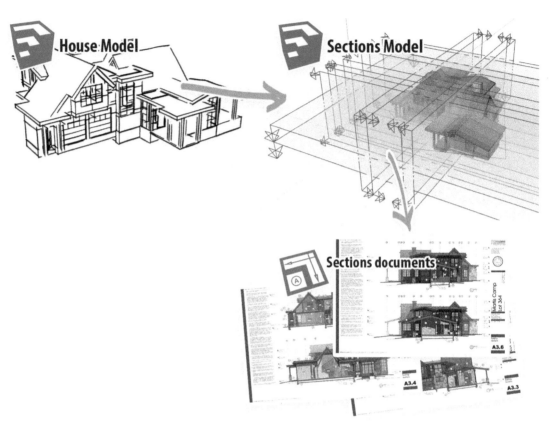

Sections template model

When you first open the Sections.skp template, it might look a little overwhelming (**Figure 7-46**). If you take it one step at a time, everything will make sense. Notice that there are a pair of scenes for each section, labeled alphabetically. One scene is intended to be rendered in raster mode in LayOut, the other is intended to be rendered as vector.

The template includes two front facing sections (A & B), two right facing sections (C & D), two rear facing sections (E & F), and two left facing sections (G & H). Again, this is a template, so if you need more or fewer sections in your particular project, you will need to add or delete them. (**Figure 7-47**)

The building sections template includes preset scenes and section cuts for you to adjust to your model.

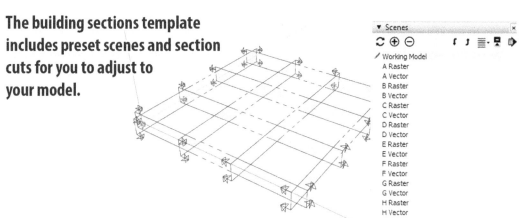

Figure 7-47
The sections template includes preconfigured section planes and scenes.

Before you import your model, take a minute to think about layers. Remember that whenever you import a model, all of that model's layers will be imported too. Also, whenever you create a new layer in SketchUp, that layer will be active by default in all of your existing scenes that save layers. So if you think about that for a second, you will realize that if you import your building model, there may be layers appearing in your preset scenes that you do not want to be seen.

The best way around this is to use the plugin recommended earlier called **Auto-hide Layer www.sketchupbook.com/layer**. This plugin will prevent any new layers from being added to your existing scenes while activated. Alternatively, you can go through each scene and update them manually, after you have imported the building model.

Once you have imported your model, you will review each section, one at a time, and set them up for the scenes you will need in LayOut.

To configure the sections model, follow these steps: (Figure 7-48)

1. In the Sections.skp template, go to **File > Import**, and insert your model somewhere near origin. (Make sure you are in the Working Model scene so that you can toggle style properties without affecting the other scenes.)

2. Each section plane is assigned to its corresponding layer. For example, the section plane that is active in the two Section A scenes is assigned to the SP_A layer. To identify which section plane is associated with which layer, you will want to isolate the layers. To do this, go to the **Layers panel**, click on layer SP_B, then **SHIFT+click** on SP_K to select all except SP_A. Uncheck the box to hide all of the section plane layers except for section A.

3. Use the **Move tool** (**M**) to reposition section plane A through your model where you would like to display a section cut. (If you can not see any section planes in your model, make sure section plane visibility is turned on, **View > Section Planes**.) Also, you can quickly toggle the active section cut by **double-clicking** on the section plane

with the **Select tool** (**SPACE**). Repeat this process for each section plane. Isolate the layer, then move the section plane into position.

4. Use one of the section cut methods from the previous chapter titled Section Cuts to create linework of the section cut for each section, then assign that linework to its corresponding layer in the **Entity Info dialog**. The linework and the section plane should be assigned to the same layer.

Figure 7-48
Section planes need to be moved into place to intersect your model.

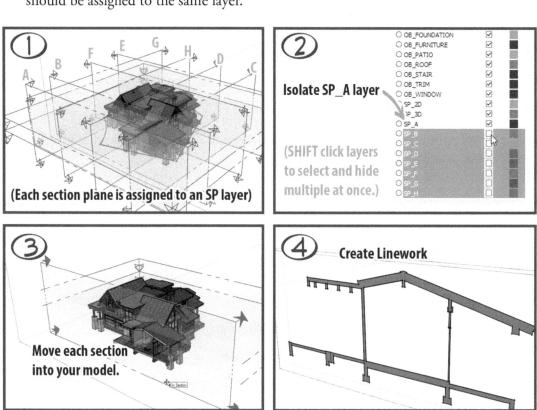

The scenes are preconfigured so that the saved camera position will be aligned with the corresponding section plane. It is likely that you will need to re-center the camera on your particular model. There are multiple scenes which share the same camera position, so it can be helpful to reset their camera positions all at once.

To set the camera property of multiple scenes at once, follow these steps: (Figure 7-49)

1. **Double-click** on one scene to activate it, then adjust your camera position to match your desired view. CTRL+click (Command+click on Mac) on each additional scene that you want to share the same camera perspective. Uncheck the camera position property, then check the camera position box once more to save the new position to those scenes. (You could click the **Update button** instead, then uncheck all the properties other than Camera, but this method is faster since you are only updating a single property.)

2. You will also need to update Fog on each of the raster scenes, one by one. Because each section plane intersects the model at a different depth (in relationship to the camera position), you will not be able to use the same fog settings for each scene. Activate each raster scene and update the fog settings one by one.

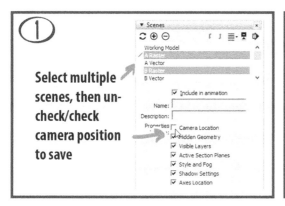

Figure 7-49
Set camera properties to multiple scenes at once.

Creating Additional Sections

If you are adding more section planes to the model, use the existing section planes and scenes as templates to follow in order to configure them correctly. Create a new layer for the section plane and linework, for example SP_I. (Do not forget, any time you add a new layer to your model, it will be visible in all existing scenes unless you use the **Auto-hide Layer plugin www.sketchupbook.com/layer**.)

> **TIP** Although it is not necessary to assign the section planes to a layer, it makes things a little easier to manage, and allows you to identify which section plane is related to which scene by its assigned layer. Technically, active section planes remain active even if their assigned layer is turned off.

After creating the linework for the section, you will need to create a scene for the raster viewport and a scene for the vector viewport. The easiest way to do this is to copy scene properties from an existing scene.

To copy properties from an existing scene, follow these steps: (Figure 7-50)

1. After adding a new layer, section cut, and creating linework for the section, activate the working model scene. Then, isolate the section plane you want by turning off all the other section plane layers. Hide any other layers you do not want in your raster scene. **Double-click** on the section plane to activate it.

2. Save a new scene just so the correct active section plane and layers are saved, then **double-click** on a different scene that shares the same camera position and style settings that you want for your new scene.

Figure 7-50
Scene properties can be copied from other scenes in the model.

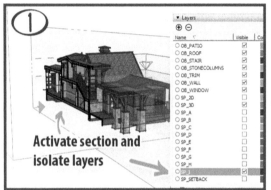

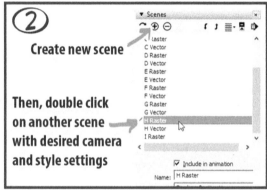

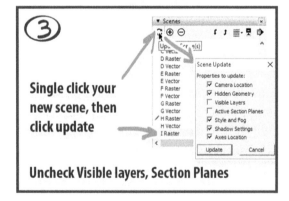

3. **Single-click** on your newly created scene in the **Scenes panel.** Click the **Update button** in the **Scene panel**, then uncheck the Active Section Planes and Camera Location property.

Construction Details

This will be the most time consuming on your first few projects, but you will begin to see a big advantage when you adapt your existing details for multiple projects. The detail pages include viewports to separate detail models, which illustrate specific construction assemblies. (**Figure 7-51**)

Instead of modeling your project at a high level of detail, you can build separate models from which you can use to produce detail drawings. This helps keep your main models lightweight and flexible, while providing a blank canvas for you to model construction assemblies. This allows you the opportunity to get creative with your detail models, showing a cut-away view of a certain assembly.

Figure 7-51
The Construction Details pages.

Each viewport will be placed on the Raster Viewport layer, and all annotations will be placed on the Page Notes layer. Once all the viewports are positioned, you can delete or hide the entities on the GUIDES layer. (**Figure 7-52**)

Raster Viewports (Multi)

LayOut Template	A4-Assemblies.layout, A8-Exterior Details.layout, A9-Interior Details.layout
Model	Multiple detail models as needed.
Visible Objects	All objects visible
Camera	Camera > Perspective
Style	"Raster", Fog on, Shadows on

Figure 7-52
The Construction Details layers.

Details Layers

Detail tags, labels
(Viewports) Detail models

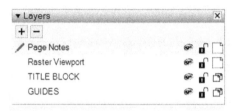

There are three separate LayOut templates for each set of details you will need to include in your project.

✓ **A4-Assemblies** - Wall, floor, and roof assemblies.

✓ **A8-Exterior Details** - Exterior details.

✓ **A9-Interior Details** - Interior Details.

One of the best ways to increase your efficiency while modeling is to model at a lower level of detail. Can you imagine if you had to model every single stud in a project? How long would it take you to make a change to a window or door position? Instead, you model a representation of the wall using basic shapes in order to increase speed and enable easy changes to the design.

However, in construction documents you need to include detailed drawings of various construction assemblies as they occur in the building. So how do you create viewports of detailed construction assemblies while modeling at a low level of detail in your main model? You build separate detail models. (**Figure 7-53**)

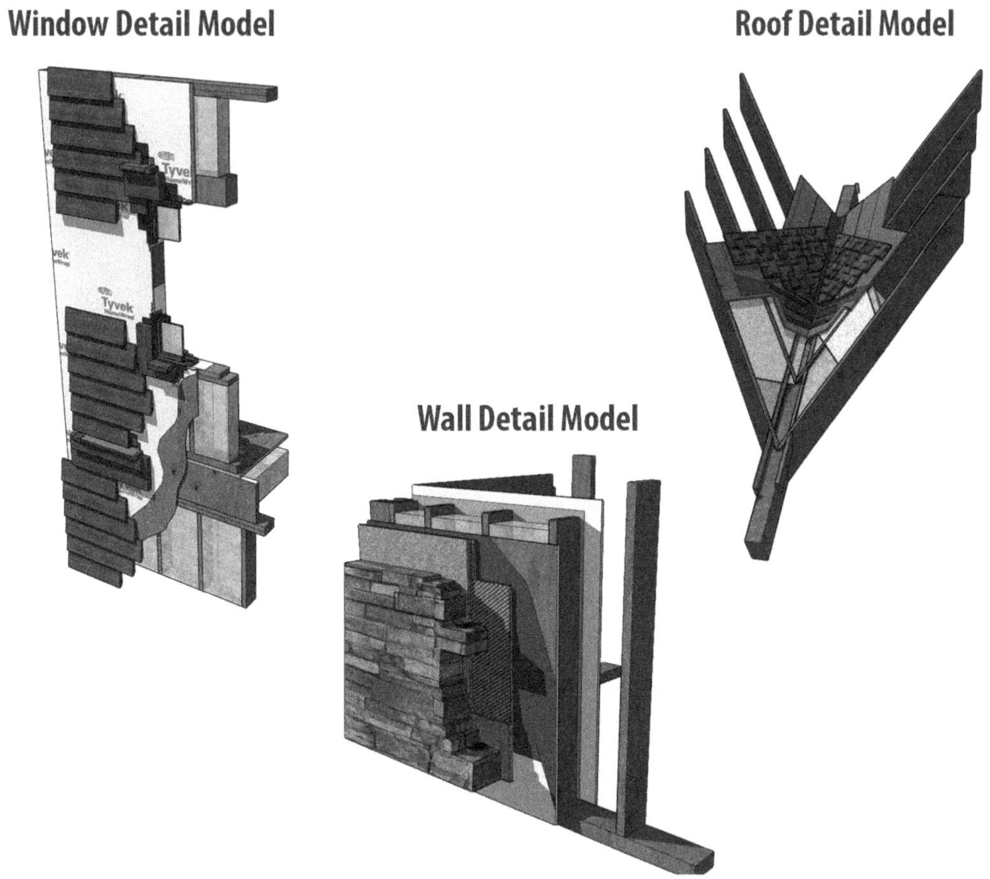

Window Detail Model

Roof Detail Model

Figure 7-53
Sample detail
models.

Wall Detail Model

In a detail model, you have the freedom to stagger building materials as you model them to create a cut-away view of the construction assembly. This is one of the big advantages to having your detail models separate from your main model. You would not be able to create cut-away views if they were part of your main model.

Detail models can also be reused on multiple projects. You may have standard details that you use often, or you may have to tweak some of them to fit the specific requirements of the project. Other times, you may need to build a detail model from scratch. You will be able to add it to your private library to be used on future projects.

Most times, a single detail model can be used to create more than one viewport. For example, this one garage door model is used to create a header, jamb, and threshold viewport. (**Figure 7-54**)

Figure 7-54
One detail model being used for multiple detail viewports.

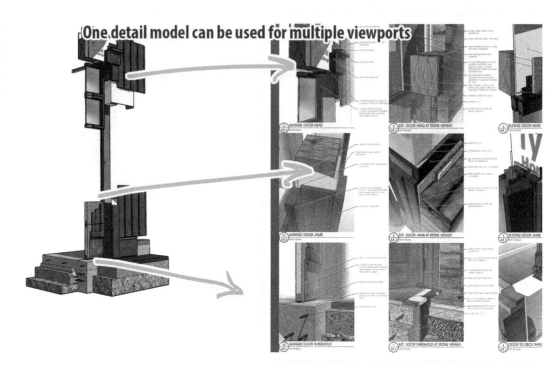

When setting up your scenes inside a detail model, you do not need to worry about creating two scenes for each viewport. A single scene is usually all that is needed. Shadows and fog can help bring focus to specific parts of the model.

Detail template and scrapbooks

To help with creating detail pages in LayOut, the A4-Assemblies.layout template includes detail tags and guide boxes arranged in a grid. When you create a viewport, you just snap to the guide box. Once you have created all of your viewports, hide the guide layer. (**Figure 7-55**)

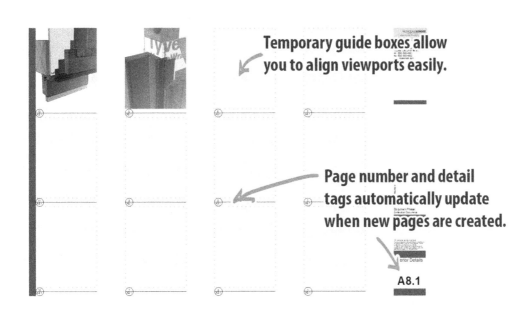

Temporary guide boxes allow you to align viewports easily.

Page number and detail tags automatically update when new pages are created.

A8.1

Figure 7-55
The detail template includes guide boxes to help you align viewports.

The page numbers on the page and the detail tags use Auto-Text, so when you duplicate a page, the page number updates automatically. If you use a different prefix for your detail pages besides "A8", go to **File > Document Setup > Auto-Text**, and change the <PageSet> Auto-Text variable.

It can be rather tedious creating these detail pages since you are likely to have to import multiple SketchUp models, and select the proper scenes for each one. Once you have built up a library of detail models, you should take the time to create your own custom scrapbooks with common detail viewports already configured to their appropriate scene (**Figure 7-56**). There are numerous advantages to doing this:

✓ **Viewport Size** - The viewports you grab from the scrapbook should already be sized exactly how you want them, saving you a step for each model you would have had to import.

✓ **Organization** - You can arrange the detail viewports on multiple pages within the scrapbook, making it easier to find the detail viewport you are looking for. The scrapbook allows for quick access to your details, instead of having to search for them through the **File > Import** menu.

✓ **Scene Selection** - Instead of having to assign a scene to each viewport you copy, you can just set up your scrapbooks so they display multiple viewport copies of a particular model, each assigned to a different scene. Import the exact scene you want directly from the scrapbook, saving you time from having to select it manually.

✓ **Customization** - Whenever a viewport is placed from inside LayOut, a temporary copy of the associated SketchUp model is embedded inside the LayOut file, whether or not you have the original SketchUp model linked to the file. If you need to make any job-specific customizations to the detail model, you can just **right-click** the viewport > **Open With SketchUp**. Once you save the changes, the SketchUp model is embedded back into LayOut. This is sometimes faster and easier than trying to manage project-specific folders of custom detail models.

✓ **Annotations** - If you group the annotations with the viewport in the scrapbook, you will be able to insert them with the viewport onto your page, saving you from the redundancy of having to recreate them for each project.

Figure 7-56
Use scrapbooks to organize your detail models.

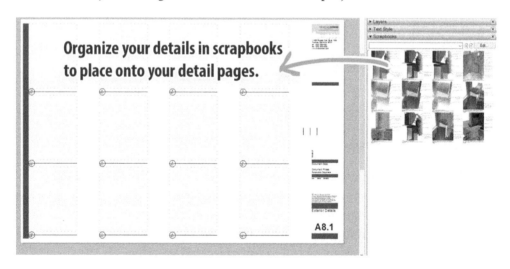

Interior Elevations

For any interior spaces that require elevations, such as kitchens or baths, you will create the interior elevations document (**Figure 7-57**). Very similar to how you created the building sections model, you will import your building model into a separate model that will be used to create the interior elevation scenes.

In LayOut, you will create a clipping mask around your viewports to isolate the boundaries of the viewport around fixed objects such as cabinets, beams, walls, floors or ceilings.

Figure 7-57
The Interior Elevations pages.

The layers in the Interior Elevations document are self-explanatory. The viewports go on the Raster Viewport layer, dimensions go on the Dimensions layer, and all other notes go on the Page Notes layer. (**Figure 7-58**)

Raster Viewports (Multi)

LayOut Template	A4-Assemblies.layout
Model	Interior Elevations.skp Multiple viewports as needed.
Visible Objects	All objects visible
Camera	Camera > Parallel Projection Align camera to each interior elevation required.
Style	"Raster", Fog on, Shadows on

Interior Elevations Layers

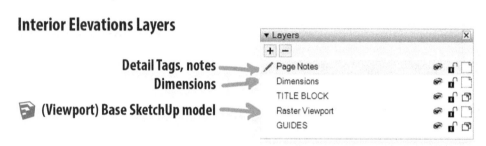

Detail Tags, notes —
Dimensions —
(Viewport) Base SketchUp model —

Interior elevations focus on specific rooms and spaces within a building. Scenes are created using the same workflow for preparing building sections. Import your building model into a dedicated interior elevations model, then create section cuts and scenes as needed.

The template model provided for interior elevations does not include preset scenes or section cuts, because it is less predictable to know where you will need to add a section to your model. It is actually faster to just add the section planes manually as needed, and create the scenes as you go along.

Although you could very well just open a blank model and import your building model into that, we still provide the template file so it becomes established in your project folder.

Clipping Masks

Once you have created the interior elevations model, prepared scenes, and inserted those scenes into LayOut viewports, you will want to create a clipping mask around the viewport in LayOut to create a profile around the boundaries of the space, hiding the rest of the model. (**Figure 7-59**)

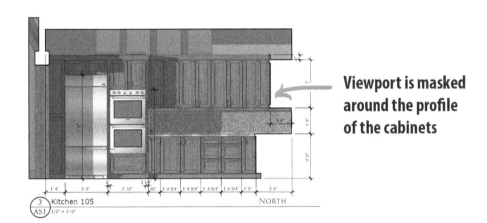

Viewport is masked around the profile of the cabinets

Figure 7-59
A clipping mask lets you create a new boundary around a viewport.

To create a clipping mask, follow these steps: (Figure 7-60)

Step by Step

1. With the **Line tool** (**L**) active, turn off Fill & Pattern in the **Shape Style panel**. Draw a shape around the viewport where you would like to define the boundary. Use **Object Snap** to snap to points in the model. Make sure you finish by clicking back to the starting point so the stroke is completed around the entire perimeter of the shape. Otherwise, you will have a segment without the stroke.

2. Select both the viewport and the shape you just made. **Right-click > Make Clipping Mask**. The viewport will be masked by the boundaries of the shape, and they will be treated as one object.

3. Use the **Shape Style panel** to add a stroke to the viewport if needed.

Figure 7-60
How to create
a clipping
mask.

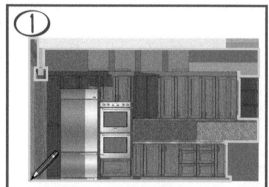

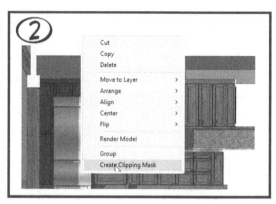

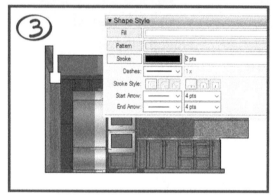

Figure 7-61
Interior
elevations
with clipping
masks
applied.

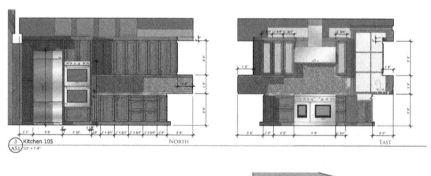

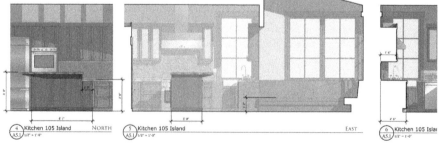

MPE Plans

At this point, you will not need to create any more models or prepare any additional SketchUp scenes. The rest of the documents you create will use existing models for the viewports but will communicate different information. The MPE drawings include mechanical, plumbing, and electrical (power & signal plans/lighting plans). (**Figure 7-62**)

You can copy your floor plan viewports and your reflected ceiling plan viewports to create this sheet set. You will then use LayOut scrapbook symbols to represent various electrical fixtures, lights, fans, etc. The **Line tool** (L) can then be used to draw curved lines to represent electrical connections between the various fixtures.

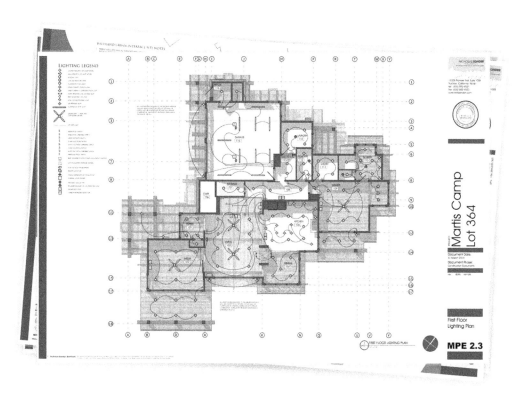

Figure 7-62
The MPE lighting plans.

The plumbing plans are created on top of a set of floor plan viewports placed on the Raster and Vector Viewport layers, and uses the **Line tool** (L) to draw paths to represent plumbing lines placed on the Page Notes layer. Room names are copied from the floor plan documents and placed on the Room Notes layer. (**Figure 7-63**)

Figure 7-63
Plumbing
plans.

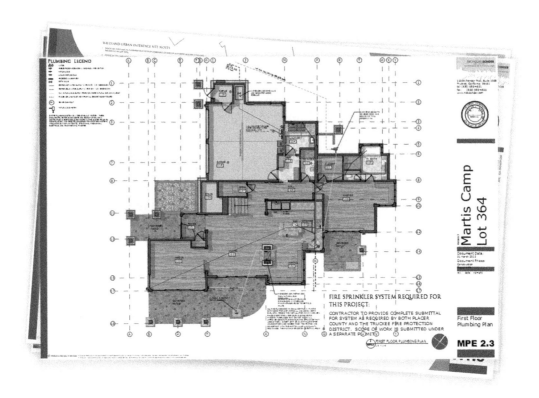

Creating plumbing diagrams in LayOut is a fast way to coordinate plumbing. If you wanted to have more precise coordination of plumbing, there is no reason why you could not model that in SketchUp. You would simply have to plan out the scenes you would need to create the viewports, and make sure you organized your model layers in a way that allowed you to isolate the plumbing.

Figure 7-64
The MPE
layers.

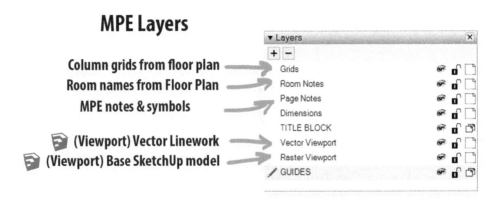

LayOut Tips

You already know how to import basic viewports of the various models that make up your project. In this section, we will review various LayOut specific tasks that you will need to know in order to complete a set of construction documents. Although we are not going to review every single tool in LayOut since you should already have a basic understanding of LayOut's toolset, we will provide many shortcuts and workflow enhancements for you to apply to many of the tools you already use.

Text

Text boxes are treated as LayOut shapes. What this means is that you can apply a fill, pattern, or stroke to a text box just like you can with any other LayOut shape. (**Figure 7-65**)

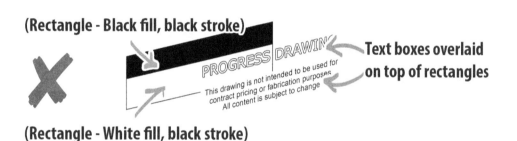

(Rectangle - Black fill, black stroke)

PROGRESS DRAWING
This drawing is not intended to be used for contract pricing or fabrication purposes. All content is subject to change

Text boxes overlaid on top of rectangles

(Rectangle - White fill, black stroke)

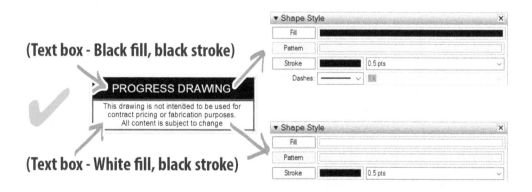

(Text box - Black fill, black stroke)

PROGRESS DRAWING
This drawing is not intended to be used for contract pricing or fabrication purposes. All content is subject to change

(Text box - White fill, black stroke)

Figure 7-65
Text boxes are treated as shapes and can have fill, stroke, and pattern applied to them.

Many times, people will create separate shapes behind text boxes in order to have a solid fill behind the text or a border around the text. This is not necessary because you can apply both of those things to the text box itself. This makes your document simpler, and can sometimes prevent you from having to create extra groups.

 Here are some other tips when working with the **Text tool** (**T**) in LayOut:

✓ Hidden in the list tab in the **Text Style panel** are some features which allow you to create various lists inside your text boxes.

✓ You can align multiple columns within a single text box by indenting using the tab key. Just be careful when doing this because if you change the font size it may push your indentations out of alignment. A better way may be to create a separate text box for each column of text.

✓ You can apply different text styles to characters within a single text box.

✓ Dragging a text box creates a bounded text box. Clicking to place a text box creates an unbounded text box. You can toggle whether a text box is bounded or unbounded at anytime by **right-clicking** it, or by toggling it in the **Text Style panel**.

Label Tool

The **Label tool** in LayOut can create a number of differently styled labels and can extract data from your SketchUp model to display in the label. (**Figure 7-66**)

Depending on how you click when you create a label, you can create a straight, elbowed, curved, or compound curved label leader. Labels are controlled by the **Shape Style panel**, just like any other object in LayOut. You can change the end point style, stroke, color, text box fill, etc. The label text is controlled by the **Text Style panel**.

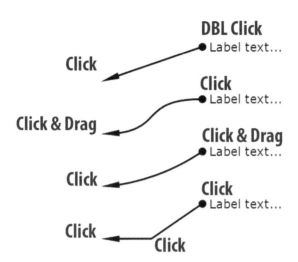

Figure 7-66
The types of
label leaders
you can draw
in LayOut.

✓ If you anchor a label on a SketchUp viewport, you will be able to extract optional data from the model such as component name, or face area.

✓ Aligning multiple labels will only move the label text, not the anchor point.

✓ **Double-click** on a label to edit where leader snaps to label text, or to edit the leader curve.

✓ Convert label leader type by **right-clicking** on it.

✓ Hold **CTRL** (**Option** on Mac) while creating a label to flip the text orientation.

Dimensions

Creating dimensions in LayOut is as simple as clicking at the starting point, end point, and the dimension line position. You are probably already familiar with how to change the dimension style using the **Shape Style panel**.

One of the reasons you created a raster viewport and a vector viewport was to make the task of placing dimensions extremely easy. As you know, LayOut can sometimes be a little over-excited when trying to find snapping points. By creating a simplified vector viewport, you reduce the number of available points, ensuring that you are snapping to the correct point.

Before inserting dimensions, turn off the raster viewport layer and snap your dimensions to the vector viewport.

Once you have set the first dimension, additional dimensions along the same linear path are easy. Simply **double-click** at the end point of the next dimension, and it will measure to the end point of your last dimension and align it to the same offset. (**Figure 7-67**)

Figure 7-67
Double-click to quickly create dimensions.

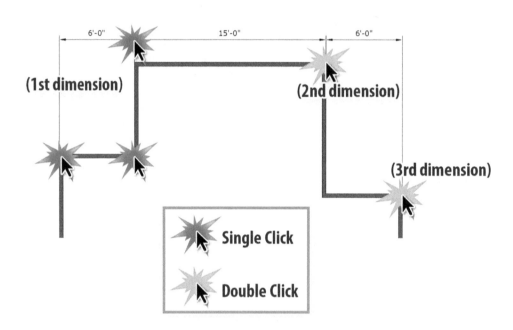

Smart Grouping

Just like in SketchUp, LayOut allows you to group objects together to provide another level of structural organization within your document. Just select two or more objects > **right-click** > **Group**. You can even have groups within groups. However, groups are not required in the same way as SketchUp because of the way LayOut's layer system behaves. In LayOut, objects assigned to a layer can be protected by hiding or locking the layer, unlike SketchUp.

Still, groups provide a very useful utility for collecting objects and can be used in conjunction with layer assignments to help you organize your document. Here are the main uses for groups inside LayOut:

✓ **Proximity** - Use groups on objects that will always be moved or copied together and have the same proximity to each other. Symbols and labels made up of multiple

LayOut shapes and text should be grouped so you can move them without having to make a multi-selection every time. Grids are another example of a set of objects that can be grouped together.

✓ **Scrapbook objects** - Scrapbook objects are stamped into your document by group. When creating scrapbooks, think about whether you want to stamp individual objects into your document, or if you should group multiple objects together to stamp into your document in one step. For example, symbols that are created from multiple shapes should be grouped together.

✓ **Object type** - One way to use groups is to collect all similar types of objects. For example, you might contain all room labels inside a group on a floor plan. This would provide a way to select all of a certain type of object and move or change properties in one simple step. However, the layers system in LayOut provides all of that functionality so this is not entirely necessary and can be considered redundant.

Whenever you create a group which contains text that will need to be updated whenever it is inserted onto a page, do not bury the text box within multiple sets of groups because you will waste time opening and closing groups. For example, detail tags should have the description, detail number, and scale text boxes directly under the first group, so you only need to open one group to edit any of those text boxes.

When entering multiple sets of groups, it is helpful to zoom in first in order to make the selection area larger. Sometimes you will find yourself opening the wrong group or text box due to overlapping selection areas of different objects. Zooming in can reduce the chance of that from happening. When exiting groups, LayOut seems to respond fastest by tapping the **ESC** key on your keyboard instead of clicking outside the group.

Scrapbooks

If you understand the advantage of using templates, then you can understand the value of scrapbooks. Scrapbooks are libraries of pre-made LayOut entities that are quickly accessible to stamp onto your LayOut pages. (**Figure 7-68**)

Figure 7-68
Select
scrapbooks
from the drop-
down menu
and navigate
its pages
to find the
desired object.

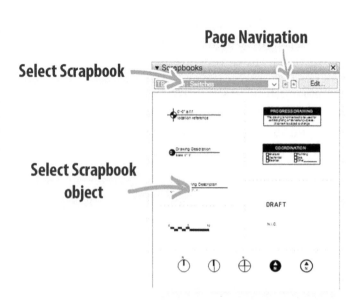

SketchUp includes a number of default scrapbooks, and you can even customize your own. For example, when you go to add grid lines to your model, you do not need to create the grid symbol from scratch. You can find a number of pre-made grid lines in the scrapbook, for instance under the TB-Simple folder (**Figure 7-69**). Just click on the element you want to grab, then click on your document to stamp it. You can continue to stamp, or just press **ESC** to cancel.

Figure 7-69
Scrapbook
items are
selected by
the way they
are grouped.

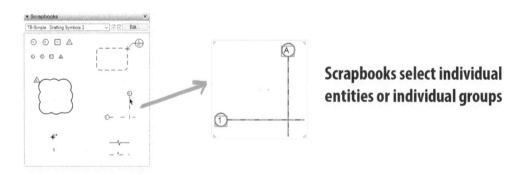

Notice that the grid line is simply made up of three objects: a circle, a dashed line, and a text box. There is nothing special about scrapbook objects, they are simply LayOut entities grouped together. You could draw this symbol from scratch if you would like, and it would be no different from the symbol you just stamped into your document. The value behind scrapbooks is the ability to quickly access commonly used objects that you would like to place in your documents.

Using Scrapbooks

Scrapbooks can be used for virtually anything (**Figure 7-70**), but you primarily want to use scrapbooks for common symbols or text, and anything not physically represented in the SketchUp model. There can be some discretion as to what you decide to put in the model and what you decide to insert in LayOut.

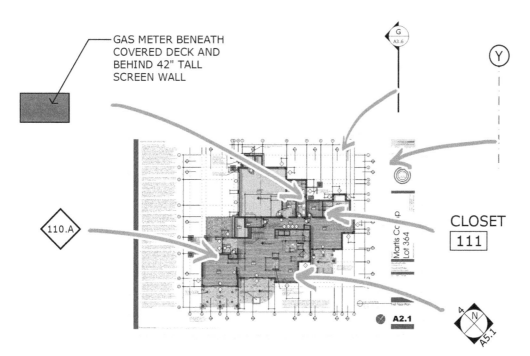

Figure 7-70
Examples of objects that can be saved as scrapbook items.

For example, as we have discussed previously, trees symbols can be inserted directly in your SketchUp model as a part of the 3D tree component placed on the SP_2D layer. The advantage of this is that wherever there is a tree in your model, a tree symbol will appear in the viewport as long as it is set up properly. If you do not want to go through the hassle of setting up tree components to do that, you could just insert tree symbols into LayOut directly from the tree scrapbook (**Figure 7-71**). The disadvantage is that you will need to manually place and locate each one, and you will need to resize the symbol accordingly.

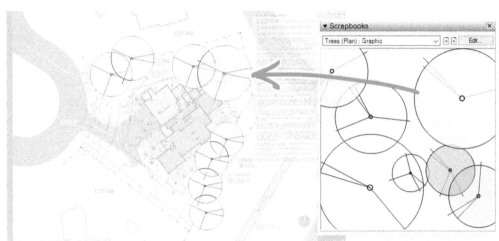

Figure 7-71
Trees can be
placed on the
page from a
scrapbook.

A similar approach could be taken with electrical objects. You could, in theory, create a library of electrical SketchUp components that have a 3D object group on SP_3D, and a flat symbol group placed on the SP_2D layer that only shows up in plan view. You could then set up a special scene that will display the electrical symbols and import it into LayOut.

The advantage to this approach is that you are able to coordinate everything directly in the model, instead of having a disconnect between the model and LayOut by inserting scrapbook elements manually. However, this can get messy pretty quickly, especially when you have multiple switch and outlet configurations, or when you have two objects very close to each other and their symbols start to overlap. Not to mention the challenges you will face when you are dealing with different page sizes in LayOut and need to display a scaled symbol.

Here are some other common uses for Scrapbooks:

✓ Stamp common symbols onto your document, such as electrical outlets, switches, sheet tags, elevation markers, etc.

✓ Prepare general notes for various conditions; then grab the appropriate text block and drop it into your document as needed.

✓ SketchUp viewports can be part of a scrapbook. Useful for commonly used construction assembly details.

✓ You can sample styles from scrapbook objects using the eyedropper.

Creating your own Scrapbooks

You create a scrapbook in the same way you create any other LayOut document. The main difference is that when you save it, you select **File > Save As Scrapbook**. There is actually nothing special about a scrapbook file; it is just a regular LayOut file.

In fact, any LayOut file can be placed in a scrapbook, it just needs to be saved in the correct folder. By selecting Save As Scrapbook, LayOut will allow you to select one of your scrapbook folder locations to save it in, without having to search your computer for the scrapbook folder locations. You can customize or add folders to your scrapbook library by going to **Edit > Preferences > Folders (Figure 7-72)**. All LayOut files that are located inside these folders will appear in your **Scrapbooks panel**. Adding an easily accessible folder location to your scrapbook makes it easier to customize your scrapbook LayOut files.

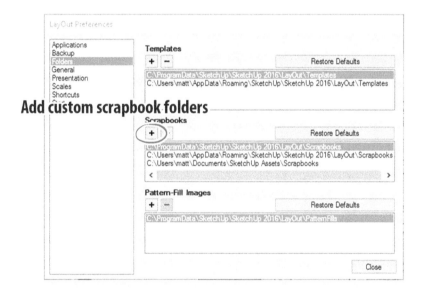

Figure 7-72
Add custom scrapbook folder locations.

The first thing to think about when creating a scrapbook is the paper size. The paper size and ratio of your scrapbook document is important because it sets the visual scale of the objects when viewed from the **Scrapbooks panel (Figure 7-73)**. The ratio of the page height and width will affect how the scrapbook is viewed in the **Scrapbooks panel**. In other words, the scrapbook page will fill the space you provide the **Scrapbooks panel**, while keeping its aspect ratio. A square ratio tends to work well by default, but it really depends on how you personally have your trays configured, and if you like to keep your

Scrapbooks panel compact, tall, or in its own tray.

To change the paper size of a LayOut document, go to **File > Document Setup > Paper.**

Figure 7-73
Scrapbooks
are restricted
by the
size of the
Scrapbooks
panel.

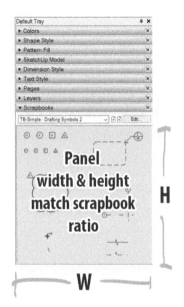
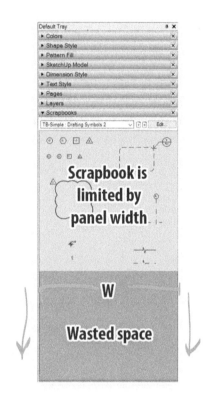

If you like to have your **Scrapbooks panel** tall, as shown on the right image above (**Figure 7-73**), you need to make sure you size your scrapbook paper size to fit that rough height and width ratio.

If you work on a computer with multiple monitors, another solution is to create a custom tray just for your scrapbooks. By doing this, you can undock the scrapbook into its own window, and place it in a secondary monitor where you can resize the panel so your scrapbook pages are much larger. This makes it much easier to see and select scrapbook objects. (On Mac, you can detach the Scrapbook panel and resize it.)

To create a dedicated panel for scrapbooks, follow these steps: (Figure 7-74)

1. Go to **Window > New Tray**.

2. Type in a tray name and check the Scrapbooks box to include the **Scrapbooks panel** in this new tray. (Panels can only exist in one tray at a time, so if the **Scrapbooks panel** is currently in another tray, it will be removed from it and placed in this one.)

3. Click and drag the tab at the bottom of the default tray to detach the panel from the LayOut window, and place it in another monitor. Click and drag the sides of the tray to expand the width. Click and drag the tray, then the panel, in order to increase the height.

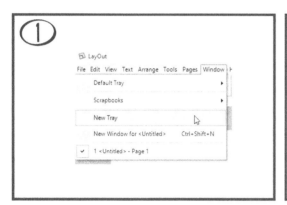
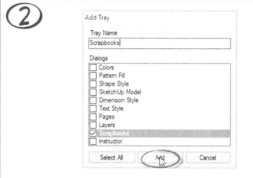

Figure 7-74
Undock the Scrapbooks panel to place it in another monitor.

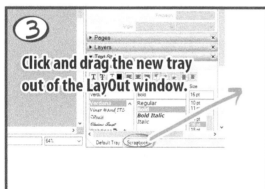
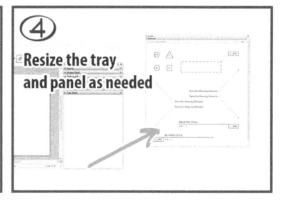

In addition to the proper ratio, you also want to select a paper size that displays each scrapbook element at an appropriate scale for viewing in the **Scrapbooks panel**. For example, if you are working on a scrapbook with small symbols that are about 1/2" in size, it would not make sense to use a page size of 10" x 10", because when the scrapbook is scaled down in the panel, the symbols will appear too small to identify or select.

Instead, use a paper size of about 5" x 5". Instead of trying to fit all the symbols on a single page, create multiple pages and organize the symbols so each page is a different category (**Figure 7-75**). The symbols will be easier to identify in the **Scrapbooks panel**, and they will be better organized through the use of pages.

Figure 7-75
Size scrapbook pages so they appear large enough to see in the Scrapbooks panel, using multiple pages if needed.

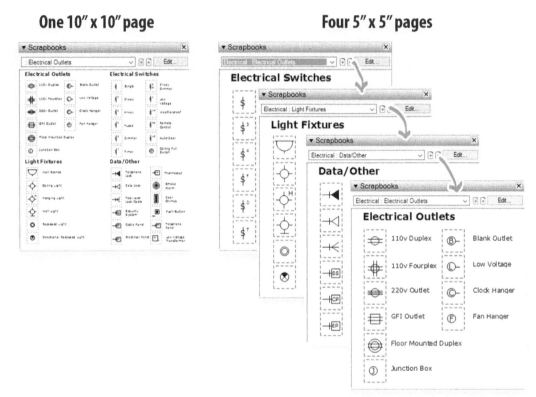

Keep the following in mind when building a scrapbook file:

✓ **Pages** - A scrapbook file can include multiple pages. When you add new pages to the LayOut document, those pages will be accessible in the **Scrapbooks panel** using the page toggle buttons.

✓ **Groups** - When you select an object from a scrapbook, it will select a single entity or a single group. So if you are creating a symbol made up of multiple shapes, you need to make sure you group those shapes together so they are sampled from the scrapbook as a single object.

✓ **Locked layers** - You may want to include text labels in your scrapbook documents to help you identify objects on the page when viewing from the

Scrapbooks panel. However, you do not want these labels to be sampled from the scrapbook. Any layers that are locked when saving the scrapbook will not be able to be sampled from inside the **Scrapbooks panel**.

Implementation

We have reviewed the entire process of designing, revising, and documenting a custom project in SketchUp and LayOut from concept to completion. You should be able to take these workflows and concepts and apply them to any type of construction.

We encourage you to adapt this workflow to fit your own preferences. Change the templates, create new ones, try different methods for preparing section cuts. Over time, you will build a library of detail models that you can adapt to each project. Your window and door component library will expand as well.

After using this workflow on a few projects, the entire process will become even faster and easier to use, allowing you to bring focus back to the design. Remember the key characteristics of this workflow:

✓ **Level of Detail** - Build your 3D models to the minimum level of detail required for the phase of design you are in, while adding important visual details to help convey the design intent.

✓ **Multiple files** - Split projects into multiple SketchUp and LayOut files for more control and flexibility.

✓ **Build a library** - Create components that you can reuse on future projects. Save components that you've downloaded from other sources. Organize them in folders for quick access.

✓ **Use templates** - Using templates in both SketchUp and LayOut save you time, increase consistency, and provide better project organization.

SketchUp is a powerful design tool when used in a thoughtful, well-organized manner. We hope this book has enabled you to have more fun designing, and released you from some of the technical limitations of traditional drafting.

Index

Are you looking for a more in-depth guide on creating SketchUp models for LayOut?

Go to www.sketchuptolayout.com for information on:

SketchUp to LayOut

The essential guide to creating construction documents using SketchUp & LayOut.

by Matt Donley

✓ Available in PDF, ebook, and paperback.

✓ Learn how to have full control over the look of your models in LayOut.

✓ Video course available.

Lightning Source UK Ltd.
Milton Keynes UK
UKHW050649131122
412125UK00002B/2